EXPLORING Financial Literacy

THIRD EDITION

Judi Deatherage

Publisher
The Goodheart-Willcox Company, Inc.
Tinley Park, IL
www.g-w.com

Copyright © 2025
by
The Goodheart-Willcox Company, Inc.

Previous editions copyright 2020, 2012 (under the title *Becoming Money $mart*)

All rights reserved. No part of this work may be reproduced, stored, or transmitted in any form or by any electronic or mechanical means, including information storage and retrieval systems, except as permitted by U.S. copyright law, without the prior written permission of The Goodheart-Willcox Company, Inc.

ISBN 979-8-88817-182-0

1 2 3 4 5 6 7 8 9 – 25 – 28 27 26 25 24 23

The Goodheart-Willcox Company, Inc. Brand Disclaimer: Brand names, company names, and illustrations for products and services included in this text are provided for educational purposes only and do not represent or imply endorsement or recommendation by the author or the publisher.

The Goodheart-Willcox Company, Inc. Safety Notice: The reader is expressly advised to carefully read, understand, and apply all safety precautions and warnings described in this book or that might also be indicated in undertaking the activities and exercises described herein to minimize risk of personal injury or injury to others. Common sense and good judgment should also be exercised and applied to help avoid all potential hazards. The reader should always refer to the appropriate manufacturer's technical information, directions, and recommendations; then proceed with care to follow specific equipment operating instructions. The reader should understand these notices and cautions are not exhaustive.

The publisher makes no warranty or representation whatsoever, either expressed or implied, including but not limited to equipment, procedures, and applications described or referred to herein, their quality, performance, merchantability, or fitness for a particular purpose. The publisher assumes no responsibility for any changes, errors, or omissions in this book. The publisher specifically disclaims any liability whatsoever, including any direct, indirect, incidental, consequential, special, or exemplary damages resulting, in whole or in part, from the reader's use or reliance upon the information, instructions, procedures, warnings, cautions, applications, or other matter contained in this book. The publisher assumes no responsibility for the activities of the reader.

The Goodheart-Willcox Company, Inc. Internet Disclaimer: The Internet resources and listings in this Goodheart-Willcox Publisher product are provided solely as a convenience to you. These resources and listings were reviewed at the time of publication to provide you with accurate, safe, and appropriate information. Goodheart-Willcox Publisher has no control over the referenced websites and, due to the dynamic nature of the Internet, is not responsible or liable for the content, products, or performance of links to other websites or resources. Goodheart-Willcox Publisher makes no representation, either expressed or implied, regarding the content of these websites, and such references do not constitute an endorsement or recommendation of the information or content presented. It is your responsibility to take all protective measures to guard against inappropriate content, viruses, or other destructive elements.

Image Credits. Front cover: TarikVision/Ivan Lukyanchuk

Financial Capability— What Does It Mean to You?

As a young adult, one of the most important keys to your success will be financial capability. *Financial capability* is the ability to combine financial knowledge with the attitude, skills, and behaviors needed to use money wisely in a person's own life.

Financial literacy is knowledge about basic topics related to finance, such as making, spending, and saving money. As a young person, you will need to learn how to make wise financial decisions at an early age. Wise financial decisions will help you lead a productive life, as well as enable you to be a positive contributor to your community.

Exploring Financial Literacy will provide you with opportunities to learn about financial literacy topics and how they impact your life now, as well as how they will influence your future. As you read about each new topic, jump in and see how the information applies to you as a student. Learn how to make your money work for you and how to plan for your career and your future. Have fun as you begin the journey and explore financial literacy!

About the Author

Judi Deatherage is a retired business education teacher with a passion for educating teens about money. She received her bachelor degree from Eastern Kentucky University and her master degree from the University of Cincinnati. During her teaching career, Ms. Deatherage taught accounting and finance courses to high school and college students. She was the recipient of Ashland Oil's Golden Apple Award for Teachers and is listed in *Who's Who Among America's Teachers*. Ms. Deatherage is the author of a trade book, *Who Wants to be a Millionaire?*, which focuses on basic principles of financial literacy for teens. After retiring, she worked part-time in an accounting office, keeping up to date on current tax laws. She lives in northern Kentucky with her husband, near her children and grandchildren.

Reviewers

The author and publisher wish to thank the following industry and teaching professionals for their valuable input into the development of *Exploring Financial Literacy*.

Aaron Barker
High School Business Teacher
Springboro High School
Springboro, Ohio

Leann Bennett
Personal Finance Teacher
Pinnacle View Middle School
Little Rock, Arkansas

Joan Birdsell
Business Education Teacher
Drake-Anamoose High School
Drake, North Dakota

Lexie Centers
7th and 8th Grade Financial Literacy Teacher
Gregg Middle School
Summerville, South Carolina

Dianna Dance-Lewis
Family and Consumer Science Teacher
County of Henrico Public School
Henrico, Virginia

Christina M. Drauden
8th Grade Math Teacher
Linda Jobe Middle School
Mansfield, Texas

Mary Eisert
Family and Consumer Science/ Language Arts Teacher
Wea Ridge Middle School
Lafayette, Indiana

David A. Hamner
Career/Business Education Teacher
Aventura City of Excellence School
Aventura, Florida

Jana Locke
Department Head—Special Education
Marshall High School
Marshall, Missouri

Melissa Manly
Reading Specialist, Personalized Learning Teacher
Northern Summit Academy Shasta
Anderson, California

Nancy B. Martin
Social Studies/Personal Finance Teacher
Andover Middle School
Andover, Kansas

Annette Morrell
Family and Consumer Science Teacher
Ririe Junior Senior High School
Ririe, Idaho

Jennifer Nicholls
Family and Consumer Science Teacher
Shenendehowa Central Schools/ Koda Middle School
Clifton Park, New York

Jenny Watson
Family and Consumer Science Teacher
Southeast Middle School
Kernersville, North Carolina

Credentialing Partners and Support

Goodheart-Willcox appreciates the value of industry credentials, certifications, and accreditation. We are pleased to partner with leading organizations to support students and programs in achieving credentials. Integrating industry-recognized credentialing into a career and technical education (CTE) program provides many benefits for the student and for the institution. By achieving third-party certificates, students gain confidence, have proof of a measurable level of knowledge and skills, and earn a valuable achievement to include in their résumés. For educators and administrators, industry-recognized credentials and accreditation validate learning, enhance the credibility of programs, and provide valuable data to measure student performance and help guide continuous program improvement.

Exploring Financial Literacy is correlated to the National Standards for Personal Financial Education offered by Jump$tart.

Jump$tart Coalition for Personal Financial Literacy

Goodheart-Willcox is pleased to partner with the Jump$tart Coalition for Personal Financial Literacy to correlate *Exploring Financial Literacy* with their National Standards in K–12 Personal Finance Education. The Jump$tart Coalition works to raise awareness about the importance of financial literacy and the need for financial education, especially among youth; fosters collaboration among financial literacy stakeholders; and promotes and supports effectiveness in financial education endeavors. For more information about Jump$tart, please visit www.jumpstart.org.

Explore Financial Literacy

Almost every aspect of your life is affected by financial literacy in some way. Each time you earn money from a part-time job or spend money on your favorite gym shoes, you make financial decisions.

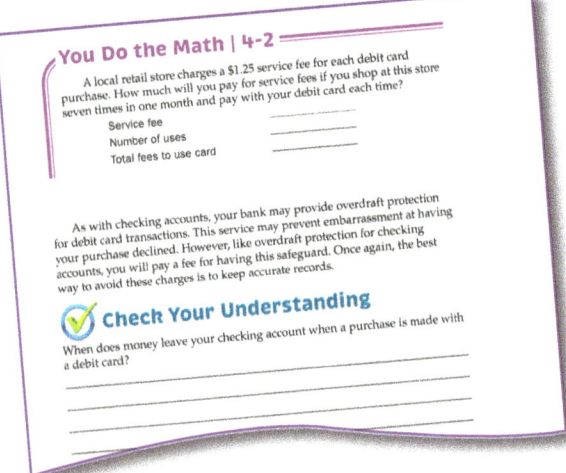

How easy is this? Each chapter section teaches financial literacy concepts. After learning a concept, you immediately apply it.

- **You Do the Math** activities walk you through math examples, so you learn by doing.
- **Check Your Understanding** questions help you assess content you have covered before moving on to the next concept.

How does this apply to me? Throughout this text, features highlight how financial literacy can impact your life.

- **Are You Financially Responsible?** asks if you are prepared to create a financial plan and look ahead to your future.
- **Dollars and Sense** features share common-sense information about how to use your money wisely.

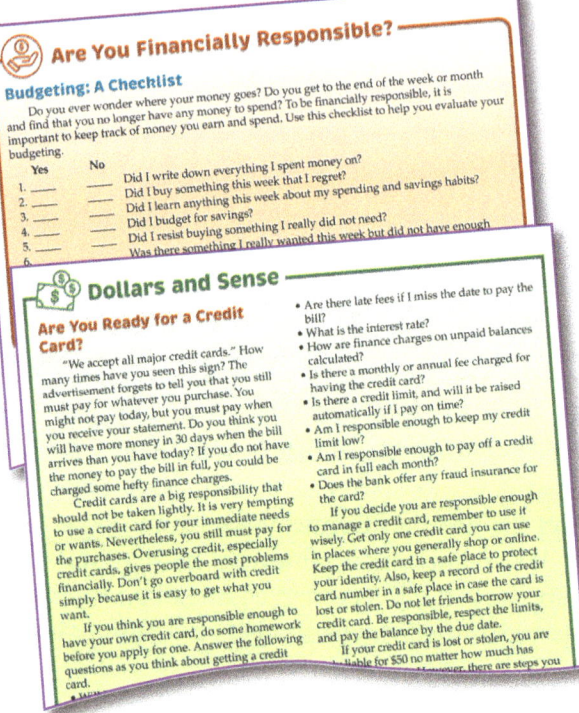

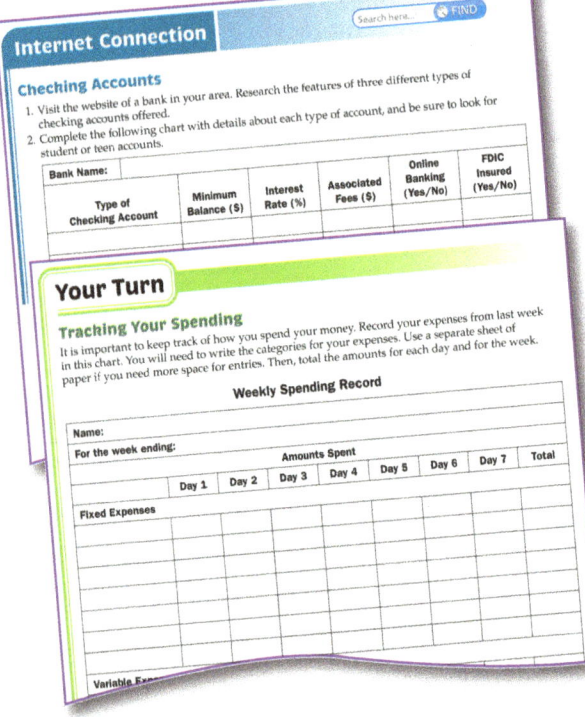

What about a challenge? Learning about finance raises new challenges for you to tackle. Opportunities are presented for you to apply what you learn about how to manage your money.

- **Internet Connection** enables you to practice your research skills while learning about important financial literacy concepts.
- Hands-on **Your Turn** activities provide opportunities to apply what you have learned.

Chart Your Progress

Learning to be financially literate is fun. This text provides you with tools to help you in your quest for a bright financial future. Setting a path to financial security now can lead to success in the future.

- Each chapter opens with **What is Your Financial IQ?** questions so you can review what you already know about the subject matter.
- The **Essential Question** at the beginning of each chapter will engage you to uncover the important points presented in the content.

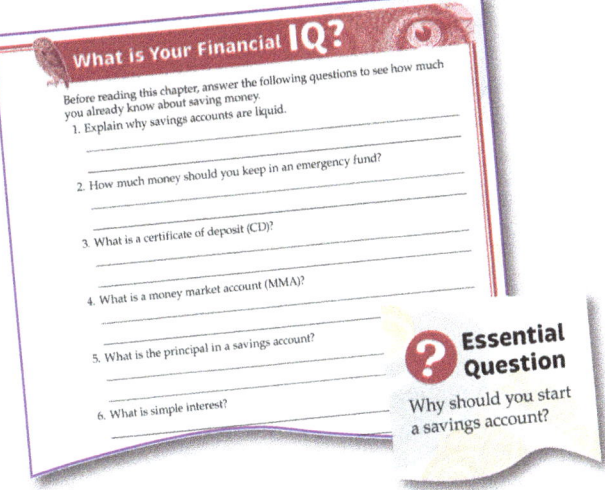

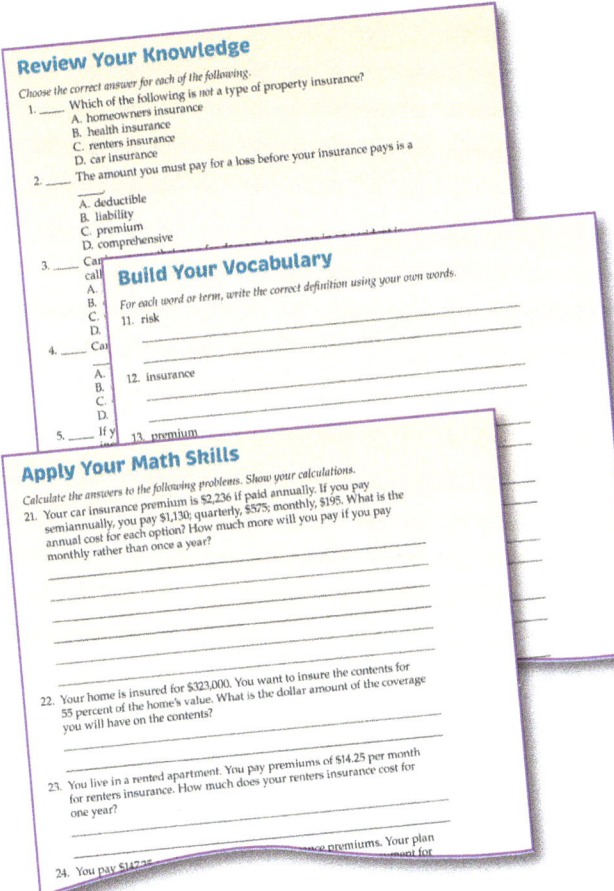

Assess what you learned. Multiple opportunities are provided to confirm learning as you explore the content. *Formative assessment* includes the following:

- **Review Your Knowledge** questions cover basic concepts presented in the chapter so you can evaluate your understanding of the chapter material.
- **Build Your Vocabulary** reviews key terms presented in the chapter and challenges you to demonstrate your understanding of financial literacy terms.
- **Apply Your Math Skills** problems reinforce the math concepts and formulas covered in the chapter so you can practice applying math skills to financial situations.

Get ready for life as a financially capable individual. You will need good literacy skills as you plan for your future.

- Each chapter opens with a **Reading Prep** activity so you can improve your literacy skills.
- **Learning Outcomes** provide goals to help you read and understand the content in each chapter.

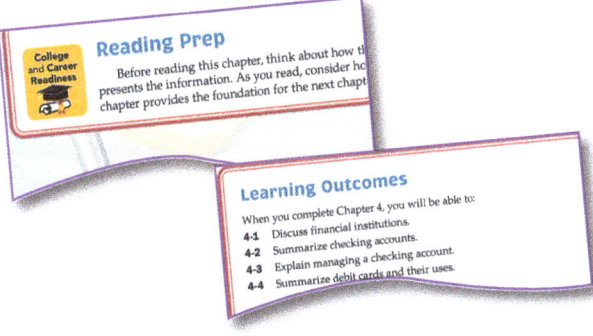

TOOLS FOR STUDENT AND INSTRUCTOR SUCCESS

Student Tools

Student Text

Exploring Financial Literacy is written specifically for teens and discusses how to become financially capable. The material covered in the text—including saving money, managing credit, buying a car, and renting an apartment—emphasizes what young people need to know to create a successful financial plan for their lives.

Online Textbook

Online student text, along with rich supplemental content, brings digital learning to the classroom.

G-W Digital Companion

E-flash cards and vocabulary exercises allow interaction with content to create opportunities to increase achievement.

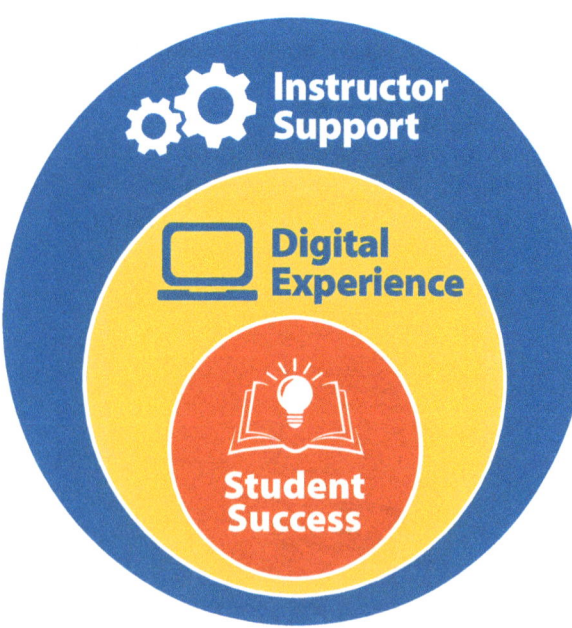

Instructor Tools

LMS Integration

Integrate Goodheart-Willcox content within your Learning Management System for a seamless user experience for both you and your students. LMS–ready content in Common Cartridge® format facilitates single sign-on integration and gives you control of student enrollment and data. With a Common Cartridge integration, you can access the LMS features and tools you are accustomed to using and G-W course resources in one convenient location—your LMS.

G-W Common Cartridge provides a complete learning package for you and your students. The included digital resources help your students remain engaged and learn effectively:

- **Digital Textbook**
- **Drill and Practice** vocabulary activities

When you incorporate G-W content into your courses via Common Cartridge, you have the flexibility to customize and structure the content to meet the educational needs of your students. You may also choose to add your own content to the course.

For instructors, the Common Cartridge includes the Online Instructor Resources. QTI® question banks are available within the Online Instructor Resources for import into your LMS. These prebuilt assessments help you measure student knowledge and track results in your LMS gradebook. Questions and tests can be customized to meet your assessment needs.

Online Instructor Resources

- The **Instructor Resources** provide instructors with time-saving preparation tools such as answer keys, editable lesson plans, and other teaching aids.
- **Instructor's Presentations for PowerPoint®** are fully customizable, richly illustrated slides that help you teach and visually reinforce the key concepts from each chapter.
- Administer and manage assessments to meet your classroom needs using **Assessment Software with Question Banks**, which include hundreds of matching, completion, multiple choice, and short answer questions to assess student knowledge of the content in each chapter.

See www.g-w.com/exploring-financial-literacy-2025 for a list of all available resources.

Professional Development

- Expert content specialists
- Research-based pedagogy and instructional practices
- Options for virtual and in-person Professional Development

Contents

CHAPTER 1 Planning: Your Financial Future Begins Here 1

CHAPTER 2 Earning: Wages from Your Job 15

CHAPTER 3 Budgeting: Using Your Money Wisely 42

CHAPTER 4 Banking and Checking: Managing Your Money 63

CHAPTER 5 Saving: Setting Aside Money for Your Future. 84

CHAPTER 6 Credit: Buy Now, Pay Later 103

CHAPTER 7 Insurance: Protecting Your Assets 132

CHAPTER 8 Education: Funding Your Future 157

CHAPTER 9 Loans and Leases: Paying for Cars and Housing 180

CHAPTER 10 Investing: Making Your Money Work for You 203

CHAPTER 11 Retirement and Estate Planning: Looking Toward Your Future. 236

Glossary 258
Index 264

CHAPTER 1

Planning: Your Financial Future Begins Here

Essential Question

What does it mean to plan for your financial future?

Learning Outcomes

When you complete Chapter 1, you will be able to:
- **1-1** Define financial literacy.
- **1-2** Summarize financial goals.
- **1-3** Discuss needs and wants.
- **1-4** Explain what it means to build wealth.

Key Terms

financial literacy
financial capability
financial plan
financial goal
need
want
value
priority
FOMO
wealth
net worth
asset
liability

Reading Prep

To *skim* is to glance through material quickly to get an overview. It is also known as *prereading*. Before reading this chapter, skim the text by reading the first sentence of each paragraph. Use this information to create an outline for the chapter before you read it.

What is Your Financial IQ?

Before reading this chapter, answer the following questions to see how much you already know about financial literacy.

1. What is financial literacy?
   _____
   _____

2. What is the purpose of a financial plan?
   _____
   _____

3. Name one of your financial goals.
   _____
   _____

4. How often do you spend money on things you really need?
   _____
   _____

5. How often do you spend money on things you want?
   _____
   _____

6. Name something you value.
   _____
   _____

7. What are your priorities?
   _____
   _____

8. What does it mean to be wealthy?
   _____
   _____

9. Is there anything you could give up spending money on now to begin saving money?
   _____
   _____

10. How do you save for something you want?
    _____
    _____

1-1 Financial Literacy

You, as a teen or young adult, have been using money for much of your life. Do you think about where your money goes or how you spend it? Do you think about saving it? You have a responsibility to use money wisely. You are accountable for your future.

An important key to your success will be financial literacy. **Financial literacy** is knowledge about basic topics related to finance, such as making, spending, and saving money. To succeed in a modern economy, you need to learn to make wise financial decisions at an early age. **Financial capability** is the ability to combine financial knowledge with the attitude, skills, and behaviors needed to use money wisely in a person's own life. Financial capability will help you lead a productive life and aid you in contributing positively to your community.

Creating a financial plan is the first step in planning your financial future. A **financial plan** is a set of goals for acquiring, saving, and spending money. The plan also includes actions or strategies for achieving the goals. Do you want to just "get by" and live from paycheck to paycheck or be free from financial worry? Will you leave your financial security up to chance or follow a plan? A financial plan helps you control your financial situation and achieve your goals.

> **FYI**
> According to the World Bank, approximately one in ten people worldwide live on less than $2 per day, and nearly half on less than $5.50 daily.

✅ Check Your Understanding

Why is it important to have a financial plan?

_____
_____
_____

Internet Connection

Money Tips for Teens

1. Using the Internet, research *money tips for teens*. Find and read two articles.
2. List the title and complete source information for each article.

   Article 1:
   _____
   _____

   Article 2:
   _____
   _____

3. On a separate sheet of paper, write a paragraph or bulleted list that summarizes the information contained in the articles.

1-2 Financial Goals

Financial goals are an important element of a financial plan. A *goal* is something a person works toward or strives to achieve. A **financial goal** is a measurable objective related to acquiring or spending money. Strategies for achieving your financial goals will be included in your financial plan. They can be short-term or long-term.

A financial *short-term goal* is an objective related to money that you want to achieve in six months or less. You may have simple short-term financial goals, such as buying a new video game or a gift for your friend's birthday. Other short-term financial goals might be to earn money and purchase new school clothes.

A financial *long-term goal* is an objective related to money that you want to achieve in the future. Long-term goals are generally set for six months or for several years. Your long-term financial goals might include saving for college, a car, or your first home.

A financial plan can help you think about how and when you want to achieve your goals. Most people do not have enough money to meet all their goals without creating a plan for using money. Suppose you have a goal of buying a car when you turn 16. If you wait until your birthday to try meeting your goal, you may not have enough money saved. However, if you create a plan, you can begin taking steps to meet this goal, such as getting a part-time job.

Financial literacy is having the ability to understand basic topics related to finance, such as making, spending, and saving money. *How would you describe your level of financial literacy?*

Blue Planet Earth/Shutterstock.com

Your financial goals will change throughout your life. Goals you set after your high school or college graduation may be quite different from the goals you will set after you start working and have a career. A financial plan is a work in progress and should be updated regularly as you meet goals and progress in your education and career.

✓ Check Your Understanding

Why is it important to set financial goals?

_____

_____

_____

_____

Dollars and Sense

SMART Goals

The first step in creating a financial plan is setting goals for acquiring, saving, and spending money. Well-defined financial goals follow the SMART goal model. SMART is an acronym for:
- specific
- measurable
- attainable
- relevant
- timely

Use the SMART goal model to set short-term and long-term financial goals. Creating SMART goals will help you make wise decisions and eventually reach financial security.

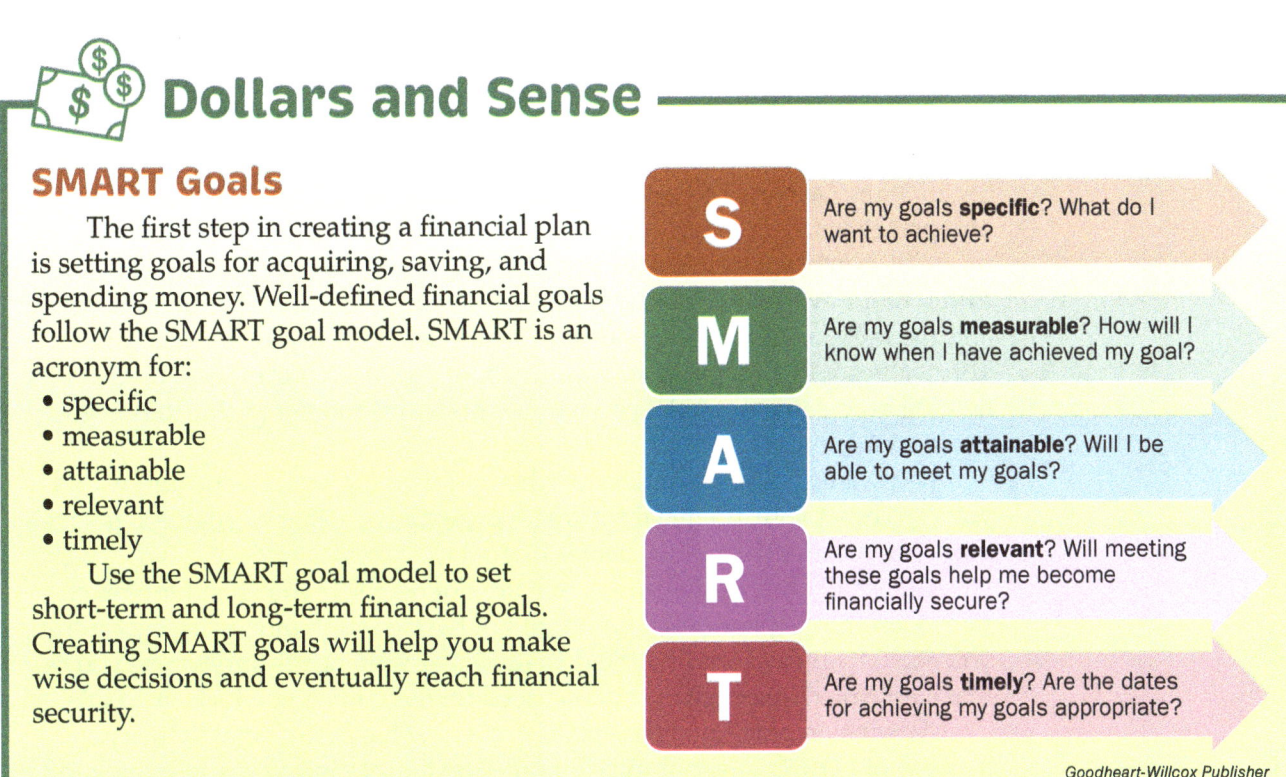

S — Are my goals **specific**? What do I want to achieve?

M — Are my goals **measurable**? How will I know when I have achieved my goal?

A — Are my goals **attainable**? Will I be able to meet my goals?

R — Are my goals **relevant**? Will meeting these goals help me become financially secure?

T — Are my goals **timely**? Are the dates for achieving my goals appropriate?

Goodheart-Willcox Publisher

1-3 Needs and Wants

Before you can set financial goals, you must determine your needs and wants. A **need** is something a person must have to survive. Examples are food, water, shelter, and clothing. One of your financial goals may be to have enough money to pay for your basic needs. In addition to needs, most people have many wants. A **want** is something a person desires but is not necessary for survival. Examples of wants include smartphones, cars, and designer clothes.

A financial long-term goal is something you want to achieve in the future, like traveling. *What financial long-term goals do you have for yourself?*

Sergey Novikov/Shutterstock.com

In many cases, wants are related to values. A **value** is a belief about ideas and principles a person thinks is important. For example, a value for you might be honesty. One for someone else might be trustworthiness. They are different for everyone. Have you thought about your values? Your experiences and the ideas and beliefs of your family and friends may affect your values. Your values will affect how you think about and use your money. If you value helping others, for example, you may want to give money to charities or to those who are in need.

By considering your values and then prioritizing your needs and wants, you can direct your financial future. A **priority** is a value or goal that is given more importance than other values or goals.

Almost all of us desire things that are not needs. If you spend too much money on things you want, you might not have enough money to pay for things you need. By understanding the difference between needs and wants, you can make informed, reasonable choices based on the money you have available.

Many never reach their financial goals or achieve financial security because of **FOMO**—fear of missing out. The temptation to spend money for things we don't really need to keep up with everyone else follows many people well into adulthood.

Check Your Understanding

What is the difference between needs and wants? How do values and FOMO play a role in determining which is which?

_____

_____

_____

Your Turn

Values and Goals

Before creating a financial plan, consider your values. Then, you can set realistic financial goals.

1. In the table that follows, list five values that are important to you. State how each value influences you in earning, saving, or spending money.

Value	Influence

2. Part of creating a financial plan is setting short-term and long-term goals. List five short-term goals you would like to achieve. Remember to consider your values when setting goals. State actions needed to achieve these goals and include the amount of money that may be necessary.

Short-Term Goals	Actions and Money Needed

3. List five long-term goals you would like to achieve. Remember to consider your values when setting goals. State actions needed to achieve these goals and include the amount of money that may be necessary.

Long-Term Goals	Actions and Money Needed

Are You Financially Responsible?

Needs and Wants: A Checklist

Do you ever think about what you really need and what you want? Use this checklist to help you consider your needs and wants.

	Yes	No	
1.	___	_X_	Do I need to buy designer clothes to feel accepted or fit in?
2.	___	_X_	Do I need to buy a car to get to school?
3.	___	_X_	Do I need to save money for college?
4.	___	_X_	Do I need to buy the latest streaming device?
5.	___	_X_	Do I need to go out for pizza every week with my friends?
6.	___	_X_	Do I have to borrow money to make it through the week?
7.	___	_X_	Do I need to buy the newest video games?
8.	___	_X_	Do I need to buy special sports equipment for my team?
9.	___	_X_	Do I need the newest smartphone?
10.	_X_	___	Have I experienced FOMO?

FYI: Liabilities, such as unpaid loans or credit card debt, reduce a person's net worth.

1-4 Building Wealth

Wealth, as it relates to finances, is a plentiful supply of money or valuable goods. A wealthy person may be called *prosperous* or *affluent*. A person who is wealthy should not have to worry about paying bills and meeting basic needs and is basically financially secure. However, even a wealthy person probably doesn't have enough money to buy everything desired. Very few people can buy everything they want.

As you begin a financial plan, you should understand the concept of net worth. **Net worth** is the difference between what is owned and what is owed. In order to build your wealth, you must own more than you owe. An **asset** is an item of value that is owned, such as a tablet computer or money in a savings account. A **liability** is a debt that is owed, like an unpaid bill. Net worth is found by listing all assets and then subtracting liabilities from the assets.

$$\text{assets} - \text{liabilities} = \text{net worth}$$

Consider the following example. If your total assets are $1,785 and your total liabilities are $968, what is your net worth?

Assets	$1,785.00
Liabilities	− 968.00
Net Worth	$817.00

You Do the Math | 1-1

If your total assets are $3,940 and your total liabilities are $1,232, what is your net worth?

Assets	_____
Liabilities	_____
Net Worth	_____

Where do you want to be financially in twenty or thirty years? Do you want to be on your way to becoming a millionaire, or already a millionaire? What determines if a person is a millionaire? Is it having $1 million or more in the bank? Not necessarily. An individual may have money in a bank and other assets that total $1 million or more. However, to be a millionaire, a person must have a *net worth* of $1 million or more, not just $1 million in assets. For example, if you own a house worth $1 million, does that make you a millionaire? Not if you have a $900,000 mortgage on it!

Many people who earn large salaries or make money from investments never become millionaires because they incur a large amount of debt or spend everything they make. Some highly paid sports stars, lottery winners, and famous actors end up broke in later years because they did not have a financial plan.

Building wealth is not as difficult as you may think. However, it does not happen overnight and is rarely a matter of luck. It requires careful planning and wise decision-making, and is possible even with a moderate income. Right now, you may not be thinking beyond going to college or getting your first job. However, teens and young adults have a great advantage in their ability to build wealth. That advantage is youth. *Time* is on your side.

FYI: Ideally, the older you are, the more your net worth should be. Your assets should increase while your liabilities decrease. A general guideline to strive for is as follows: 10% × your age × your annual income after taxes = your net worth.

 ## Check Your Understanding

How is it possible to have a large amount of assets but only a modest net worth?

_____
_____
_____

Your Turn

Net Worth

You probably have some assets. Perhaps you have a smartphone, cash, money in a savings account, jewelry, sports equipment, musical instruments, or other items of value. As part of your financial plan, first determine your net worth.

1. List the assets you own and the amount each one is worth. Be aware that many items you own are probably no longer worth their purchase prices. List an amount for which you could probably sell the item. List the amounts of money you have in cash or in bank accounts. Use an additional sheet of paper if you need more space for entries.

Assets	Amounts
	$
	$
	$
	$
	$
	$
	$
	$
Total Value of Assets	$

2. List any liabilities you have and the amount of each one. Use an additional sheet of paper if you need more space for entries.

Liabilities	Amounts
	$
	$
	$
	$
Total Amount of Liabilities	$

3. Subtract your total liabilities from your total assets to find your net worth.

Assets $ _____
Liabilities $ _____
Net Worth $ _____

Chapter 1 Review and Assessment

Summary

1-1 **Define financial literacy.**

Financial literacy is having the ability to understand basic topics related to finance, such as making, spending, and saving money.

1-2 **Summarize financial goals.**

A financial goal is a measurable objective related to acquiring or spending money. Financial goals can be short-term or long-term. A short-term goal is something you want to achieve in six months or less. A long-term goal is something you want to achieve in the future.

1-3 **Discuss needs and wants.**

A need is something a person must have to survive. A want is something a person desires but is not necessary for survival. In many cases, wants are related to values.

1-4 **Explain what it means to build wealth.**

Wealth is a plentiful supply of money or valuable goods. Someone who is wealthy has enough money to be financially secure.

Review Your Knowledge

Choose the correct answer for each of the following.

1. ____ What is financial literacy?
   A. a set of goals for acquiring, saving, and spending money
   B. the ability to understand basic topics related to finance, such as making, spending, and saving money
   C. a plentiful supply of money or valuable goods
   D. having enough money for your basic needs and modest wants without work being a necessity

2. ____ Having a ____ helps you be in control of your financial situation and achieve your goals.
   A. priority
   B. net worth
   C. financial independence
   D. financial plan

3. ____ Which of the following is an example of a short-term financial goal?
   A. I want to buy a house in ten years.
   B. I want to save as much money as possible.
   C. I want to buy a guitar in six months.
   D. I want to retire at 50.

4. ____ Which of the following is an example of a long-term financial goal?
   A. I want to spend next week's allowance at the mall.
   B. I want to save as much money as possible.
   C. I want to buy a guitar in six months.
   D. I want to save $4,000 before starting college in two years.
5. ____ Which of the following is a need?
   A. shelter
   B. designer clothes
   C. television
   D. smartphone
6. ____ What is a want?
   A. something essential for living
   B. an expense
   C. something important to an individual
   D. something someone would like to have but does not need to live
7. ____ A ____ is a value or goal that is given more importance than other values or goals.
   A. short-term goal
   B. long-term goal
   C. priority
   D. trade-off
8. ____ What is wealth?
   A. the difference between what is owned and what is owed
   B. a plentiful supply of money or valuable goods
   C. the value of the option you give up when you make one choice over another
   D. when a certain value or goal is given more importance than other values or goals
9. ____ Net worth is the difference between ____ and ____.
   A. assets, wealth
   B. priorities, assets
   C. assets, liabilities
   D. liabilities, wealth
10. ____ The desire to have what everyone else has is called ____.
    A. needs
    B. values
    C. FOMO
    D. wealth

Build Your Vocabulary

For each word or term, write the correct definition using your own words.

11. financial literacy

   _____

   _____

12. short-term goal

   _____

   _____

13. long-term goal

14. need

15. want

16. value

17. priority

18. net worth

19. asset

20. liability

Apply Your Math Skills

Calculate the answers to the following problems. Show your calculations.

21. You own a laptop worth $500 and have $250 in a savings account. What are your total assets?

22. You need to pay $39.99 for your monthly cell phone bill. You also owe your friend $10. What are your total liabilities?

23. Use the amounts of total assets and total liabilities from the previous questions to calculate your net worth.

24. If your assets total $2,648 and your liabilities total $720, what is your net worth?

25. If your assets total $12,365 and your liabilities total $6,924, what is your net worth?

CHAPTER

Earning: Wages from Your Job

Essential Question
Why is it important to understand how pay is calculated?

Learning Outcomes
When you complete Chapter 2, you will be able to:
- **2-1** Calculate gross pay.
- **2-2** Calculate amounts for mandatory deductions and determine net pay.
- **2-3** Identify voluntary deductions.
- **2-4** List examples of employee benefits.

Key Terms
wage	federal income taxes	net pay
gross pay	allowance	direct deposit
time sheet	Social Security	retirement account
overtime wage	Medicare	insurance
salary	state income taxes	charitable contribution
deduction	local income taxes	employee benefit

Reading Prep
Before reading this chapter, read the list of key terms. What clues do these terms provide about the topics you will study?

What is Your Financial IQ?

Before reading this chapter, answer the following questions to see how much you already know about earnings.

1. Why should you check to see if your pay is calculated correctly?
   _____
   _____

2. What is the difference between a wage and a salary?
   _____
   _____

3. How many hours must a person work per week before the overtime rate is paid?
   _____
   _____

4. Why are federal, state, and local income taxes deducted from a person's pay?
   _____
   _____

5. Why are Social Security and Medicare taxes deducted from a person's pay?
   _____
   _____

6. What is the difference between gross pay and net pay?
   _____
   _____

7. Does your state government collect income taxes from wages?
   _____
   _____

8. Would it be advantageous to live in a state that does *not* collect income taxes? Why or why not?
   _____
   _____

9. Name a service funded by state, local, or federal tax dollars.
   _____
   _____

10. Why do employers offer benefits to their employees?
    _____
    _____

2-1 Earnings

There is a great feeling that comes with getting your first job and earning your own money. All your efforts and hard work to find a job have finally been rewarded! You may already have done baby-sitting or yard work to earn some money and have had that experience. Earning money is a step toward financial security. Although the term *paycheck* is still widely used, you're not likely to receive a paper check. Earnings will probably be deposited in your bank or onto a debit card issued by the company if you don't have a bank account.

How do you know if your employer has given you the correct amount of pay for your work? Do you take for granted that the amount is accurate? It is important that you learn how to verify the pay you are getting is the correct amount.

> **FYI**
> Know how to calculate your gross and net pay. You should be able to check it online or on paper.

Wages

If you are working while you are in school, you are probably being paid an hourly wage. A **wage** is a dollar amount paid per hour worked. Employers are required by law to pay workers a minimum wage with certain exceptions, such as servers who receive tips. Visit the US Department of Labor website to check your state's minimum wage.

The amount you earn is not the amount you will receive. Taxes will reduce the amount of your pay. The total amount of earnings is called **gross pay**. Gross pay is also known as *gross earnings* or *gross wages*. To calculate gross pay, multiply the hourly wage by the number of hours worked.

hourly wage × hours worked = gross pay

For example, a local restaurant offers summer employment paying $10.50 per hour. If you work 23 hours in one week, how much will you earn? Always round to the nearest cent.

Hourly wage	$10.50
Number of hours worked	× 23
Gross pay	$241.50

You Do the Math | 2-1

You worked 17.5 hours in a week. Your wage is $11.25 per hour. What is your gross pay for the week?

Hourly wage	11.25
Number of hours worked	17.5
Gross pay	196.88

✓ Check Your Understanding

What is the formula for calculating gross pay?

_____
_____
_____

Employers must follow US Department of Labor rules when hiring teens. The basic rules of the Fair Labor Standards Act (FLSA) allow teens who are 14 or 15 years old to work a total of 3 hours per day and 18 hours per week during school weeks unless enrolled in a work experience or career exploration program. During non-school weeks, teens in this age group can work a total of 8 hours per day and 40 hours per week. The FLSA does not limit the number of hours or times of day for workers 16 years and older. Each state may have additional rules for teens, so check online to see if your state is more restrictive. A **time sheet** is a record of the time work began, the time work ended, and any breaks taken. An example of a time sheet is shown in Figure 2-1. An employer may require you to fill out a time sheet, but it's more likely you will record this automatically from your phone or on a register if you work in a store or a restaurant. Keep track of the hours you work on your phone or by hand to make sure you are paid for the correct number of hours worked.

Figure 2-1 This is an example of a typical time sheet. *Why might you want to keep a record of your hours worked when you begin working?*

TIME SHEET

Week Ending	3/6/--		Name	Maria Diaz	
Day	Date	Time In	Time Out	Less Lunch or Breaks	Hours Worked
Sunday	2/28/--				
Monday	3/1/--	4:00 p.m.	6:45 p.m.	.25	2.5
Tuesday	3/2/--	3:45 p.m.	7:00 p.m.	.25	3.0
Wednesday	3/3/--	4:30 p.m.	6:30 p.m.	0	2.0
Thursday	3/4/--	4:00 p.m.	7:30 p.m.	.5	3.0
Friday	3/5/--	3:45 p.m.	6:30 p.m.	.25	2.5
Saturday	3/6/--	10:30 a.m.	4:00 p.m.	1.00	4.5
Weekly Total Hours					17.5

Goodheart-Willcox Publisher

Your Turn

Time Sheet

Complete the following time sheet and calculate total hours worked. Use the week ended October 16 of the current year.

Monday: Arrive 3:30 p.m., break for 15 minutes at 6:00 p.m., leave at 8:15 p.m.
Thursday: Arrive 4:00 p.m., no break, leave at 7:30 p.m.
Saturday: Arrive 10:00 a.m., lunch break for 30 minutes, afternoon break for 15 minutes, leave at 6:45 p.m.

TIME SHEET

Week Ending			Name		
Day	Date	Time In	Time Out	Less Lunch or Breaks	Hours Worked
Sunday					
Monday		3:30 PM	8:15 PM	15	4.5
Tuesday					
Wednesday					
Thursday		4:00 PM	7:30 PM		3.5
Friday					
Saturday		10:00 AM	6:45 PM	45	8
Weekly Total Hours					16

Overtime

Forty hours a week is considered a standard workweek. If you work more than 40 hours in a week, you will probably earn overtime wages. An **overtime wage** is the amount paid for working more than 40 hours. The standard overtime hourly wage is 1.5 times the hourly rate.

Hourly wage × 1.5 = hourly overtime wage

> **FYI** Some employers pay an overtime wage of double the hourly wage for hours worked on holidays or in other special situations.

For example, you earn $12.70 an hour. If you work more than 40 hours in one week, what is your hourly overtime wage?

Hourly wage	$12.70
Times 1.5	× 1.5
Hourly overtime wage	$19.05

Your overtime wage is $19.05 per hour for each hour you work over normal hours.

You Do the Math | 2-2

You earn $11.90 per hour. If you work more than 40 hours in one week, what is your hourly overtime wage?

Hourly wage	_____
Times 1.5	_____
Hourly overtime wage	_____

To calculate gross pay for the week, add your regular pay for the 40 hours to your overtime pay. For example, your hourly wage is $9.80. In one week, you work 43 hours. What is your gross pay?

Step 1. Calculate regular earnings.

Hourly wage	$9.80
Regular hours worked	× 40
Regular weekly wages	$392.00

Step 2. Calculate the hourly overtime wage.

Hourly wage	$9.80
Times 1.5	× 1.5
Hourly overtime wage	$14.70

Step 3. Calculate overtime wages.

Hourly overtime wage	$14.70
Overtime hours	× 3
Overtime wages	$44.10

Step 4. Calculate gross earnings.

Regular earnings	$392.00
Overtime earnings	+ $44.10
Gross pay	$436.10

Chapter 2 Earning: Wages from Your Job   21

You Do the Math | 2-3

You earn $11.75 per hour. In one week, you worked 45 hours. What is your gross pay?

Step 1. Calculate regular earnings.

    Hourly wage   _____

    Regular hours worked   _____

    Regular weekly wages   _____

Step 2. Calculate the hourly overtime wage.

    Hourly wage   _____

    Times 1.5   _____

    Hourly overtime wage   _____

Step 3. Calculate overtime wages.

    Hourly overtime wage   _____

    Overtime hours   _____

    Overtime wages   _____

Step 4. Calculate gross earnings.

    Regular earnings   _____

    Overtime earnings   _____

    Gross pay   _____

✓ Check Your Understanding

How is gross pay calculated when you work more than 40 hours in one week?

_____

_____

_____

_____

Tips

In some jobs, you can expect to earn tips as a part of your income. A *tip* is money given to a worker in addition to the cost of the service provided. It is also called a *gratuity*. People who earn tips are typically paid a smaller hourly rate because of the tips they are expected to receive. An example is restaurant servers. Other examples of employees who receive tips are hairstylists and cab drivers.

Tips are often given in cash. However, businesses that accept credit or debit cards allow customers to add tips to their electronic payments instead of leaving cash. The business then automatically includes those tips as part of the employee's gross pay for that week.

FYI
Tips are calculated by the customer based on a percentage of the bill. It is customary to tip 15 to 20 percent based on the quality of service.

For example, you work as a server in a restaurant. You earn $8.25 per hour plus tips. If you work 18 hours in a week and earn $43.40 in tips, what is your gross pay?

Hourly wage	$8.25
Hours worked	× 18
Wages	$148.50
Tips	+ $43.40
Gross pay	$191.90

You Do the Math | 2-4

You worked 23 hours in a week as a server in a restaurant. You earn wages of $8.90 per hour and $63.20 in tips. What is your gross pay?

Hourly wage	_____
Hours worked	_____
Wages	_____
Tips	_____
Gross pay	_____

✓ Check Your Understanding

Why might employees who earn tips not receive minimum wage?

_____
_____
_____
_____

Salaries

Employees in some jobs are paid a salary rather than hourly wages. A **salary** is payment for work expressed as a fixed annual figure. Employees who are paid a salary are not typically paid for any overtime hours they work.

A salary is not paid in one lump sum but may be paid weekly, biweekly (every two weeks), semimonthly (twice per month), or monthly. To calculate gross pay for each pay period, divide the annual salary by the number of payments per year.

annual salary ÷ 52 payments = weekly gross pay
annual salary ÷ 26 payments = biweekly gross pay
annual salary ÷ 24 payments = semimonthly gross pay
annual salary ÷ 12 payments = monthly gross pay

Assume you have been offered a job with an annual salary of $63,950. You will be paid weekly. What is your gross pay each week?

Annual salary	$63,950.00
Number of payments	÷ 52
Weekly gross pay	$1,229.81

You Do the Math | 2-5

You are offered an annual salary of $73,600.00. You will be paid biweekly. What your gross pay each pay period?

Annual salary	_____
Number of payments	_____
Biweekly gross pay	_____

Check Your Understanding

What is the formula for determining monthly pay if you earn an annual salary? Weekly? Biweekly? Semimonthly?

_____

_____

_____

Internet Connection

Salaries

1. Visit a job-search website such as Monster, Indeed, or ZipRecruiter. Use the website's search function to find available positions in your city or state.
2. Select five job postings that state an annual salary. Determine the monthly, semimonthly, biweekly, and weekly gross pay for each one.

Position	Annual Salary	Monthly Gross Pay	Semimonthly Gross Pay	Biweekly Gross Pay	Weekly Gross Pay

2-2 Mandatory Deductions

Lisa F. Young/Shutterstock.com

Employers must follow US Department of Labor rules when hiring teens.

Why would the government set rules for the number of hours a young person can work?

If you have a job, you may be surprised to see how much is deducted from your pay before you receive it. A **deduction** is an amount subtracted from gross pay. Some deductions are *mandatory*, or *required*. Federal income taxes, Social Security taxes, and Medicare taxes are examples.

Federal Income Taxes

A *tax* is a financial charge or levy that individuals and some organizations pay to fund the services of a government. **Federal income taxes** are taxes on income collected by the US government. These taxes are used to provide for national security and many projects such as interstate highways and grants for education.

The Internal Revenue Service (IRS) provides tax tables for employers. Tax tables are used to determine the amount to be deducted from an employee's pay. Examples of these tables are shown in Figure 2-2. Tax tables are updated each year, and increase as your income level increases. Deducting taxes directly from gross pay eases the burden for taxpayers, preventing the need to pay a large sum to federal and state governments at tax time. Not paying taxes, or paying late, may result in hefty fines and penalties.

The amount deducted from gross pay for federal income tax is determined by a person's earnings, marital status, and any withholding allowances claimed. An **allowance** is a condition for which a person qualifies, reducing the amount of income taxes withheld. An allowance is also called an

Excerpts from Federal Withholding Tables

Wage Bracket Method Tables for Income Tax Withholding
MARRIED Persons—WEEKLY Payroll Period
(For wages paid through December 31, 20–)

If the wages are—		And the number of allowances is—					
At least	But less than	0	1	2	3	4	5
		The amount of income tax to be withheld is—					
$290	$300	$5	$0	$0	$0	$0	$0
$300	$310	$6	$0	$0	$0	$0	$0
$310	$320	$7	$0	$0	$0	$0	$0
$320	$330	$8	$0	$0	$0	$0	$0
$330	$340	$9	$0	$0	$0	$0	$0
$340	$350	$10	$1	$0	$0	$0	$0
$350	$360	$11	$2	$0	$0	$0	$0
$360	$370	$12	$3	$0	$0	$0	$0
$370	$380	$13	$4	$0	$0	$0	$0
$380	$390	$14	$5	$0	$0	$0	$0
$390	$400	$15	$6	$0	$0	$0	$0
$400	$410	$16	$7	$0	$0	$0	$0
$410	$420	$17	$8	$0	$0	$0	$0
$420	$430	$18	$9	$1	$0	$0	$0
$430	$440	$19	$10	$2	$0	$0	$0
$440	$450	$20	$11	$3	$0	$0	$0
$450	$460	$21	$12	$4	$0	$0	$0
$460	$470	$22	$13	$5	$0	$0	$0
$470	$480	$23	$14	$6	$0	$0	$0
$480	$490	$24	$15	$7	$0	$0	$0
$490	$500	$25	$16	$8	$0	$0	$0
$500	$510	$26	$17	$9	$1	$0	$0
$510	$520	$27	$18	$10	$2	$0	$0
$520	$530	$28	$19	$11	$3	$0	$0
$530	$540	$29	$20	$12	$4	$0	$0

Wage Bracket Method Tables for Income Tax Withholding
SINGLE Persons—WEEKLY Payroll Period
(For wages paid through December 31, 20–)

If the wages are—		And the number of allowances is—					
At least	But less than	0	1	2	3	4	5
		The amount of income tax to be withheld is—					
$125	$135	$5	$0	$0	$0	$0	$0
$135	$145	$6	$0	$0	$0	$0	$0
$145	$155	$7	$0	$0	$0	$0	$0
$155	$165	$8	$0	$0	$0	$0	$0
$165	$175	$9	$0	$0	$0	$0	$0
$175	$185	$10	$1	$0	$0	$0	$0
$185	$195	$11	$2	$0	$0	$0	$0
$195	$205	$12	$3	$0	$0	$0	$0
$205	$215	$13	$4	$0	$0	$0	$0
$215	$225	$14	$5	$0	$0	$0	$0
$225	$235	$15	$6	$0	$0	$0	$0
$235	$245	$16	$7	$0	$0	$0	$0
$245	$255	$17	$8	$0	$0	$0	$0
$255	$265	$18	$9	$1	$0	$0	$0
$265	$275	$19	$10	$2	$0	$0	$0
$275	$285	$20	$11	$3	$0	$0	$0
$285	$300	$21	$13	$4	$0	$0	$0
$300	$315	$23	$14	$6	$0	$0	$0
$315	$330	$25	$16	$7	$0	$0	$0
$330	$345	$27	$17	$9	$1	$0	$0
$345	$360	$28	$19	$10	$2	$0	$0
$360	$375	$30	$20	$12	$4	$0	$0
$375	$390	$32	$22	$13	$5	$0	$0
$390	$405	$34	$24	$15	$7	$0	$0
$405	$420	$36	$26	$16	$8	$0	$0

Goodheart-Willcox Publisher; Source: Department of the Treasury, Internal Revenue Service

Figure 2-2 These tables show excerpts from federal tax tables. *Why do you think tax tables are updated every year?*

exemption. For example, people for whom you are financially responsible, such as children, will qualify you for an allowance. Your parents or guardians probably claim you as an allowance.

Allowances are claimed on a *Form W-4 Employee's Withholding Allowance Certificate* tax document, which is shown in Figure 2-3. You will complete this form for your employer when you begin a new job. The form has a worksheet that will help identify allowances. The fewer allowances you claim, the more taxes will be deducted from your gross pay. Some people claim zero allowances, allowing them to get a larger tax refund when they file their income tax return. As a student, you will probably claim one or zero allowances.

Assume you earn $135 per week at your part-time job. You are single and claim zero allowances. How much will be withheld from your pay for federal income taxes?

Step 1. Use the tax table for single persons provided in Figure 2-2.
Step 2. Find $135. The column heads show "At least $135 But less than $145."
Step 3. Find the column for zero (0) allowances.
Step 4. The amount of tax is $6.

You Do the Math | 2-6

Your gross pay is $187.65. You are single and claim zero allowances. How much will be withheld from your pay for federal income tax?

Step 1. Use the tax table for _____ persons.
Step 2. Find the column needed for $187.65. The column heads show "At least _____ But less than _____."
Step 3. Find the column for _____ allowances.
Step 4. The amount of tax is _____.

Figure 2-3 Employees should complete a Form W-4 when starting a new job. As a single teen, you would only be required to fill out Step 1 and Step 5. *Why do you think someone might choose to have more money withheld by the federal government?*

✓ Check Your Understanding

For what purposes are federal income taxes used?

___

Your Turn

Federal Income Taxes

Using the tax tables shown in Figure 2-2, find weekly withholding for federal income tax for each employee.

Employee Number	Marital Status	Weekly Gross Pay	Number of Allowances	Federal Income Tax
1	M	$511.70	2	
2	S	341.35	0	
3	M	598.40	3	
4	M	609.00	5	
5	S	382.50	1	

FYI
The first monthly Social Security payment of $22.54 was issued in 1940. The average monthly payment in 2023 was around $1,827.

Social Security Taxes

Social Security is a social insurance program operated by the US government that provides income for individuals whose earnings are reduced or stopped because of retirement, disability, or death. The program was created under the *Federal Insurance Contribution Act (FICA)*. You will begin paying these taxes when you start working. Social Security taxes are deducted from your pay to help fund the payments you may receive if you retire or become disabled.

The current rules for Social Security state that people who were born after 1960 reach full retirement at age 67. However, you may receive reduced benefits beginning at age 62. The longer you wait to claim benefits, the larger the monthly payment will be. Rules may change by the time you qualify. Current information can be found on the Social Security Administration's website (www.ssa.gov).

Social Security tax is calculated as a percentage of your gross pay. Your employer will match the amount deducted from your gross pay. In 2023, the rate was 6.2 percent of your gross pay up to $160,200, but this increases each year. If you are self-employed, you will be required to pay both shares of Social

Security taxes, or 12.4 percent. The formula for calculating Social Security tax is as follows.

gross pay × Social Security tax rate = Social Security tax

For example, your gross pay is $135. How much will be withheld for Social Security?

Gross pay	$135.00
Social Security tax rate	× .062
Social Security tax withheld	$8.37
Social Security matched by employer	$8.37

You Do the Math | 2-7

How much will be withheld for Social Security on earnings of $187.65?

Gross pay	_____
Social Security tax rate	_____
Social Security tax withheld	_____
Social Security matched by employer	_____

✓ Check Your Understanding

Why are Social Security taxes deducted from your pay?

_____
_____
_____

Medicare Taxes

Medicare is a federal program that pays for certain healthcare expenses for older citizens and those with disabilities. It is funded by payroll taxes deducted from workers' gross pay. Medicare and Social Security taxes together are known as *FICA taxes*. Medicare should not be confused with *Medicaid, CHIP* (Children's Health Insurance Program), or *SNAP* (Supplemental Nutrition Assistance Program), which are government programs designed for low-income families or those with disabilities and are not funded through payroll taxes. These social programs may be beneficial if you temporarily lose your job and/or your health insurance.

Medicare tax is calculated as a percentage of your gross pay. As with Social Security, your employer matches the amount that is deducted from your gross pay. In 2022, the rate was 1.45 percent. There is no limit on wages that are taxed for Medicare. There will likely be some changes in the tax rate and both programs during your lifetime. The formula for calculating Medicare tax is as follows.

gross pay × Medicare tax rate = Medicare tax

FYI As with Social Security taxes, your employer pays Medicare taxes for you equal to the amount you pay.

For example, your gross pay is $135. How much will be withheld for Medicare?

Gross pay	$135.00
Medicare tax rate	× .0145
Medicare tax withheld	$1.96
Medicare matched by employer	$1.96

You Do the Math | 2-8

How much will be withheld for Medicare on earnings of $187.65?

Gross pay	_____
Medicare tax rate	_____
Medicare tax withheld	_____
Medicare matched by employer	_____

✓ Check Your Understanding

For what purposes are Medicare taxes used and how is Medicare different from Medicaid?

_____
_____
_____

State and local taxes are deducted from a worker's paycheck to pay for services such as education. *How is the money collected from taxes used in your community?*

Diego Cervo/Shutterstock.com

State Income Taxes

State income taxes are taxes on income collected by a state government. The taxes are used to pay for services such as roads and education. Employers may use a percentage or a tax table to determine the amount of state taxes to withhold for employees. Tax tables vary by state. In the following examples, a percentage is used to calculate state taxes. The formula for calculating state income tax is as follows.

$$\text{gross pay} \times \text{state tax rate} = \text{state income tax}$$

For example, your gross pay is $135. Your state income tax rate is 3 percent. How much will be withheld for state taxes?

Gross pay	$135.00
State income tax rate	× .03
State income tax withheld	$4.05

You Do the Math | 2-9

Your gross pay is $187.65. Your state income tax rate is 6 percent. How much will be withheld for state income tax?

Gross pay	_____
State income tax rate	_____
State income tax withheld	_____

Check Your Understanding

For what purposes are state income taxes used?

_____
_____

Internet Connection

State Income Taxes

1. Conduct an Internet search for *states that collect income tax*.
2. In the table that follows, list five states that *do* collect state income taxes in Column 1. List five states that *do not* collect state income taxes in Column 2.

5 States That Collect Income Tax	5 States That Do Not Collect Income Tax

continued

Internet Connection (continued)

3. Look up your state to check if it collects income taxes. If so, record the percentage or state if tax tables are used.

_____
_____
_____

> **FYI**
> When you file yearly tax returns, you may get back some or all of the amounts withheld from your pay for federal and state taxes. You will not receive any refunds for Social Security or Medicare taxes.

Local Income Taxes

Local income taxes are taxes on income collected by a local government, such as a county or city. Local taxes collected are used for police departments, schools, county or city roads, libraries, recreational facilities, and other services. These taxes are a percentage of gross pay. Typical amounts are from 0.5 percent to 2 percent of gross pay. You may be required to pay more than one local tax (such as city and county). The formula for calculating local income tax is as follows.

gross pay × local tax rate = local income tax

For example, your gross pay is $135. The local income tax rate is 1.5 percent. How much will be withheld for local income tax?

Gross pay	$135.00
Local income tax rate	× .015
Local income tax withheld	$2.03

You Do the Math | 2-10

Your gross pay is $187.65. The local income tax rate is 0.75 percent. How much will be withheld for local income tax?

Gross pay _____
Local income tax rate _____
Local income tax withheld _____

✓ Check Your Understanding

For what purposes are local income taxes used?

_____
_____
_____

Net Pay

Net pay is gross pay minus payroll deductions. This is the amount that will be directly deposited into your bank or onto a debit card. The formula for calculating net pay is as follows.

gross pay − total deductions = net pay

The following example shows how to calculate net pay. Assume mandatory deductions are as follows: $6.00 for federal income tax; $8.37 for Social Security tax; $1.96 for Medicare tax; $4.05 for state income tax; and $2.03 for local income tax.

Gross pay		$135.00
Federal income tax	$6.00	
Social Security tax	8.37	
Medicare tax	1.96	
State income tax	4.05	
Local income tax	2.03	
Total deductions		− 22.41
Net pay		$112.59

> **FYI**
> Unemployment taxes are paid by employers to help provide benefits for workers who are laid off. There should *never* be a deduction from your paycheck for unemployment taxes.

You Do the Math | 2-11

Your gross pay is $187.65. Your mandatory deductions are as follows: $11.00 for federal income tax; $11.63 for Social Security tax; $2.72 for Medicare tax; $11.26 for state income tax; and $1.41 for local income tax. Calculate your net pay.

Gross pay		_____
Federal income tax	_____	
Social Security tax	_____	
Medicare tax	_____	
State income tax	_____	
Local income tax	_____	
Total deductions		_____
Net pay		_____

✓ Check Your Understanding

How is net pay calculated?

_____
_____
_____

Figure 2-4 A pay slip shows gross pay, deductions, and net pay. *Can you think of reasons to maintain a record of your earnings and deductions?*

Pay Slip

JAKE'S SKATEBOARDS
82 HUDSON HOLLOW ROAD
FRANKFORT, KY 40601-0082

EARNINGS STATEMENT

Employee Information
Joe Park
225 West Second Street
Frankfort, KY 40601-0225

Social Security Number
123-45-6789

Pay Period
4/09/-- to 4/20/--

Pay Date
4/27/--

Rate	Hours	Gross Pay	Deductions	Total	YTD Total
$11.50	30	$345.00	Federal tax	$18.06	$444.16
			State tax	$13.80	$339.38
			Social Security tax	$21.39	$526.04
			Medicare tax	$5.00	$123.03
YTD Gross Pay	**YTD Deductions**	**YTD Net Pay**	**Total**	**Deductions**	**Net Pay**
$8,484.50	$1,432.61	$7,051.89	$345.00	$58.25	$286.75

Goodheart-Willcox Publisher

You should be able to go online or on your phone to pull up information (sometimes labeled a *pay slip* or *pay stub*) from each pay period showing gross pay, deductions and net pay that looks similar to Figure 2-4. It may be emailed to you and may include year-to-date figures. The phrase *year-to-date* indicates the totals of your pay and deductions since the beginning of the year. Keep in mind if you collect tips, those tips are added to gross pay and therefore, subject to all taxes.

Your employer will ask for your bank information to use direct deposit. **Direct deposit** is a transfer of net pay to a checking or savings account. If you do not have a bank account, your net pay will be deposited to a debit card you can use to make purchases. (More about how debit cards work in Chapter 4.)

Dollars and Sense

Using Direct Deposit or Debit Cards

Most employers offer or require direct deposit for employees Some governmental payments, such as for Social Security, are also made by direct deposit.

Why Use Direct Deposit?

Employers save time and money by not having to issue individual paper checks. Your money is quickly credited to your account when your employer issues the deposit, allowing you immediate access to your money.

How Do You Set Up Direct Deposit?

The process for setting up direct deposit is easy. Your employer will provide a form to complete showing your account number and the bank's routing number.

How Do You Use Debit Cards?

Your employer will provide a card and instruct you on how to use it.

2-3 Voluntary Deductions

You may request that additional deductions be withheld from your pay. Some of these might be for retirement accounts; health, life, or disability insurance; or charitable contributions. These deductions may be a set amount or a percentage of your gross pay. Voluntary deductions should be deducted from gross pay only if the employee agrees in writing to have those deductions.

A **retirement account** is a personal investment account specifically set up to provide income during retirement, when a person is older and no longer employed. Money is deducted from your pay and put into these accounts through direct deposit. (See Chapter 11.)

Insurance is a service that is purchased to protect against financial loss. *Health insurance* protects against financial loss due to illnesses or injuries. It pays part or all the costs of medical bills. It is one of the most common types of voluntary deductions. Your employer may pay for part of your health insurance if you agree to pay the remainder. Your part of the insurance cost would be deducted from your gross pay. If you are offered health insurance through your employer, you generally will get a better policy at a lower cost with a group than you could on your own. Other types of insurance may also be deducted from your gross pay if you choose. These may include life, dental, vision, and disability insurance. (See Chapter 7.)

Many people believe it is important to give back and to act with social responsibility. *Social responsibility* is behaving with sensitivity to social, environmental, and economic issues. *Philanthropy* is the act of giving money, goods, or services to meet the needs of others. You might find that you want to support causes that are important to you by choosing to donate money. A **charitable contribution** is a donation of money or gifts to a nonprofit organization. For example, you might choose to give to a library, museum, church, or food pantry.

Your employer may collect and forward donations for selected organizations. If you choose to make regular donations, you may be able to have them deducted from your pay and sent to that organization.

When voluntary deductions are made, the amounts are totaled and subtracted from your gross pay. For example, assume your weekly gross pay is $617.85. You elect to put 10 percent of your gross pay into your retirement account. You also elect to donate $5 per pay period to a charity. Your portion of the cost for health insurance is $23 per pay period. What is the total amount of these voluntary deductions?

Gross pay	$617.85
Rate for retirement account	× .10
Retirement deduction	$61.79
Retirement deduction	$61.79
Health insurance	23.00
Contribution to charity	+ 5.00
Total voluntary deductions	$89.79

FYI: Andrew Carnegie, for whom Carnegie Hall is named, said, "It is more difficult to give money away intelligently than earn it in the first place."

FYI: Volunteering your time may be just as important as giving money to worthwhile causes. Many schools now require students to volunteer a number of hours during the school year. Some businesses even allow employees to have paid time off for volunteering.

You Do the Math | 2-12

Your monthly gross pay is $1,762.35. You elect to have 8 percent put into a retirement account. You also elect to donate $25 per pay period to a charity. Your portion of the cost for health insurance is $117.85 per pay period. What is the total amount of these voluntary deductions?

Gross pay	_____
Rate for retirement account	_____
Retirement deduction	_____
Retirement deduction	_____
Health insurance	_____
Contribution to charity	_____
Total voluntary deductions	_____

✓ Check Your Understanding

Explain voluntary deductions and list several examples.

_____
_____
_____

2-4 Employee Benefits

An **employee benefit** is a service or item of value employees receive from employers in addition to earnings. Employee benefits are also called *fringe benefits*. Benefits are offered to attract employees and encourage them to continue to work for a company.

When you are hired for your first job, ask if you are eligible for benefits. Some companies may only offer them to full-time employees. Examples of employee benefits include the following:

- **Paid time off.** Employers may offer sick days, vacation days, holidays, and personal days for their employees. Employees can take these days, with pay, when they follow company policies.
- **Gym memberships.** Most employers encourage employees to live a healthy lifestyle. Some companies will pay for gym memberships for employees or may have a gym facility available in their building.
- **Free beverages in the cafeteria.** Many employers provide free coffee, water, or other beverages in the break room or cafeteria. This can save an employee a lot of money over a year.

Each company offers different benefits to employees. However, companies are not required to provide them for workers. For those companies that do provide benefits, they can be a great incentive for employees to come to work every day.

Check Your Understanding

Why do employers offer benefits to their employees?

_____

_____

_____

Internet Connection

Federal Employment Forms

1. The first day of a new job will be spent completing necessary forms for your employment. Use the Internet to locate the following forms. Print a copy of each and practice completing the forms. Do not use your Social Security number. Use 123-45-6789 instead.
   A. The *Form I-9 Employment Eligibility Verification* is used to verify an employee's identity and authorization to work in the United States. Both citizens and noncitizens are required to complete this form.
   B. The *Form W-4 Employee's Withholding Allowance Certificate* tax document is used to claim allowances for tax withholding. The fewer allowances you claim, the more taxes will be deducted from your gross pay. As a student, you will probably claim one or zero allowances.
2. At the end of the year, your employer will provide you with a *Form W-2 Wage and Tax Statement* to use when filing income tax returns. This form summarizes all wages and deductions for the year for an individual employee. Use the Internet to locate a current example of this form.
   A. What information is contained on this form?

   _____

   _____

   _____

   B. How do you think this information can be useful?

   _____

   _____

   _____

Working from Home

Many employees now work from home without having to go into an office. Some worked completely offsite during the pandemic of 2020 and continue to do so. Even if an employee works away from the office, there may be times in-person attendance is mandatory for special meetings, meeting clients, travel, etc. Those who do both are sometimes called *hybrid employees*.

Of course, working from home will probably not be possible for teens. However, it may be an option for you in later years. Costs may be reduced for both you and your company, but you may also miss the interaction with fellow workers.

Check Your Understanding

What are the advantages and disadvantages of working from home?

_____

_____

_____

Are You Financially Responsible?

Verify Your Pay: A Checklist

When you start working, it is up to you to make sure you are being paid the correct amount and that your deductions are accurate. If you are currently employed, review your latest pay slip using this checklist. If you are not yet employed, it is especially important to review your first pay slip when you begin working or after a change in pay.

Yes	No	
1. ____	____	Is my name spelled correctly?
2. ____	____	Is my address accurate?
3. ____	____	Is my employee number accurate?
4. ____	____	Is the time period recorded correctly?
5. ____	____	Is the amount withheld for taxes reasonable considering the number of allowances I selected?
6. ____	____	Was I paid for the correct number of hours worked?
7. ____	____	Check the math. Is the net pay correct?
8. ____	____	Did I elect to have any voluntary deductions? If so, are they accurate?
9. ____	____	Are the year-to-date earnings correct?
10. ____	____	If my pay is deposited directly into my bank, is it noted accurately on the pay slip?

Chapter 2 Review and Assessment

Summary

2-1 Calculate gross pay.
To calculate gross pay, multiply the hourly wage by the number of hours worked. If you work more than 40 hours in a week, you will probably earn overtime wages. To calculate the gross pay for a salaried position, divide the annual salary by the number of payments per year.

2-2 Calculate amounts for mandatory deductions and calculate net pay.
Social Security, Medicare, and federal, state, and local income taxes are calculated as a percentage of gross pay. To calculate each type of tax, multiply the gross pay amount by the tax rate. The formula for calculating net pay is gross pay − total deductions = net pay.

2-3 Identify voluntary deductions.
Voluntary deductions are withheld from your pay as a set amount or a percentage of gross pay. These amounts may be for items such as insurance, a retirement plan, or charitable contributions.

2-4 List examples of employee benefits.
An employee benefit is a service or item of value employees receive from employers in addition to earnings. Examples include paid time off, gym memberships, and free beverages.

Review Your Knowledge

Choose the correct answer for each of the following.

1. ____ What is gross pay?
   A. the amount paid for working beyond the standard workweek
   B. the total amount of earnings minus payroll deductions
   C. the total amount of earnings
   D. a dollar amount paid per hour worked

2. ____ Most employers pay an overtime rate after you have worked ____ regular hours in a week.
   A. 30
   B. 35
   C. 40
   D. 45

3. ____ Which of the following is an example of a mandatory deduction?
   A. state income tax
   B. insurance premiums
   C. charitable contributions
   D. retirement contributions

Copyright Goodheart-Willcox Co., Inc.
May not be reproduced or posted to a publicly accessible website.

4. _____ What is Social Security?
   A. behaving with sensitivity to social, environmental, and economic issues
   B. a federal program that pays for certain healthcare expenses for older citizens and those with disabilities
   C. income provided by the US government for working beyond the standard workweek
   D. a social insurance program operated by the US government that provides income for individuals whose earnings are reduced or stopped because of retirement, disability, or death

5. _____ Net pay is _____.
   A. total wages earned
   B. the amount deposited in your bank or on a debit card
   C. Social Security wages
   D. Medicare wages

6. _____ Taxes on income collected by the US government are _____ income taxes.
   A. federal
   B. state
   C. local
   D. voluntary

7. _____ Which of the following is an example of a voluntary deduction?
   A. local income tax
   B. state income tax
   C. FICA taxes
   D. insurance premiums

8. _____ A personal investment account set up for use when a person is older and no longer employed is a(n) _____.
   A. insurance premium
   B. retirement account
   C. direct deposit
   D. allowance

9. _____ A(n) _____ is a donation of money or gifts to a nonprofit organization.
   A. charitable contribution
   B. gratuity
   C. allowance
   D. tip

10. _____ A(n) _____ is a service or item of value employees receive from employers in addition to earnings.
    A. overtime wage
    B. employee benefit
    C. deduction
    D. contribution

Build Your Vocabulary

For each word or term, write the correct definition using your own words.

11. wage

12. time sheet

13. salary

14. deduction

15. allowance

16. Medicare

17. state income taxes

18. local income taxes

19. direct deposit

20. insurance

Apply Your Math Skills

Calculate the answers to the following problems. Show your calculations.

21. You earn $10.75 per hour and worked 31 hours. What is your gross pay?

22. Your wages are $12.25 per hour. What is your hourly overtime wage?

23. You earn $11.85 per hour and worked 46 hours in a week. What is your gross pay?

24. You earn $7.95 per hour plus tips. If you work 26 hours this week and collect $26.35 in tips, what is your gross pay?

25. If your biweekly gross pay is $1,495.00, what is your annual salary?

26. You apply for a position that pays $62,000.00 annually. What would be your gross pay per week?

27. Your weekly gross pay is $264.24. You are single and claim zero allowances. How much will be withheld for federal income taxes? Use the tax tables shown in Figure 2-2.

28. Your gross pay is $568.93. How much is withheld for Social Security taxes if the tax rate is 6.2 percent?

29. Your gross pay is $683.47. How much is withheld for Medicare taxes if the tax rate is 1.45 percent?

30. Your state income tax rate is 6 percent. How much is withheld for state income taxes if your gross pay is $721.52?

31. The county in which you live has a local tax rate of 1.75 percent. How much is withheld if your gross pay is $311.89?

32. Your weekly gross pay is $792.50. You are married and claim one allowance. Use the tax tables shown in Figure 2-2 to determine the amount of federal income tax. In addition to federal income taxes, you must also pay 6.2 percent for Social Security taxes, 1.45 percent for Medicare taxes, and 4 percent for state income taxes. What is your net pay?

33. Your gross pay is $327.68. You want your employer to deduct 8 percent of your gross pay for your retirement account and $27 for a charitable contribution. What is the total amount of your voluntary deductions?

34. You earn $12.50 per hour and your friend earns $11.95 per hour. If you both work 22 hours this week, how much more than your friend will you earn?

35. You are offered a health insurance plan through your employer. The total cost per pay period is $465. You are required to pay 25 percent of the cost. How much will be deducted from your check for health insurance?

CHAPTER 3
Budgeting: Using Your Money Wisely

Essential Question
Why would you need to create a budget?

Learning Outcomes

When you complete Chapter 3, you will be able to:

- **3-1** Explain the purpose of a budget.
- **3-2** Discuss income.
- **3-3** Explain the difference between fixed and variable expenses.
- **3-4** Calculate discretionary income.
- **3-5** List steps to create a monthly budget.

Key Terms

budget
income
expense
pay yourself first
fixed expense
variable expense
discretionary income

Reading Prep

Before reading this chapter, review the table of contents for this text. As you read, consider how this chapter fits into the "bigger picture" presented by this text.

What is Your Financial IQ?

Before reading this chapter, answer the following questions to see how much you already know about budgeting.

1. What is a budget?

2. How do you think using a budget could help you manage your money?

3. How do you keep track of the money you receive?

4. How do you keep track of the money you spend in a typical day or week?

5. What is a charitable contribution?

6. What is a fixed expense?

7. What is a variable expense?

8. What does it mean to "pay yourself first" when managing your money?

9. What is discretionary income?

10. What steps are involved in creating a budget?

3-1 Budgets

After you learn some of the basics of financial planning, the next step toward your financial plan is to create a budget. What is a budget? A **budget** is a plan for the use of money based on goals, income, and expenses. It is an estimate of categories of expected income and expenses for a given period of time. A budget may be prepared for a week, month, or longer period such as a year. It is a useful tool that can help you keep track of your money and spend it wisely.

In chapter 1, you set short-term and long-term financial goals. They were based first on your values, then on your needs and wants. These goals will help guide you as you create your budget. Go back and look at the goals you set. Make sure they are appropriate so you can use them to create your budget.

✓ Check Your Understanding

What is the purpose of a budget?

_____
_____
_____

A budget is a plan for the use of money over time based on goals, income, and expenses. *Describe the system you use to keep track of money you earn and money you spend.*

Iakov Filimonov/Shutterstock.com

3-2 Income

When planning a budget, an important step is to estimate your income. **Income** is money received from any source, such as pay from a job, a birthday gift, or an allowance. You can estimate your income for a budget based on what you typically receive each month.

For example, Carlos tracked his last month's income, as shown in Figure 3-1. He will use this as an estimate for the budget he will create for next month.

To estimate your income, track the income you had last month and record the amount in a chart similar to the one shown in Figure 3-1. Write each source of income, such as job, yard work, or allowance. Then, total the amounts. This will serve as an estimate of your income when you create a budget for the next month.

As a teen, your income is probably not very high. However, after you graduate and begin a career, your income should increase. Learning to manage your income now will help you as you make more money in the future.

✓ Check Your Understanding

Explain how to estimate income.

_____

_____

_____

Monthly Income

Carlos Acosta For the Month of September, 20--	
Source	**Amount**
Part-time job	$585.00
Babysitting	35.00
Yard work for neighbors	45.00
Allowance	40.00
Gifts	25.00
Total Income	**$730.00**

Goodheart-Willcox Publisher

Figure 3-1 Carlos kept track of his income for a month using this table. *Explain why you think it is important to list each source of income separately.*

Your Turn

Tracking Your Income

Review your income from last month and record the amounts in this chart. Write categories for your income in the Source column and each amount in the Amount column. Total the Amount column.

Monthly Income

Name:	
For the month of:	
Source	**Amount**
Total Income	$

3-3 Expenses

After you have estimated your income, you are ready to estimate expenses. An **expense** is an amount paid for goods or services. Do you pay for your school lunches? Clothes? Your cell phone? Entertainment? These are examples of expenses. Examples of expenses for adults are mortgage or rent payments and car payments.

You probably do not have many expenses beyond those for your personal needs. However, when you graduate and go to college or begin a full-time job, you will find there will be many more expenses to consider. Rent, utilities, groceries, and other expenses will need to be tracked. Getting in the habit of tracking your spending now will help make it easier when your expenses are greater.

When creating a budget, do not forget to allow for savings as well as spending. The phrase **pay yourself first** means you should budget for savings *before* you budget for spending. If you do not plan to save money in your budget, you probably will not have money left over to save. Record savings as an expense to help you get into the routine of saving money every month.

You may also want to budget for charitable contributions. A **charitable contribution** is a donation of money or gifts to a nonprofit organization or private foundation. Making charitable contributions is often an act of social responsibility. **Social responsibility** is behaving with sensitivity to social, environmental, and economic issues. When deciding how much to give, look at your income and expenses to see what you can afford to contribute. Donations you make to a qualified charity in the form of both money and property are often tax deductible when you file your income taxes as an adult. You will need to keep proof of your donations to take advantage of this.

Be responsible in your giving. Research organizations before you make a donation. This is especially a good idea if you are donating online. Make sure contributions go to the cause, not into the pockets of those who run the charity.

> **FYI**
> While you are young, you may not have a lot of money to give. A donation of your time can be just as valuable to a charity as a monetary contribution. Community groups, animal shelters, elderly neighbors, food pantries, and other organizations often need volunteers. Make the most of those opportunities. Some may lead to a career later in life.

✓ Check Your Understanding

How does a charitable contribution demonstrate social responsibility?

_____
_____
_____

Internet Connection

Charities

1. Visit the Better Business Bureau website and perform an Internet search for *charitable contributions*.
2. Select three charities to which you might consider contributing. Record their names in the table.
3. Research how much of each dollar goes to the actual charity recipients or activities and how much goes to administrative expenses and salaries. Record this information in the table.

Charity	Percent to Charity	Percent to Administration

Categorizing Expenses

Expenses are categorized as either fixed or variable. A **fixed expense** stays the same each month, such as the amount paid for a monthly bus pass or a cell phone data package. Record savings as a fixed expense to help you get into the routine of saving money every month. Depending on your personal budget, you might also choose to categorize charitable contributions as a fixed expense.

Exploring Financial Literacy

A **variable expense** changes from month to month. Examples include amounts paid for school lunches, entertainment, and personal care items.

✓ Check Your Understanding

List two examples of fixed expenses and two examples of variable expenses that you may have during a month.

_____

_____

_____

Your Turn

Categorizing Expenses

Expenses can be fixed or variable. Think about the expenses listed in the table that follows. Decide whether each expense would be fixed or variable. Put an X in the appropriate column for each expense in the table.

Expense	Fixed	Variable
Bus pass for school		
Car insurance		
Cell phone plan		
Clothing		
Eating out with friends		
Gas for the car		
Gifts		
Personal care		
Haircuts		
Monthly gym membership dues		
Movie tickets		
Music downloads		
Other entertainment		
Savings		
School lunches		

Copyright Goodheart-Willcox Co., Inc.
May not be reproduced or posted to a publicly accessible website.

Tracking Expenses

Do you know where your money goes? If you are like many others, you spend money but do not always remember what you spent it on. If you want to build wealth and have a solid financial plan, start paying attention to how you spend your money. The best way to do this is to create a record of what you spend. If you track your spending for several days or weeks, you will get an idea of how much you should plan for expenses in your budget.

To create a weekly spending record, write the amounts you spend for fixed and variable expenses each day. Then, total the amounts for each day and for the week. An example of a weekly spending record for Carlos Acosta is shown in the following chart. This spending record is for the week ending September 10.

Weekly Spending Record

Carlos Acosta
For the week ending September 10, 20--

Amounts Spent	Day 1	Day 2	Day 3	Day 4	Day 5	Day 6	Day 7	Total
Fixed Expenses								
Bus fare to work		2.40		2.40		2.40		7.20
Savings deposit	20.00							20.00
Total Fixed Expenses	20.00	2.40	0.00	2.40	0.00	2.40	0.00	27.20
Variable Expenses								
School lunches	3.75	4.35	4.15	3.85	4.10			20.20
Birthday gift for sister						25.00		25.00
School music fee				22.00				22.00
Entertainment			17.65					17.65
Lunch with friends							14.45	14.45
New T-shirt							19.85	19.85
Total Variable Expenses	3.75	4.35	21.80	25.85	4.10	25.00	34.30	119.15
Total Expenses	23.75	6.75	21.80	28.25	4.10	27.40	34.30	146.35

You Do the Math | 3-1

The weekly spending record for Carlos Acosta for the week ending September 17 is shown in the chart that follows. How much has Carlos spent this week? Total the amounts for each day and for the week.

Weekly Spending Record

Carlos Acosta For the week ending September 17, 20--								
Amounts Spent								
	Day 1	Day 2	Day 3	Day 4	Day 5	Day 6	Day 7	Total
Fixed Expenses								
Bus fare to work		2.40	2.40	2.40				
Savings deposit	15.00							
Total Fixed Expenses	15.00	2.40	2.40	2.40	0.00	0.00	0.00	
Variable Expenses								
School lunches	4.00	3.85	4.75	3.70	3.95			
School workbook		27.60						
Entertainment	19.50							
Lunch with friends						13.40		
New shoes						53.70		
Total Variable Expenses	23.50	31.45	4.75	3.70	3.95	67.10	0.00	
Total Expenses								

Check Your Understanding

Explain how to create a weekly spending record.

_____
_____
_____

Your Turn

Tracking Your Spending

It is important to keep track of how you spend your money. Record your expenses from last week in this chart. You will need to write the categories for your expenses. Use a separate sheet of paper if you need more space for entries. Then, total the amounts for each day and for the week.

Weekly Spending Record

Name:								
For the week ending:								
	\multicolumn{8}{c}{Amounts Spent}
	Day 1	Day 2	Day 3	Day 4	Day 5	Day 6	Day 7	Total
Fixed Expenses								
Variable Expenses								
Total Expenses								

3-4 Discretionary Income

> **FYI**
> Money remaining after expenses are paid is also referred to as a *surplus*. When there is not enough income to pay all expenses, this is called a *deficit*. These terms are commonly used on news programs about government spending.

After you total your expenses and subtract the total from your income, hopefully you will have money left over. This extra money is called discretionary income. **Discretionary income** is money that remains after you have paid for regular or needed expenses. It is also called *disposable income*. This is money you can deposit in savings or use to plan for emergencies or leisure activities.

It is important to calculate your discretionary income each month. Doing so helps you know how much money you will have after all your expenses have been paid. If you do not track your income and expenses using a budget, you may find that you have no discretionary income. To calculate discretionary income, subtract your total fixed and variable expenses from your income.

income – fixed and variable expenses = discretionary income

For example, Carlos wants to calculate his discretionary income. His expenses for the week ending September 10 are $146.35. What will Carlos' monthly expenses be if he spends this amount every week? His monthly income shown in Figure 3-1 states that he has $730.00 in income. What will his discretionary income be?

Step 1. Calculate monthly expenses.

Weekly expenses	$146.35
Number of weeks	× 4
Total monthly expenses	$585.40

Step 2. Calculate discretionary income.

Monthly income	$730.00
Monthly expenses	– 585.40
Discretionary income	$144.60

Creating a budget includes estimating income as well as expenses. An expense is an amount paid for goods or services. *Why do you think a budget begins with estimated amounts?*

You Do the Math | 3-2

Carlos' weekly expenses during the following week ending September 17 were $156.65. What will Carlos' monthly expenses be if he spends this amount every week? His monthly income shown in Figure 3-1 states that he has $730.00 in income. What will his discretionary income be?

Step 1. Calculate monthly expenses.

Weekly expenses _____

Number of weeks _____

Total monthly expenses _____

Step 2. Calculate discretionary income.

Monthly income _____

Monthly expenses _____

Discretionary income _____

✓ Check Your Understanding

Why is it important to calculate your discretionary income each month?

_____
_____
_____
_____

3-5 Creating a Budget

After tracking spending for a few weeks, you will see a pattern. This pattern of spending will help you decide how much you need for entertainment, lunch, and other items you purchase during the week. It will also help you identify changes you want to make to your spending habits.

Once you have an idea of how much you need for specific items, you are ready to create a budget. A budget is a reminder to spend your money on things you really need or want. It helps in creating a financial plan because it forces you to think ahead about how you want to spend your money before you actually spend it.

To create a budget, follow these steps.
- Select a time period for the budget, such as one month.
- List the amounts of estimated income for the period and total them. These estimates will be based on actual income you had last month.
- List the estimated fixed and variable expenses for the period and total them. These estimates will be based on actual expenses you had last month.

- Subtract the total expenses from the total income to find discretionary income.

If the discretionary income amount is a negative number, reduce expenses.

There is no set format for a budget. The example in Figure 3-2 shows a budget for a typical teen.

When you have completed your budget, you have taken a big step in planning for your future. By keeping track of your income and planning what you will spend, you will have some control over your finances.

Figure 3-2 This example shows a sample budget for Carlos Acosta. *How can discretionary income be used to help you meet your financial goals?*

Carlos Acosta
Budget
For the Month of October, 20--

Estimated Income		
Pay from part-time job	585.00	
Babysitting	35.00	
Yard work for neighbors	45.00	
Allowance	40.00	
Gifts	25.00	
Total Estimated Income		730.00
Estimated Expenses		
Fixed		
Savings	100.00	
Charitable contribution	20.00	
Bus fare to work	28.00	
Total Fixed		148.00
Variable		
School lunches	80.00	
School supplies/fees	22.00	
Entertainment	70.00	
Clothing	80.00	
Eating out	60.00	
Miscellaneous	40.00	
Total Variable		352.00
Total Estimated Expenses		−500.00
Estimated Discretionary Income		$230.00

Goodheart-Willcox Publisher

Advice for Budgeting

Keep track of the amounts spent each week.
Transfer that information to a budget each month.
Pay yourself first.
Be disciplined.
Stay organized.
Review the budget regularly.
Make changes when necessary.

Goodheart-Willcox Publisher

Figure 3-3 Budgeting will help you have some control over your finances. *Why do you think some people have a hard time following a budget?*

A budget is a working document that needs to be reviewed often. You will need to update your budget when your income or expenses change. The advice in Figure 3-3 can help you follow your budget.

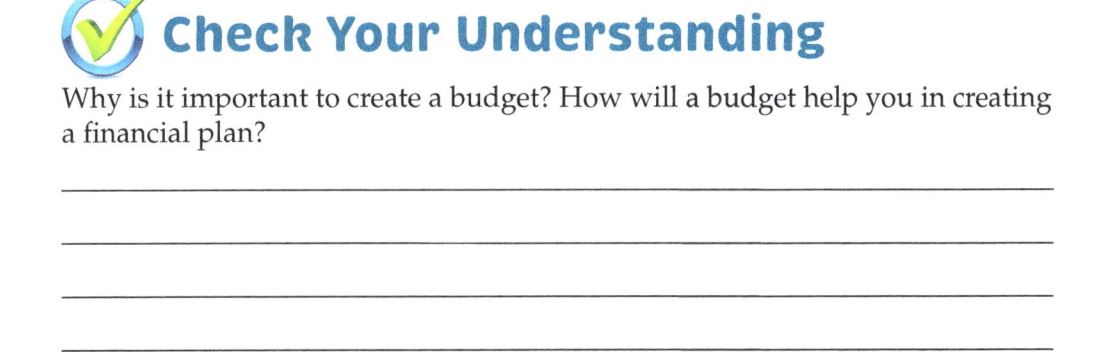

✓ Check Your Understanding

Why is it important to create a budget? How will a budget help you in creating a financial plan?

_____

_____

_____

_____

Your Turn

Creating a Budget

1. Use your information for estimated income and expenses to create a budget for one month. Use spreadsheet software or write the information on paper if you do not have access to a computer. Refer to Figure 3-2 as an example for the column headings, labels, and types of information to enter.
2. Save the budget file as directed by your teacher. Use a unique name for your file. For example, if your name is Mason Parker, save the file as MParkerNovBudget. Each month, you will be able to update the budget amounts as needed.

Internet Connection

Money Management Software

1. Using the Internet, search for *money management software*. Find five different programs. Record the name and the cost of each one in the table that follows.

Name of Software	Cost

2. If your teacher permits, download free money-management software and create a budget. How could you use this software to help with your own budgeting?

_____

_____

Dollars and Sense

Budgeting

Budgeting is an important part of financial planning. It will guide your future spending and help you become financially responsible. By learning how to create a budget now, you will be able to make better decisions for saving and spending money in the future.

Being organized is important when creating your budget. If you do not keep receipts and other records, it will be difficult to track your spending accurately. This might cause you to omit expenses when you create your monthly budget. In that case, your budget would not be accurate.

There are many ways of keeping track of income and expenses. Things you can do each day or week to prepare for your budget include the following.

- Each time you spend money, or use a debit card, record these payments on your daily spending chart.
- When you get paid, record the amount of payment at the top of your spending chart, along with any money taken out of your bank account or any gifts received.
- If you have access to a computer at home, you may want to keep track of this information on a spreadsheet or use money-management software.

Are You Financially Responsible?

Budgeting: A Checklist

Do you ever wonder where your money goes? Do you get to the end of the week or month and find that you no longer have any money to spend? To be financially responsible, it is important to keep track of money you earn and spend. Use this checklist to help you evaluate your budgeting.

	Yes	No	
1.	____	____	Did I write down everything I spent money on?
2.	____	____	Did I buy something this week that I regret?
3.	____	____	Did I learn anything this week about my spending and savings habits?
4.	____	____	Did I budget for savings?
5.	____	____	Did I resist buying something I really did not need?
6.	____	____	Was there something I really wanted this week but did not have enough money to buy?
7.	____	____	Did I run out of money this week?
8.	____	____	Did I have to borrow money to make it through the week?
9.	____	____	Did I spend my monthly budget on needs?
10.	____	____	Did I spend my monthly budget on wants?

Chapter 3 Review and Assessment

Summary

3-1 **Explain the purpose of a budget.**

A budget is a plan for the use of money based on goals, expenses, and expected income. A budget can help you keep track of your money and spend wisely. It estimates categories of expected income and expenses for a given period of time.

3-2 **Discuss income.**

Income is money received from any source. To estimate income, write the amount and the source of each income. Then, total the amounts.

3-3 **Explain the difference between fixed and variable expenses.**

A fixed expense is one that stays the same each month, while a variable expense is one that changes from month to month. Tracking expenses will give you an idea of how to plan for expenses in your budget.

3-4 **Calculate discretionary income.**

Money that remains after you have paid for regular or needed expenses is discretionary income. To calculate discretionary income, subtract total fixed and variable expenses from income.

3-5 **List steps to create a monthly budget.**

To create a budget, select a time period for the budget. List the amounts of estimated income for the period and total them. List the estimated fixed and variable expenses for the period and total them. Subtract the total expenses from the total income to find discretionary income. If the discretionary income amount is a negative number, reduce expenses.

Review Your Knowledge

Choose the correct answer for each of the following.

1. ____ You can track expected income and expenses for a given period using a(n) ____.
   A. financial goal
   B. investment
   C. budget
   D. deficit

2. ____ Your ____ will guide you as you create your budget.
   A. goals
   B. age
   C. disposable income
   D. spending

3. ____ Money you receive for working at a job is an example of ____.
   A. income
   B. an expense
   C. discretionary income
   D. a financial goal

4. ____ You paid $22.50 for a haircut. This amount represents a(n) ____.
   A. income
   B. expense
   C. goal
   D. charge

5. ____ Last week, you paid $4.50 for lunch on Monday, $3.00 for lunch on Tuesday, and $3.85 for lunch on Wednesday. The amounts you paid for lunch are ____.
   A. fixed expenses
   B. variable expenses
   C. discretionary expenses
   D. discretionary income

6. ____ You take weekly music lessons that cost $35.00 per week. This is an example of a(n) ____.
   A. fixed expense
   B. variable expense
   C. voluntary expense
   D. income

7. ____ What does the phrase *pay yourself first* mean?
   A. set aside money for all your wants in your budget
   B. write yourself a check for spending money every week
   C. set aside money to save as part of your budget
   D. set aside money after all expenses are met

8. ____ How is discretionary income calculated?
   A. income – fixed and variable expenses = discretionary income
   B. income – fixed expenses = discretionary income
   C. fixed and variable expenses – income = discretionary income
   D. fixed expenses – variable expenses = discretionary income

9. _____ What is the first step when creating a budget?
   A. Subtract the total expenses from the total income.
   B. List the amounts of income and total them.
   C. List the fixed and variable expenses.
   D. Select a time period for the budget.
10. _____ When should you update your budget?
   A. when income increases
   B. when income decreases
   C. when expenses change
   D. all of the above

Build Your Vocabulary

For each word or term, write the correct definition using your own words.

11. budget

12. fixed expense

13. variable expense

14. charitable contribution

15. discretionary income

Apply Your Math Skills

Calculate the answers to the following problems. Show your calculations.

16. The weekly spending record for Alice Wong for the week ending October 7 is shown in the chart that follows. How much has Alice spent for the week? Total the amounts for each day and for the week. Write your answers in the chart.

\multicolumn{9}{c}{**Weekly Spending Record**   **Alice Wong**   **For the week ending October 7, 20--**}
Amounts Spent								
	Day 1	Day 2	Day 3	Day 4	Day 5	Day 6	Day 7	Total
Fixed expenses								
Bus fare	2.50	2.50	2.50	2.50	2.50			
Savings deposit			25.00					
Total fixed expenses	2.50	2.50	27.50	2.50	2.50			
Variable expenses								
School lunches	3.35	3.95	3.40	4.20	4.25			
School supplies	12.50		4.50		6.00			
E-book purchases		3.00		7.75				
Meals with friends			12.25			13.80	9.85	
Clothes and shoes					22.50	27.60		
Total variable expenses	15.85	6.95	20.15	11.95	32.75	41.40	9.85	
Total expenses								

17. Latoya's expenses for a typical week are $125.00. Her monthly income is $590.00. What will Latoya's monthly expenses be if she spends this amount every week?

_____

_____

18. What will Latoya's discretionary income be? Will she have enough money to cover her expenses?

_____

_____

19. After you graduate and get a full-time job, your earnings and expenses will increase. Assume you are sharing an apartment with a friend and have the income and expenses listed in the chart that follows. What are your total expenses? How much will you have for discretionary income?

Monthly Income and Expenses	
Net pay	$3,000.00
Savings	12% of net pay
Donations to charity	35.00
Rent (your share)	455.00
Utilities	98.00
Internet service	60.00
Cell phone plan	25.00
Car payment and insurance	480.00
Groceries	235.00
Gas	130.00
College tuition, fees, and books	295.00
Health insurance and personal care	350.00
Payment on a credit card balance	120.00
Clothes	110.00
Miscellaneous expenses	100.00

_____

_____

_____

_____

20. You decide to make a weekly donation to a local charity. You categorize the donation as a fixed expense in your monthly budget. If you donate $25 per week, what is the total monthly fixed expense amount for your budget?

_____

_____

CHAPTER 4
Banking and Checking: Managing Your Money

Essential Question:
Why might a teen have a checking account?

Learning Outcomes

When you complete Chapter 4, you will be able to:
- **4-1** Discuss financial institutions.
- **4-2** Summarize checking accounts.
- **4-3** Explain managing a checking account.
- **4-4** Summarize debit cards and their uses.

Key Terms

financial institution
bank
liquidity
automated teller machine (ATM)
emergency fund
Federal Deposit Insurance Corporation (FDIC)
credit union
savings and loan association (S&L)
checking account
service fee
endorsement
payee
check
overdraft
overdraft protection
check register
debit card

Reading Prep

College and Career Readiness

Before reading this chapter, think about how the author presents the information. As you read, consider how this chapter provides the foundation for the next chapter.

What is Your Financial IQ?

Before reading this chapter, answer the following questions to see how much you already know about bank accounts.

1. What do you think *liquidity* means when it refers to a bank account?

2. What is the purpose of the Federal Deposit Insurance Corporation (FDIC)?

3. What is a savings and loan association?

4. What is the purpose of a checking account?

5. List some advantages of using electronic banking.

6. Explain the term *overdraft*.

7. Why is it important to keep track of amounts spent from your checking account?

8. What do you think is an *advantage* of using a debit card?

9. What do you think is a *disadvantage* of using a debit card?

10. What is an ATM used for?

4-1 Financial Institutions

Individuals look to financial institutions for a safe place to keep money and for help managing it. A **financial institution** provides services related to money. Some of the most common services they offer include:
- checking accounts
- savings accounts
- certificates of deposit
- loans
- money market accounts

When you go to a financial institution to open an account, you will need to provide proof of your identity as you complete the application forms. Bring photo identification with you, such as a state ID. You will also need your Social Security number.

You will be requested to sign a signature card for the account. An example of a signature card is shown in Figure 4-1. This will be used to confirm your signature on financial documents when needed.

Banks

Most teens are familiar with the services of banks. A **bank** is a financial institution that receives, lends, exchanges, and safeguards money, controlled by the Federal Reserve System. Banks provide easy access to your money through checking or savings accounts, and may offer safe deposit boxes to store valuable items.

Signature Card

Submit one card to establish an optional check redemption privilege, which allows you to write checks against your account.	
Name of Account	
Account Number	Date
The registered owner(s) of this account must sign below. By signing this card, the signatory(ies) agree(s) to all the terms and conditions set forth on the reverse side of this card.	
Signature	Signature
Signature	Signature
Institutional Accounts: ❏ Check here if any two signatures are required on checks ❏ Check here if only one signature is required on checks	Joint Tenancy Accounts: ❏ Check here if both signatures are required on checks ❏ Check here if only one signature is required on checks

Goodheart-Willcox Publisher

Figure 4-1 A signature card is completed when a bank account is opened. *For what reasons might a bank need to confirm your signature?*

A sign stating, "Insured by FDIC" should be displayed within a financial institution. *How can you be sure your money is protected by FDIC insurance?*

Haslam Photography/Shutterstock.com

FYI

The mission of the FDIC is to keep the financial system in the United States stable. It also seeks to promote public confidence in the system. FDIC insurance began in January of 1934. The original amount of coverage was for deposits up to $2,500.

Liquidity refers to the ease with which an asset can be converted into cash without losing value. Most bank accounts are liquid. You can withdraw money at any time, usually through an **automated teller machine (ATM)**. Some ATMs also allow users to make deposits and transfer money between accounts.

You should not have to pay a fee to use an ATM that is owned by your bank. However, you will probably pay a fee if you use an ATM from a bank other than your own. Fees of $2 to $6 per withdrawal add up quickly. You could easily have $15 to $20 in fees each month in addition to your monthly service fees. Keep some of your money in a no-risk bank account to be used in emergency situations. An **emergency fund** consists of three to six months' basic living expenses kept in a liquid account for unexpected situations. If you lose your job or are injured and cannot work, this fund can be used for daily necessities.

✓ Check Your Understanding

Why should you have a bank account?

_____
_____
_____

Banks also offer protection for your money. The ==Federal Deposit Insurance Corporation (FDIC)== is an independent agency created by the federal government to protect consumers by insuring their deposits at most banks and other financial institutions. FDIC insurance coverage is limited to $250,000 per depositor, per insured bank. This means you would be able to withdraw your funds up to $250,000 even if the bank were to close, guaranteed by the federal government. Make sure your bank is a member of FDIC, indicated by a sign. There are many online-only banks, too. Research carefully before using an online-only bank, and make sure it is insured by the FDIC.

✓ Check Your Understanding

Why is it important for your bank to be a member of the FDIC?

_____

_____

_____

Other Financial Institutions

Other types of financial institutions offer many of the same services as a bank. Two examples are credit unions and savings and loan associations. However, they are more specialized and may not have the complete range of services that a full-service bank will have.

A ==credit union== is a nonprofit financial cooperative owned by and operated for the benefit of its members. Members of credit unions share something in common. For example, they may all be in the same profession, such as teachers. Typically, you must be a member to use the services of a credit union. Interest rates on loans may be lower at a credit union than at a regular bank. Deposits in most credit unions are insured by the *National Credit Union Share Insurance Fund (NCUSIF)* up to $250,000 per account.

A ==savings and loan association (S&L)== is a financial institution that earns money to pay interest on accounts by issuing home mortgages. Interest rates on savings are generally higher at a savings and loan association than at a regular bank. The FDIC also insures accounts at savings and loan associations up to $250,000.

✓ Check Your Understanding

Who may use the services of a credit union?

_____

_____

_____

4-2 Checking Accounts

A primary service that banks offer is checking accounts. A **checking account** is a liquid bank account that allows the owner to make deposits, make online payments or transfers, write checks, and withdraw money. These accounts are called checking accounts, even though you will rarely need to write a paper check. Using a checking account is a convenient, safe way to make payments and keep track of spending.

When opening a checking account, shop around. Some checking accounts pay interest. *Interest* is money paid for the use of money. However, these accounts often require a minimum balance, such as $500 to $1,000, to remain in the account at all times.

Most banks have basic or student accounts with minimal or no service fees. A **service fee** is an amount you must pay the bank for having an account. However, if you have a minimum direct deposit each month, such as your net pay, the service fee may be waived. Banks will require a parent or guardian's signature for a teen account.

✓ Check Your Understanding

Why might you want to have a checking account?

_____

_____

_____

Internet Connection

Checking Accounts

1. Visit the website of a bank in your area. Research the features of three different types of checking accounts offered.
2. Complete the following chart with details about each type of account, and be sure to look for student or teen accounts.

Bank Name:					
Type of Checking Account	Minimum Balance ($)	Interest Rate (%)	Associated Fees ($)	Online Banking (Yes/No)	FDIC Insured (Yes/No)

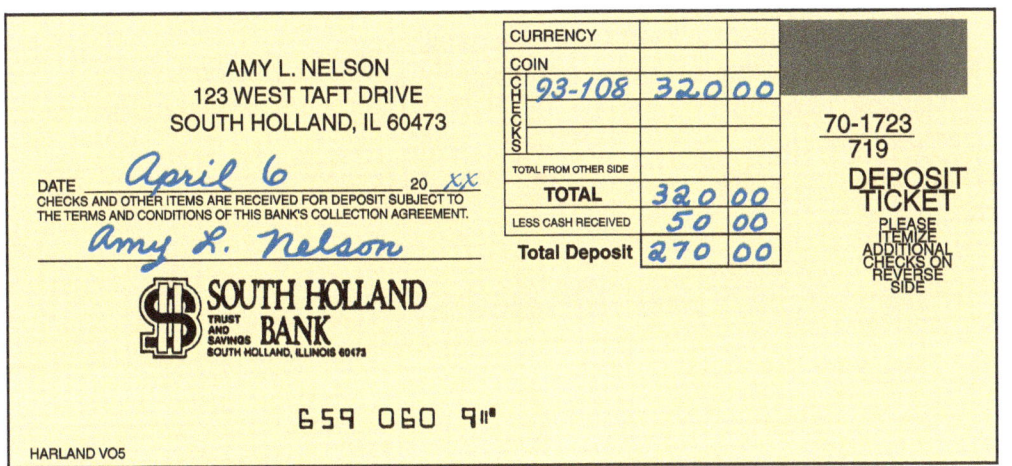

Figure 4-2 A completed deposit slip may look like the one in this example. *What are some of the possible problems that can arise from making a mistake on a deposit slip?*

Deposit Slip

Goodheart-Willcox Publisher

Making Deposits

Before you use a checking account, you must deposit money in the account. To deposit money in a checking account, you may need to complete a deposit slip if you are making the deposit in person at the bank. A sample deposit slip is shown in Figure 4-2. Your bank should also allow you to deposit a paper check using your smartphone.

If you are depositing a paper check, you must first endorse it. An **endorsement** is a signature on the back of the check to transfer ownership from the payee to the bank. The **payee** is the person, business, or organization to whom the check is written. To use a phone app to deposit a paper check, take a picture of the front and signed back of the check. Your bank may also require you to write "mobile deposit." Three ways to endorse a paper check are shown in Figure 4-3.

- A *blank endorsement* only requires the signature of the payee. A check with a blank endorsement can be cashed by anyone, and therefore should only be used if you are at the bank ready to make the deposit.

FYI: Banks typically charge a fee to cash a check if you do not have an account there, or may refuse to cash your check.

Types of Endorsements

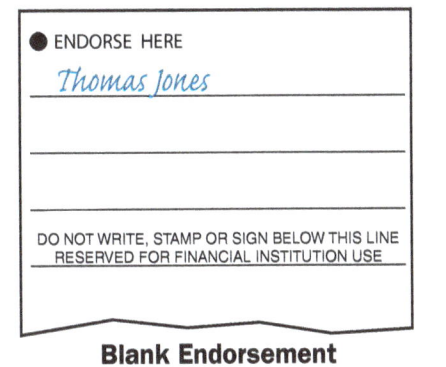

Blank Endorsement
ENDORSE HERE
Thomas Jones

Restrictive Endorsement
ENDORSE HERE
For Deposit Only
Thomas Jones

Special Endorsement
ENDORSE HERE
Pay to the order of
Kayla Reynolds
Thomas Jones

Goodheart-Willcox Publisher

Figure 4-3 Three types of endorsements are commonly used on checks. *How do different types of endorsements protect both the writer and the payee of the check?*

- A *restrictive endorsement* may be used only for the specific purpose stated in the endorsement. An example of this type of endorsement is the phrase, "For deposit only," followed by your signature.
- A *special endorsement* is used to transfer the check to someone else. The only person who can cash the check is the person named in the endorsement.

When endorsing a check, always sign your name exactly as it appears on the check.

✓ Check Your Understanding

List three ways to endorse a check.

_____
_____
_____

FYI: When you write a check, always use ink. Make sure that every line is complete so no one can change any information on the check.

Writing Checks and Transferring Money

Most payments you make from your checking account will be transferred electronically through your bank or an app such as Venmo, Zelle, Apple Pay, or PayPal. These apps are set up on your phone and are funded from your checking or savings account to pay businesses or individuals. You can also set up a recurring payment automatically, such as a car payment. Electronic deposits and payments are continuously updated and are reflected almost immediately online.

However, occasionally you may have to write a paper check. A **check** is a written order to direct the bank to pay a specific amount to the person, business, or organization to whom the check is written. When you write a check, enter the following information in the correct spaces:

- date
- name of the payee
- check amount in numbers
- check amount in words
- reason for writing the check (optional)
- your signature

Hi and Lois © 2022 Comicana Inc. Distributed by King Features Syndicate, Inc.

Completed Check

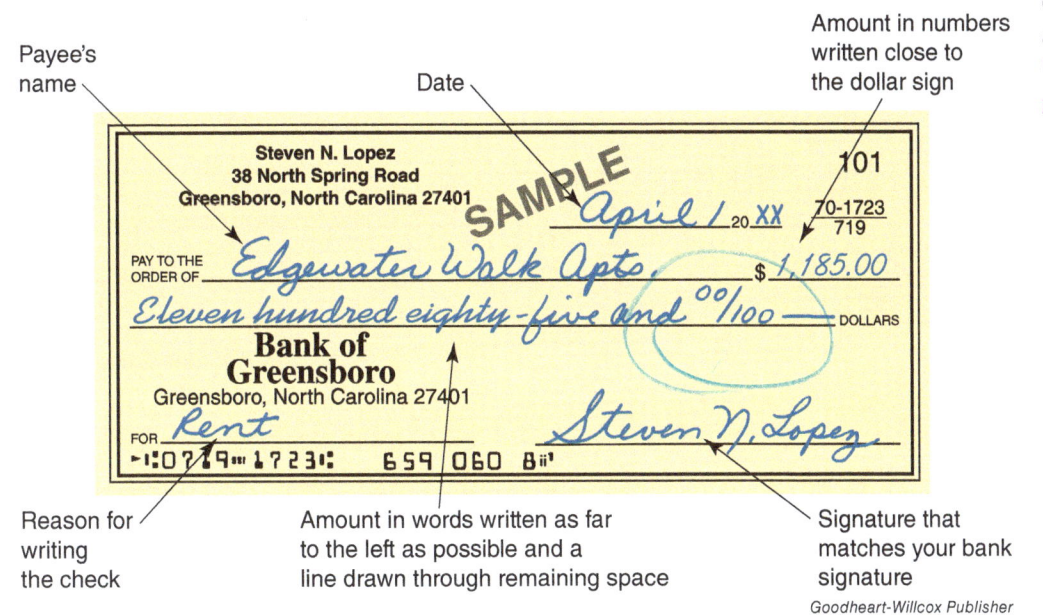

Figure 4-4 A check directs the bank to make a payment to the payee. *What reasons can you list for paying with a check?*

- Payee's name
- Date
- Amount in numbers written close to the dollar sign
- Reason for writing the check
- Amount in words written as far to the left as possible and a line drawn through remaining space
- Signature that matches your bank signature

Goodheart-Willcox Publisher

Checks must have this information to be processed. An example of a completed check is shown in Figure 4-4. All lines on a check should be completed so the check cannot be altered easily.

Never write a check or try to transfer more money than you have in your account. A check or transfer for an amount greater than the balance of the account is called an **overdraft**. Overdrafts are also known as *bounced checks*. If your bank does pay the overdrawn amount, you may be charged hefty fees. Your bank might charge $25 to $30 or more as an overdraft fee. If the bank does not pay the check, it is returned to the business or person to whom you gave it. You may have to pay $30 or more to the business for the returned check. Keep in mind that it is a criminal offense to deliberately write checks or transfer money when you do not have enough funds in your account.

Some banks offer overdraft protection. **Overdraft protection** is a banking service that ensures your check or transfer will be paid by the bank even if you do not have enough in your account to cover it. Customers sign up and pay extra for this protection. Read the terms carefully when considering signing up for overdraft protection. Some banks may provide this protection free for teen accounts. You should not need overdraft protection if you keep accurate records and always know how much money you have in your account.

WilleeCole Photography/Shutterstock.com

Some banks have basic or student accounts with minimal or no service fees. *Why do you think banks offer more than one type of checking account?*

Chapter 4 Banking and Checking: Managing Your Money 71

Copyright Goodheart-Willcox Co., Inc.
May not be reproduced or posted to a publicly accessible website.

Check Your Understanding

List the information you must write on a check for it to be processed.

_____
_____
_____
_____

Your Turn

Deposit Slips and Checks

Complete deposit slips and checks for the following transactions. Use the current year in the dates.

October 1:	Deposit check for $128.50.
October 4:	Check #104 to City Foods for $32.68 for groceries.
October 9:	Check #105 to Cinemagic for $9.25 for a movie ticket.
October 17:	Deposit of $50 cash.
October 26:	Check #106 for $12.75 to Fun Land for game.

Your Turn (continued)

Check 1:

Student Name
1234 School Street
Anytown, USA 55615

Date _____

Pay to the Order of _____ $ _____

_____ dollars

Memo _____

Account # 0009-4213-01-36-50

Goodheart-Willcox Publisher

Main St. Bank

DEPOSIT

Today's Date _____

Customer Name *(Please Print)*
_____

Sign Here *(If cash is received from this deposit)*
X _____

▼ Start your account number here

| 0 | 0 | 0 | 9 | 4 | 2 | 1 | 3 | 0 | 1 | 3 | 6 | 5 | 0 | TOTAL $ |

CASH ▶
CHECK ▶
TOTAL FROM OTHER SIDE ▶
SUBTOTAL ▶
CASH BACK ▶

Goodheart-Willcox Publisher

Student Name
1234 School Street
Anytown, USA 55615

Date 2/6/25

Pay to the Order of _____ $ _____

_____ dollars

Memo _____

Account # 0009-4213-01-36-50

Goodheart-Willcox Publisher

4-3 Managing a Checking Account

Although you will be able to check the balance in your checking account online at any time, a good way to keep track of deposits and transfers is by keeping a check register. A **check register** is a record of checking account deposits, withdrawals, online payments, transfers, checks, fees, and interest. If you record every transaction, you will always know how much you have in your account.

Each month, you will get a statement either online or by mail. The statement shows all activity in your checking account for the month. Keep your statements in a safe place where others cannot see them to avoid identity theft. Compare your bank statement with your register to be sure they match, subtract any fees charged by the bank, and add interest earned. This is called a *bank reconciliation*. If you have written a paper check, it is possible that the check has not yet been cashed and is not reflected on the bank statement; this is called an *outstanding check*. To keep an accurate check register, record your information as shown in Figure 4-5.

Check Register

Date	Type	Transaction	W/D	Deposit	Balance
9/1		Initial deposit		3,672.00	3,672.00
9/3	Auto Trans.	Ace Realty, rent	1,090.00		2,582.00
9/5	Electronic	ABC Internet	96.30		2,485.70
9/7	Electronic	City Electric	142.21		2,343.49
9/9	Electronic	Municipal Utilities, water	55.84		2,287.65
9/11	Electronic	Venmo, fund account	100.00		2,187.65
9/15	Auto Trans.	Savings account	100.00		2,087.65
9/16	Auto Dep.	Net Pay		1,295.60	3,383.25
9/18	ATM	Withdrew cash	40.00		3,343.25
9/20	Ck. 365	Gary's Garage, auto repair	327.80		3,015.45
9/23	Debit Card	Fresh Express, groceries	98.54		2,916.91
9/25	Electronic	SmartCom, cell phone	68.39		2,848.52
9/27	Debit Card	Al's Drugstore, medicine	31.73		2,816.79

Goodheart-Willcox Publisher

Figure 4-5 Record your information accurately in a check register. *What can you do to help keep your check register updated?*

Assume you deposited $78.00 into a new checking account and later made another deposit of $45.00. You then transferred $25.00 to your savings account, used your debit card for $18.65, and withdrew $40.00 at your ATM. Your bank charges a service fee of $5.50 per month. What is your ending balance at the end of the month?

Beginning balance		$78.00
Deposit		+ 45.00
Subtotal		$123.00
Transfer to Savings	$25.00	
Debit card purchase	18.65	
ATM withdrawal	+ 40.00	
Total amount of payments and withdrawals		$83.65
Service fee		− 5.50
Ending balance		$33.85

You Do the Math | 4-1

You deposited $268.45 in a new checking account. Later in the month, you made a deposit of $68.25 and used your debit card for $12.39, wrote a check for $37.62, transferred $35.00 to your savings, and withdrew $20.00 at the ATM. Your bank charges a service fee of $8 per month. What is your ending balance at the end of the month?

Beginning balance		_____
Deposit		_____
Subtotal		_____
Debit card	_____	
Check	_____	
Transfer to savings	_____	
ATM withdrawal	_____	
Total amount of payments and withdrawals		_____
Service fee		_____
Ending balance		_____

✓ Check Your Understanding

Why do you need to keep a record of your deposits and payments?

_____
_____
_____

Copyright Goodheart-Willcox Co., Inc.
May not be reproduced or posted to a publicly accessible website.

Your Turn

Check Register

Record the following entries in the check register.

April 1	Initial deposit $468.90
April 7	Used debit card to pay for T-shirt at Jeans World $14.95
April 10	Automatic Payment to Tower Calls for cell phone $29.85
April 12	ATM Cash withdrawal $40.00
April 15	Direct deposit, net pay $147.30
April 17	Check 001, Midtown Music Hall, concert ticket $45.00
April 23	Used debit card at Food Court for lunch $12.38
April 26	Used Venmo at Music World for new earbuds $121.94
April 30	Direct deposit, net pay $169.80

Date	Ck #	Transaction	Debits	Credits	Balance

Goodheart-Willcox Publisher

4-4 Debit Cards

FYI: Keep your debit card, PIN, and passwords in a safe place. When using at a retail establishment or ATM, make sure no one is looking over your shoulder.

You should receive a debit card with your checking account. A **debit card** is a card that allows you to electronically access your funds and make purchases directly from your checking account. They may also be called *bankcards* or *check cards*.

You will probably have access to a debit card and an ATM. These withdrawals should also be recorded in your check register, as shown in Figure 4-5. If you have a written record, you are not likely to overdraw your account. Debit cards can be used to access your checking account at ATMs. To use your debit card at an ATM, you must enter your personal identification number, or *PIN*, a password or numeric code used to provide security and protection on electronic transactions. You may be required to use your PIN to complete banking transactions using your debit card. Your PIN may be assigned by your bank or you may be allowed to choose it for yourself. Debit cards provide a convenient way to pay for goods and services. They can be used in most retail stores, restaurants, and for cash withdrawals from your bank account.

✓ Check Your Understanding

What are some advantages of using a debit card?

_____

_____

_____

_____

Internet Connection

Debit Cards

1. Visit the websites of three different banks in your area. Research the features of the debit cards offered by these banks.
2. Complete the following chart with details about each card.

Bank Name	Debit Card Fees	Overdraft Fees

Purchases

A debit card allows you to make purchases by swiping or inserting the card into a machine at the merchant's counter. Debit cards can also be used to make online purchases.

When you make a purchase using a debit card, the money is taken out of your checking account immediately. This is different from using a credit card because when you use a credit card, payment is not due until you receive a statement at the end of the month. It is easy to have an overdraft when using a debit card, so use your debit card wisely. Many overdrafts occur because of failure to record purchases and withdrawals.

Before making a debit purchase, ask whether the merchant charges a service fee for the use of a debit card. If there is a service fee, you will need to pay an additional amount if you pay with a debit card. The total cost of your purchase will include the service charge. Money will be taken out of your checking account immediately for the entire amount.

Copyright Goodheart-Willcox Co., Inc.
May not be reproduced or posted to a publicly accessible website.

Suppose a retail store charges a service fee of $1.50 for each debit card purchase. How much will you pay for service fees if you shop at this store four times in one month and pay with your debit card each time?

Service fee	$1.50
Number of uses	× 4
Total fees to use card	$6.00

You Do the Math | 4-2

A local retail store charges a $1.25 service fee for each debit card purchase. How much will you pay for service fees if you shop at this store seven times in one month and pay with your debit card each time?

Service fee	_____
Number of uses	_____
Total fees to use card	_____

As with checking accounts, your bank may provide overdraft protection for debit card transactions. This service may prevent embarrassment at having your purchase declined. However, like overdraft protection for checking accounts, you will pay a fee for having this safeguard. Once again, the best way to avoid these charges is to keep accurate records.

✓ Check Your Understanding

When does money leave your checking account when a purchase is made with a debit card?

_____
_____
_____
_____

Dollars and Sense

On the Lookout for Identity Theft

Identity theft is an illegal act that involves stealing someone's personal information and using that information to commit theft or fraud. An identity thief might withdraw money from your bank account or buy items using your credit card number. Identity theft is a serious crime. If you are a victim, it may cost you a great deal of money. It can also take a lot of time to correct problems with your finances caused by the crime.

You need to be very careful to protect your identity when using banking services. Banks often ask for important personal information, such as your date of birth, address, and Social Security number. Be careful not to leave the information where someone else could easily see or take it.

Your Social Security number will identify you for income taxes and various types of accounts throughout your life. Protect your Social Security number. Do not give it to anyone on the phone or online unless you are sure of their identity. There are many criminals who say they work for banks, credit card companies, the IRS, or even the Social Security Administration. Their online or phone requests may seem legitimate. However, these institutions will not ask for a Social Security number online or over the phone. The following is a list of guidelines that can be used to help protect your identity.

- Always shred or destroy any document that has your Social Security number on it. Do not just toss the documents into the trash. Keep bank statements in a safe place or shred them.
- Keep your PINs and passwords safe. Do not put them in an obvious place where someone can steal them, such as in your wallet or purse.
- The bank will give you a document that explains its privacy policy. Read the fine print and ask questions if you do not understand the policy. The bank should not give any personal or financial information about you to anyone without your approval.

Are You Financially Responsible?

Finding the Right Bank for You: A Checklist

When you are ready to open an account at the bank, do not just go to the bank that is most convenient. Shop around until you find the bank that is right for you. Much of your homework can be done online. Use this checklist to help you select the bank you will use.

	Yes	No	
1.	____	____	Do I know the type of identification I need to open a checking account?
2.	____	____	Are student checking accounts available?
3.	____	____	Do I know if interest is paid on the account?
4.	____	____	Is there a monthly service fee to have an account?
5.	____	____	Is there an overdraft fee or overdraft protection?
6.	____	____	Do I have to pay to have checks printed?
7.	____	____	Will I have to keep a minimum balance in the account?
8.	____	____	Does a debit card come with the account?
9.	____	____	Is there a charge for using an ATM?
10.	____	____	Can I check my balance, pay bills, and make transfers online with no fees?

Chapter 4 Review and Assessment

Summary

4-1 Discuss financial institutions.

A financial institution is an organization that provides services related to money. A bank is financial institution that receives, lends, exchanges, and safeguards money. The FDIC insures accounts at most banks and other financial institutions. Other types of financial institutions are more specialized than banks. Two examples are credit unions and savings and loan associations.

4-2 Summarize checking accounts.

A checking account allows the owner to make deposits, make online payments or transfers, write checks, and withdraw money. Before you use a checking account, you must deposit money in the account. After you deposit money, you can begin writing checks or transferring money. Never write a check or transfer money for more than you have in your account.

4-3 Explain managing a checking account.

A check register is a record of checking account transactions. Each month, your bank will send a statement online or by mail that shows all activity in your account. Compare it with your check register to be sure your balance is accurate.

4-4 Summarize debit cards and their uses.

A debit card allows the cardholder to electronically access funds by having the money withdrawn from a bank account. Debit cards can be used in most retail stores and restaurants and for cash withdrawals from your bank account. They can also be used at ATMs to make withdrawals.

Review Your Knowledge

Choose the correct answer for each of the following.

1. ____ Which type of financial institution is *not* insured by the FDIC?
   A. bank
   B. credit union
   C. savings and loan association (S&L)
   D. automated teller machine (ATM)

2. ____ An asset that can easily be converted to cash without losing value is said to be ____.
   A. valid
   B. insured
   C. liquid
   D. endorsed

3. _____ A(n) _____ is a written order for the bank to pay a specific amount to the person to whom it is written.
   A. endorsement
   B. debit
   C. overdraft
   D. check

4. _____ Which of the following functions can *not* be performed through an ATM?
   A. obtaining a loan
   B. making a deposit
   C. withdrawing cash
   D. checking the balance in your account

5. _____ A payee is the person, business, or organization _____.
   A. who endorses a check
   B. who signs a check
   C. to whom a check is written
   D. who cashes a check

6. _____ A check written for an amount greater than the balance of the account is called a(n) _____.
   A. overdraft
   B. post-dated check
   C. canceled check
   D. outstanding check

7. _____ What is your record of deposits, withdrawals, online payments, transfers, checks, fees, and interest called?
   A. emergency fund
   B. bank statement
   C. checking account
   D. check register

8. _____ Which of the following is *not* a use of a debit card?
   A. make a purchase in a retail store with money that is immediately taken out of your account
   B. withdraw cash at an ATM
   C. make a purchase online with money that is immediately taken out of your account
   D. make a purchase in a retail store with money that is borrowed and will be repaid later

9. _____ Which of the following is *not* typically a banking service?
   A. loans
   B. savings accounts
   C. budgeting
   D. checking accounts

10. _____ Which of the following is the limit for FDIC insurance for individual accounts?
    A. $150,000
    B. $250,000
    C. $275,000
    D. $300,000

Build Your Vocabulary

For each word or term, write the correct definition using your own words.

11. financial institution
_____
_____

12. bank
_____
_____

13. emergency fund
_____
_____

14. Federal Deposit Insurance Corporation (FDIC)
_____
_____

15. savings and loan association (S&L)
_____
_____

16. checking account
_____
_____

17. automated teller machine (ATM)
_____
_____

18. service fee
_____
_____

19. endorsement
_____
_____

20. overdraft protection
_____
_____

Apply Your Math Skills

Calculate the answers to the following problems. Show your calculations.

21. Your bank charges a monthly service fee of $7.50, plus $2.00 for ATM withdrawals at other banks. You have made two ATM withdrawals at another bank. What are your total fees for the month?

    _____

    _____

22. You make an initial deposit of $168.72 in a checking account and your net pay of $123.10 is directly deposited the following week. You use your debit card for $28.12, transfer $29.36 to a friend, withdraw $20 from an ATM, and write a check for $51.69. Your bank service fee is $6.95 per month. How much will you have in your account at the end of the month?

    _____

    _____

23. A retail store charges a service fee of $1.25 for each debit card purchase. How much will you pay in service charges for the month if you use your debit card to make two purchases from this retail store?

    _____

    _____

24. Your bank statement dated two days ago shows a balance of $325.48. However, you made a debit purchase yesterday for $32.17 and withdrew $40 in cash from an ATM this morning. What is your actual balance?

    _____

    _____

25. Your bank statement dated yesterday shows a balance of $296.85. However, your net pay of $204.13 was deposited this morning, and $98.16 was automatically transferred out of the account today. What is your correct balance?

    _____

    _____

CHAPTER 5
Saving: Setting Aside Money for Your Future

Essential Question
Why should you start a savings account?

Learning Outcomes
When you complete Chapter 5, you will be able to:
- **5-1** Identify types of savings accounts.
- **5-2** Explain simple and compound interest.
- **5-3** Apply the Rule of 72.

Key Terms
savings account
interest
savings plan
regular savings account
certificate of deposit (CD)
money market account (MMA)
time value of money
simple interest
principal
compound interest
annual percentage yield (APY)
Rule of 72

Reading Prep
Before reading this chapter, look at the chapter title. Write a short paragraph about what you already know on the topic. As you read, relate new information to your prior knowledge.

What is Your Financial IQ?

Before reading this chapter, answer the following questions to see how much you already know about saving money.

1. Explain why savings accounts are liquid.

2. How much money should you keep in an emergency fund?

3. What is a certificate of deposit (CD)?

4. What is a money market account (MMA)?

5. What is the principal in a savings account?

6. What is simple interest?

7. What is compound interest?

8. How does compound interest affect the balances in your savings accounts?

9. Explain annual percentage yield (APY).

10. What is the Rule of 72 used to calculate?

5-1 Savings Accounts

> **FYI**
> If you are having a difficult time saving, know that 40 percent of the world lives on $2 a day or less. This perspective may make it easier to avoid the temptation to spend everything you make.

You may already have a savings account. A **savings account** is a bank account used to accumulate money for future use. This type of bank account accumulates interest. **Interest** is money paid for the use of money.

Why do some people have such a difficult time putting money aside for saving? Remember FOMO from Chapter 1? Do not let the desire to have things that others have keep you from saving for your future. There is never a convenient time to save, so start saving **now**. A **savings plan** is a plan for using money to reach financial goals and increase financial security. You can save money for a specific purpose or build a reserve for unexpected expenses using savings accounts. Set goals for your savings using the SMART goal model in Chapter 1.

There are several different types of savings accounts from which to choose. You might need more than one type of account if you want some money readily accessible and other money earning a higher interest rate. Examples of savings accounts include regular savings accounts, certificates of deposit, and money market accounts.

✓ Check Your Understanding

What is an advantage of having a savings account?

_____
_____
_____

Regular Savings Accounts

A **regular savings account** is one that pays interest and allows deposits and withdrawals. These savings accounts generally offer the lowest rate of interest of all savings options, but they have the most liquidity.

Regular savings accounts provide a way to teach teens and younger children how to save money. Even though they do not earn high rates of interest, they can be an important part of a financial plan because they are liquid.

When you open a savings account, you may receive a savings account record to track activity in the account. An example of a savings account record is shown in Figure 5-1. You can also check your balance online at any time.

If you are opening your first savings account, you will want to shop for a bank that allows small balances in those accounts. Some banks charge a service fee if there is no activity in your account for several months or if you get below a minimum balance. Just as you should do with checking accounts, be sure to compare savings accounts at various banks to find the best option for you.

If you have a checking account and a savings account at the same bank, it may be a simple process to transfer money between them. You may be able to set up an automatic transfer from your checking to your savings. This is a **great** way to begin saving!

▪▪▪▪ SAVINGS ACCOUNT RECORD ▪▪▪▪

Learning Financial Institution
Anytown, USA 55615

Statement Savings Account

Account Number __00 - 1234__
Name __Student Name__
Address __1234 School Street__
    __Anytown, USA 55615__

Date	Credit/Deposits	Debit/Withdrawal	Account Balance	Memo
3/8	100 00		100 00	Initial Deposit
3/24	27 00		127 00	
4/3	32 00		159 00	
4/10		25 00	134 00	
4/30	68 00		202 00	
5/6	20 00		222 00	
5/14		12 50	209 50	
5/21	32 75		242 25	

Figure 5-1 If you have a savings account, your savings account record may look similar to this example. *What do you think you might learn about your habits by reviewing your savings account record?*

Goodheart-Willcox Publisher

✓ Check Your Understanding

What makes a regular savings account an important part of a financial plan?

_____
_____
_____

Certificates of Deposit

Banks offer many types of savings accounts. A **certificate of deposit (CD)** is a savings account that requires a deposit of a fixed amount of money for a fixed period of time. This type of account usually earns a higher rate of interest than a regular savings account because you commit to leaving your money in the bank for a specific time. A set amount is deposited, usually a minimum of $500 to $1,000 or more. You agree to leave the amount on deposit for a certain length of time. For example, you may deposit $1,500 in a CD for one year. The bank guarantees a certain interest rate for that time period.

If you withdraw the money early, you will not receive the full interest amount. You may also have to pay a significant penalty or fees for early withdrawal. You may not even get your entire deposit back if the withdrawal penalty is high. Although there are certain rules that banks must follow, the terms of CDs vary from bank to bank. Read the terms carefully so you make informed decisions about your money. Regular savings accounts and CDs at banks that are insured by the FDIC are guaranteed by the federal government for up to $250,000. See Figure 5-2 for an example of a CD.

FYI
The *maturity date* of a CD is the date when the money has been on deposit for the agreed upon amount of time. This is when you can collect the principal plus the interest earned.

Figure 5-2 A certificate of deposit usually earns a higher rate of interest than a regular savings account. *Why do you think some people use this type of account?*

Certificate of Deposit

Date Opened: 10/2/- -   Term: 1 Year   Tax ID: XXX-XX-XXXX   Number: 000-00

Account Number: 10001

Dollar Amount of Deposit: One thousand dollars — $1,000.00

STUDENT NAME
123 MAIN STREET
ANYTOWN, USA 55615

Additional Terms and Disclosures

This form contains the terms of your time deposit. It is also the Truth-in-Savings disclosure for those depositors entitled to one.
Maturity Date: This account matures 10/2/- -
(See below for renewal information.)
Rate Information: The interest rate for this account is 2.96% with an annual percentage yield of 3.0%. This rate will be paid until the maturity date specified above. Interest begins to accrue on the business day you deposit.
Interest will be compounded Daily.
Interest will be credited Quarterly.

☑ The annual percentage yield assumes that interest remains on deposit until maturity. A withdrawal of interest will reduce earnings.
☑ If you close your account before interest is credited, you will not receive the accrued interest.
The NUMBER OF ENDORSEMENTS needed for withdrawal or any other purpose is: 1.

Minimum Balance Requirement: You must make a minimum deposit to open this account of $1,000.00.
☐ You must maintain this minimum balance on a daily basis to earn the annual percentage yield disclosed.
Withdrawals of Interest: Interest ☐ accrued ☑ credited during a term can be withdrawn: Quarterly

Early Withdrawal Penalty: If we consent to a request for a withdrawal that is otherwise not permitted you may have to pay a penalty. The penalty will be an amount equal to: One-half _____ interest on the amount withdrawn.
Renewal Policy:
☑ Single Maturity: If checked, this account will not automatically renew. Interest ☐ will ☑ will not accrue after maturity.
☐ Automatic Renewal: If checked, this account will automatically renew on the maturity date.
Interest ☐ will ☐ will not accrue after maturity.

ACCOUNT OWNERSHIP: You have requested and intend the type of account marked below.
☑ Individual.
☐ Joint Account - With Survivorship.
☐ Joint Account - No Survivorship.
☐ Trust: Seperate Agreement Dated. _____

ENDORSEMENTS - SIGN ONLY WHEN YOU REQUEST WITHDRAWAL
X _____
X _____
X _____

Goodheart-Willcox Publisher

✓ Check Your Understanding

Explain the difference between a regular savings account and a certificate of deposit. Why might you want to have both?

_____
_____
_____
_____

Money Market Accounts

A **money market account (MMA)** is a savings account that typically pays higher interest than regular savings accounts. Money markets require a large minimum balance, often $5,000 or more. If the balance falls below the required minimum, the interest rate could be reduced and service fees could be charged.

Most money market accounts offer check-writing privileges. However, there may be a maximum number of checks allowed per month. The minimum amount for each check may be $100 or more.

Check Your Understanding

What are some advantages of a money market account?

_____

_____

_____

Internet Connection

Savings Accounts

1. Locate the website of a bank in your area using a search phrase such as *banks near me* or *bank* plus the name of your city. Research the features of three different types of savings accounts offered by the bank.
2. Complete the following chart with details about each type of account.

Bank Name:					
Type of Savings Account	Minimum Balance ($)	Interest Rate (%)	Associated Fees ($)	Online Banking (Yes/No)	FDIC Insured (Yes/No)

Your Turn

Account Fees

1. Review the three common types of savings accounts: regular savings accounts, CDs, and money market accounts. List the types of fees that each might charge.

Type of Account	Possible Fees
Regular Savings Account	
Certificate of Deposit	
Money Market Account	

continued

Your Turn (continued)

2. What are the potential benefits of having each of these accounts?

Type of Account	Benefits
Regular Savings Account	
Certificate of Deposit	
Money Market Account	

Are You Financially Responsible?

Finding the Right Savings Account for You: A Checklist

Make sure to shop around to find a savings account for teens. Go online to research banks in your area. Use this checklist to help you select the bank with the right savings account for you.

	Yes	No	
1.	____	____	Do I know the minimum amount needed to open a savings account?
2.	____	____	Will I have to keep a minimum balance in the account to collect interest?
3.	____	____	What is the current interest rate?
4.	____	____	Will I get a higher interest rate if I keep a higher balance?
5.	____	____	Is there a limit on the number of withdrawals per month?
6.	____	____	Can I use the ATM to make withdrawals and deposits?
7.	____	____	Can I transfer funds electronically from my checking account?
8.	____	____	Can I directly deposit a percentage of my pay from my employer?
9.	____	____	How often does the interest compound?
10.	____	____	Will I need a parent or guardian to be on the account with me until age 18?

5-2 Interest

Interest is money paid for the use of money. The value of money generally stays the same, but it loses purchasing power over a long period of time. For example, you can buy less with $1 today than you could several years ago. The **time value of money** is the idea that the value of money decreases over time if it doesn't earn interest.

Banks and other financial institutions pay customers interest to keep their money on deposit. Earning interest helps to ensure that the value of your money will increase over time instead of decrease. There are basically two types of interest used by the financial institution. Depending on the use of the money, it may be simple interest or compound interest.

Simple Interest

Simple interest is interest paid only on the original amount deposited. The original amount deposited is called the **principal**. The longer the money is kept on deposit, the more it will earn.

Assume you invest a principal of $1,000 at a simple interest rate of 5 percent. After one year, your initial savings amount will be worth $50 more than when it was deposited.

$$\text{principal} \times \text{rate} \times \text{time} = \text{interest}$$
$$\$1{,}000 \times 5\% \times 1 \text{ year} = \$50$$
$$\text{principal} + \text{interest} = \text{total}$$
$$\$1{,}000 + \$50 = \$1{,}050$$

An example of simple interest is shown in the table that follows. Each year, the principal is multiplied by the interest rate of 5 percent. The interest amount is added to the account but is not used to calculate a new principal.

Year	Beginning Balance	5% Interest	Ending Balance
1	$1,000.00	$50.00	$1,050.00
2	1,000.00	50.00	1,100.00
3	1,000.00	50.00	1,150.00
4	1,000.00	50.00	1,200.00
5	1,000.00	50.00	1,250.00

Ending balance $1,250.00
Beginning balance   − 1,000.00
Interest earned $250.00

The simple interest earned is $50 per year for a total of $250 over five years.

> **FYI**
> Interest rates are always stated as one-year percentages. To calculate interest, you must first convert the percentage to a decimal by dividing the percentage by 100. For example, an interest rate of 5 percent would be converted to .05. A rate of 3.25 percent would be .0325.

A savings plan is a plan for using money to reach financial goals and increase financial security. *Why do you think it is important to start saving money at an early age?*

Morakod1977/Shutterstock.com

You Do the Math | 5-1

You deposited $5,000 in a savings account with a simple interest rate of 6 percent. Calculate your earnings using the following table.

Year	Beginning Balance	6% Interest	Ending Balance
1	$5,000.00		
2			
3			
4			
5			

How much interest have you earned in the five-year period?

Ending balance _____

Beginning balance _____

Interest earned _____

✓ Check Your Understanding

State the formula for simple interest.

_____

_____

_____

Compound Interest

Compound interest is commonly paid on most accounts. **Compound interest** is earning interest on the principal plus the interest already earned.

Time can make a big difference in earnings when interest is compounded. For example, assume you deposited a principal of $1,000 at an interest rate of 5 percent. In one year, you will have $1,050. The next year, you will earn interest on $1,050 instead of $1,000. The interest will be $52.50 instead of $50.

Year 1: principal × rate × time = interest
$1,000 × 5% × 1 year = $50
principal + interest = total
$1,000 + $50 = $1,050

Year 2: principal × rate × time = interest
$1,050 × 5% × 1 year = $52.50
principal + interest = total
$1,050 + $52.50 = $1,102.50

Results are amazing when you keep adding to your original savings amount on a regular basis. The younger you are when you start, the more your money grows during your working years; *time is on your side*. Money earned from the compounding of interest over a period of 30 years really adds up. That is why it is called the *magic of compounding*!

To estimate how much a one-time deposit of $1,000 can grow when earning compound interest, use the following table and write your age in the blanks. This, of course, does not include any additions to your principal. Imagine what you could do with just $1,000 added each year!

FYI
The formula for compounding is $A = P(1 + r \div n)^{nt}$ where P is the original principal, r is the annual rate of interest, t is the number of years (time), and n is the number of times it is compounded in a year. A, of course, is the final amount. Remember, this assumes you are funding your account at one time, and not adding to it later.

Year	Age	5% Interest	7% Interest
Current age		$1,000	$1,000
Current age + 10 years		$1,629	$1,967
Current age + 20 years		$2,653	$3,870
Current age + 30 years		$4,322	$7,612
Current age + 40 years		$7,040	$14,975
Current age + 50 years		$11,467	$29,458

The idea is to let your money grow without using it for a period of 20 to 30 years. You do need accounts that allow you to use your money for emergencies. However, you also need long-term savings that build for your financial independence and retirement. If you choose to keep working after you reach retirement age, that is fine. You may also choose to work part-time in your retirement years. In an ideal situation, continuing to work during retirement would be a choice and not a necessity. Retirement account options are discussed in Chapter 11.

Another example of compound interest is shown in the table that follows. For each year, the beginning balance is multiplied by the interest rate of 5 percent. That amount is added to the beginning balance. The ending balance then becomes the beginning balance for the next year.

Year	Beginning Balance	5% Interest	Ending Balance
1	$1,000.00	$50.00	$1,050.00
2	1,050.00	52.50	1,102.50
3	1,102.50	55.13	1,157.63
4	1,157.63	57.88	1,215.51
5	1,215.51	60.78	1,276.29

How much interest was earned?

    Ending balance $1,276.29
    Beginning balance   − 1,000.00
    Interest earned $276.29

Without compounding, simple interest would be $50 per year, for a total of $250.

You Do the Math | 5-2

You deposited $5,000 in a saving account at an interest rate of 6 percent compounded annually. Calculate your earnings using the following table.

Year	Beginning Balance	6% Interest	Ending Balance
1	$5,000.00		
2			
3			
4			
5			

How much interest have you earned in the five-year period?

Ending balance _____

Beginning balance _____

Interest earned _____

The results may not seem impressive in the first few years; but after 25 or 30 years, the difference is astounding. If you keep adding to your savings on a regular basis, the results are even better!

Now, look at adding more to your savings along with compounding more frequently. This example shows interest compounding quarterly, which is four times per year, instead of annually, which is once per year. Suppose an initial deposit of $2,000 is compounded quarterly at 4 percent and you are depositing an additional $500 each quarter.

Step 1. principal × rate × time = interest

$2,000 × .04 × .25 (1/4 of a year) = $20

Step 2. principal + interest = new balance

$2,000 + $20 = $2,020

Step 3. new balance + deposit = 1st quarter balance

$2,020 + $500 = $2,520

(This number is also the beginning balance for next quarter.)

The following example shows how quickly money can grow over a period of three years.

Year	Quarter	Principal	Rate (4%)	Time (.25 year)	New Balance	Deposit	Quarter Balance
1	1	$2,000.00	$80.00	$20.00	$2,020.00	$500.00	$2,520.00
	2	2,520.00	100.80	25.20	2,545.20	500.00	3,045.20
	3	3,045.20	121.81	30.45	3,075.65	500.00	3,575.65
	4	3,575.65	143.03	35.76	3,611.41	500.00	4,111.41
2	1	4,111.41	164.46	41.11	4,152.52	500.00	4,652.52
	2	4,652.52	186.10	46.53	4,699.05	500.00	5,199.05
	3	5,199.05	207.96	51.99	5,251.04	500.00	5,751.04
	4	5,751.04	230.04	57.51	5,808.55	500.00	6,308.55
3	1	6,308.55	252.34	63.09	6,371.63	500.00	6,871.63
	2	6,871.63	274.87	68.72	6,940.35	500.00	7,440.35
	3	7,440.35	297.61	74.40	7,514.75	500.00	8,014.75
	4	8,014.75	320.59	80.15	8,094.90	500.00	8,594.90

You Do the Math | 5-3

Begin with a deposit of $3,500 and deposit an additional $300 each quarter. The interest rate is 5 percent compounded quarterly for a period of three years.

Year	Quarter	Principal	Rate (5%)	Time (.25 year)	New Balance	Deposit	Quarter Balance
1	1	$3,500.00					
	2						
	3						
	4						
2	1						
	2						
	3						
	4						
3	1						
	2						
	3						
	4						

Copyright Goodheart-Willcox Co., Inc.
May not be reproduced or posted to a publicly accessible website.

The **annual percentage yield (APY)** is the rate of yearly earnings from an account expressed as a percentage. It is the actual percentage earned when compounding is added to the equation. Most banks compound daily, which makes money grow more quickly. The actual yield on deposits is often higher than the stated percentage because of compounding.

✓ Check Your Understanding

How does adding to your savings on a regular basis affect the amount you have saved?

_____

_____

_____

Internet Connection

Compound Interest Calculator

1. Locate a compound interest calculator on the Internet. Search using the term *daily compound interest calculator* or the term *future value calculator*.
2. Using the table that follows and the online calculator, calculate the ending balances using the interest rates and the number of years given.

Deposit	Annual Interest Rate	Number of Years	Compounded	Ending Balance
$1,000	5%	20	Daily	
$2,000	3%	15	Daily	
$3,000	2%	25	Daily	

Note: The final ending balances may vary slightly depending on the calculator used.

5-3 Rule of 72

When creating a financial plan, savings accounts can play a role in your future finances. It can be helpful to have an idea of what your savings accounts can earn as you create financial goals.

One way to estimate future value is to use the Rule of 72. The **Rule of 72** is an equation that estimates how long it will take to double an amount of money at a fixed annual interest rate. To use the Rule of 72, divide 72 by the interest rate to find the number of years it will take to double your money. When using the Rule of 72, do not convert the interest rate to a decimal.

72 ÷ interest rate = number of years to double

The Rule of 72 gives an estimate, not the exact answer. However, it is useful for quick calculations. Naturally, the higher the interest rate, the fewer number of years it will take to double your money.

Assume that you have saved $3,000 for college. You want to know if you could double this by the time you start college in five years. A local bank is offering 4 percent interest on a savings account.

Start with	72
Divide by the interest rate	÷ 4
Number of years to double	18

The equation shows that you cannot double your money at this interest rate in five years. This is another reminder that planning for future needs or wants is essential.

You Do the Math | 5-4

If the interest rate is 3 percent, how many years will it take for you to double your money?

Start with	_____
Divide by the interest rate	_____
Number of years to double	_____

✓ Check Your Understanding

Why is the Rule of 72 useful if the answer will not be exact?

_____
_____
_____

The younger you are when you start saving, the more time your money has to grow during your working years. *What role can savings play in your financial plan?*

Prostock-studio/Shutterstock.com

Dollars and Sense

Start a Savings Plan

How do you develop a savings plan? Many people find it very difficult to save on a regular basis. We can always find *something* to buy. It takes determination to set aside money from each paycheck when you would rather use it to buy *stuff*.

The important thing to remember is to get started! Many people think they will begin saving when they have $100 to $500 to open an account. However, starting with a small amount will put you on the road to accumulating larger amounts.

Do not plan to save whatever you have left at the end of the month. Even with the best of intentions, this does not usually happen. Make it a rule to *pay yourself first*. Here are some suggestions to get into the habit of saving regularly.

- If direct deposit for savings is available to you through your employer, have a percentage of your pay deposited directly into a savings account. Use a percentage rather than a set amount. If you cannot start with 10 percent, begin with 5 or 3 percent and try to increase it over time. Using a percentage will help you automatically increase your savings as your earnings increase, while still having more to spend.
- If direct deposit for savings is not available to you through your employer, set up an automatic transfer with your bank each time your pay is deposited into your checking account, again using a percentage. If this money is not in your checking account, you will not be tempted to spend it.
- Set SMART goals to determine how long it will take to save for those goals. This will encourage you to be consistent in your saving. The reward is the satisfaction of watching your money grow!

Chapter 5 Review and Assessment

Summary

5-1 Identify types of savings accounts.

A savings account is a bank account used to accumulate money for future use. Three types of savings accounts are regular savings account, certificate of deposit (CD), and money market account (MMA).

5-2 Explain simple and compound interest.

Simple interest is interest paid only on the original amount deposited. Compound interest is interest paid on the principal plus the interest you have already earned.

5-3 Apply the Rule of 72.

The Rule of 72 is an equation that estimates how long it will take to double an amount of money at a fixed annual interest rate. To use the Rule of 72, divide 72 by the interest rate to find the number of years it will take to double your money. The Rule of 72 gives an estimate, not the exact answer.

Review Your Knowledge

Choose the correct answer for each of the following.

1. ____ Which of the following is *not* true of saving money?
   A. Money you save today could be worth more in the future if it is earning interest.
   B. Money you put in a regular savings account accumulates interest.
   C. Saving should not be part of your financial plan.
   D. Money you save can be used to start an emergency fund.

2. ____ Of the accounts listed, which type usually pays the lowest interest rate?
   A. overdraft account
   B. regular savings account
   C. certificate of deposit (CD)
   D. money market account (MMA)

3. ____ You might incur a penalty by withdrawing money before the maturity date from which of the following accounts?
   A. certificate of deposit (CD)
   B. checking account
   C. regular savings account
   D. money market account (MMA)

4. ____ For which type of account do you agree to leave your money on deposit for a certain period of time?
   A. checking account
   B. regular savings account
   C. certificate of deposit (CD)
   D. money market account (MMA)

5. ____ Of the accounts listed, which type usually requires a large minimum balance and grants check-writing privileges?
   A. checking account
   B. regular savings account
   C. money market account (MMA)
   D. certificate of deposit (CD)
6. ____ What is the time value of money?
   A. The idea that money increases in value over time.
   B. The idea that money decreases in value over time.
   C. Interest is paid only on the original amount deposited.
   D. Interest is paid on the principal plus the interest already earned.
7. ____ The original amount initially deposited into a savings account is the ____.
   A. certificate of deposit
   B. interest
   C. emergency fund
   D. principal
8. ____ What is the actual percentage earned when compounding is added to the equation?
   A. Rule of 72
   B. annual percentage yield (APY)
   C. simple interest
   D. principal
9. ____ Which of the following time periods will earn the highest annual percentage yield?
   A. yearly
   B. quarterly
   C. monthly
   D. daily
10. ____ To figure approximately how many years it will take for your savings account balance to double, you would use ____.
    A. simple interest
    B. the Rule of 72
    C. compound interest
    D. annual percentage yield (APY)

Build Your Vocabulary

For each word or term, write the correct definition using your own words.

11. savings account

    _____

    _____

12. interest

    _____

    _____

13. savings plan

14. simple interest

15. compound interest

Apply Your Math Skills

Calculate the answers to the following problems. Show your calculations.

16. You make a deposit of $375 into a savings account and leave it for 1 year. How much interest will you earn in 1 year if the simple interest rate is 2.5 percent?

17. You can earn 3 percent interest on a CD and 1.25 percent interest on a savings account. How much more interest will the CD earn for 1 year if you make a deposit of $1,650 into each account?

18. You deposited $800 into a 1-year CD that will earn 2.75 percent interest. The penalty for withdrawing the money early is 1.5 times the full-term interest plus a $30 fee. How much interest will you earn on the CD if you leave it for the full term? How much will the penalty amount be if you withdraw all the money early?

19. If you deposit $2,500 into a money market account earning 2.25 percent interest, how much interest will you earn in a year?

20. You deposited $1,500 in a savings account earning 3.5 percent simple interest. How much more interest would you earn if the bank compounds quarterly?

21. You deposit $1,750 at a rate of 2.5 percent compounded annually. What amount will you have at the end of 6 years?

22. Your initial deposit is $1,500. The interest is compounded quarterly at 5.25 percent. You add $250 each quarter for 3 years. What is the ending balance?

23. If you deposit $5,800 in a CD with a simple interest rate of 1.15 percent, what is the balance of your account after 1 year?

24. Using the Rule of 72, estimate how long it will take to double your money if you earn 6 percent annually.

25. Using the Rule of 72, estimate how long it will take to double cash in a savings account at an annual interest rate of 2 percent.

CHAPTER 6
Credit: Buy Now, Pay Later

Essential Question
What does it mean to use credit wisely?

Learning Outcomes
When you complete Chapter 6, you will be able to:
- **6-1** Discuss earning the privilege of credit.
- **6-2** Explain the role of credit bureaus.
- **6-3** Summarize the use of credit cards.
- **6-4** Summarize selecting a credit card.
- **6-5** Evaluate purchasing decisions.
- **6-6** Discuss credit card debt.
- **6-7** Define types of personal bankruptcy.

Key Terms

credit	default	revolving credit
creditworthy	credit score	comparison shopping
cosigner	credit card	decision-making
character	cash advance	trade-off
capacity	grace period	opportunity cost
capital	available credit	bankruptcy
credit bureau	finance charge	Chapter 7 bankruptcy
credit report	annual percentage rate (APR)	Chapter 13 bankruptcy
credit history		

Reading Prep
College and Career Readiness

Before reading this chapter, think about the chapter title. What does the title tell you about what you will be learning? How does this chapter relate to information you already know?

What is Your Financial IQ?

Before reading this chapter, answer the following questions to see how much you already know about credit and credit cards.

1. Explain how the use of credit is a privilege.
   _____
   _____

2. What is the role of a credit bureau?
   _____
   _____

3. What information do you think is in a credit report?
   _____
   _____

4. Why do people use credit cards?
   _____
   _____

5. What might you want to consider when selecting a credit card?
   _____
   _____

6. Is using credit free? Why or why not?
   _____
   _____

7. How can you make good decisions when making purchases?
   _____
   _____

8. Explain why it is wise to limit spending with a credit card.
   _____
   _____

9. What does it mean to declare bankruptcy?
   _____
   _____

10. What laws protect someone who has a credit card?
    _____
    _____

6-1 Credit

Many people are obsessed with *stuff*. They are the first to buy the newest smartphone, wear the latest fashion, or download the most recent music. Some people are disciplined enough to only buy what they need or can afford. Others do not seem to worry if they lack the cash for what they want. They just "pull out the plastic" and charge the purchase without thinking about how they will pay the bill.

Using credit will be an important part of your financial planning. **Credit** is an agreement in which one party lends money or provides goods or services to another party with the understanding that payment will be made later. It is important for you to learn to use credit wisely and make the right decisions as to when to charge purchases and when to pay with cash or a debit card. Using credit always ties up future income.

Many people get into financial difficulty through the overuse of credit. This may result in the lack of enough money for things needed to survive or, in some cases, the loss of assets.

How do you earn the privilege of using credit? To obtain credit, you must be creditworthy. **Creditworthy** means having the ability and willingness to repay debt. To determine whether you are creditworthy, a lender will need to evaluate information that you provide on a credit application.

A *credit application* is a form that asks for personal information about you, your job, and your current debts. You will be asked to list all your financial obligations, both the total amounts that you owe as well as the monthly payment amount for each debt. Even with a large income, too much debt may prevent a person from being approved for additional credit. Educational levels and frequent job or address changes may also influence whether credit will be extended and how much.

If you have never had credit, it may be difficult to get credit the first time you apply. You might want a loan for your first car, for example. You may need someone, such as a parent or guardian, to cosign the loan for you. A **cosigner** is a responsible person who agrees to pay the debt if you fail to pay. Keep in mind that the cosigner must also be creditworthy, or your application may be denied.

> **FYI**
> If you are applying for credit, you may be asked how many days of school you miss each year. Lenders may consider it a sign of instability if you have many absences without a good reason for them, such as illness or injury.

✓ Check Your Understanding

How can the use of credit be an important part of your financial planning?

_____

_____

_____

Your Turn

Credit Card Application

When applying for a credit card, many types of information are required. Complete the following application for a credit card. Do not use your actual Social Security number. Use 123-45-6789 instead.

CREDIT CARD APPLICATION

Personal Information

Last Name	First Name	M.I.	Suffix

Social Security Number	Date of Birth (MM/DD/YYYY)
_ _ _ – _ _ – _ _ _ _	_ _ / _ _ / _ _ _ _

E-mail Address

Current Street Address	Apt./Suite

City	State	Zip

How long have you lived here?	

Previous Street Address	Apt./Suite

City	State	Zip

How long did you live here?	

Phone Number	Type (Please Select)
(_ _ _) _ _ _ – _ _ _ _	Mobile · Home · Work

Employment Information

Employment Status (Please Select)

Full-time	Part-time	Disabled
Military	Retired	Self-employed
Student	Unemployed	Other:

Employer Name

Financial Information

Residence Status (Please Select)	Monthly Mortgage/Rent Payment
Rent	
Own	Annual Income (All Sources)
Other	

Goodheart-Willcox Publisher

Lenders look at a borrower's creditworthiness in terms of character, capacity, and capital before credit is extended. These factors are called the *three Cs of credit.*

Character

Character is a person's reputation and willingness to pay debt. Lenders evaluate your character in part with information you provide on the credit application. Businesses look for honesty and stability in those who are applying for credit. Often this means looking at the history of your debt and payments.

Capacity

Capacity, as it relates to credit, is a person's ability to pay debt. You will be evaluated based on your employment and the amount of money you earn. Do you earn enough to make the payments you agreed to make? Do you change jobs frequently? Educational levels or frequent job or address changes as measures of stability may also influence how much credit will be extended.

Capital

Capital is the assets a person has. Cash in a savings account, a house, or a car are examples of capital. Most lenders will ask you to list your assets and liabilities to determine your net worth. Are your assets enough to cover

Using credit is a privilege that must be earned. *Explain how you will be financially responsible when you get your first credit card.*

Mangostar/Shutterstock.com

the liabilities you already have? If you lost your job, would you be able to use money from your savings to pay debts? Having money to pay your creditors is another reason it is important to have three to six months' cash reserve.

✅ Check Your Understanding

How do capital and capacity differ as they relate to credit?

___

Your Turn

Three Cs of Credit

Lenders look at the three Cs of credit before credit is extended. List three questions a lender might ask about a person's character, capacity, and capital to determine whether that person is creditworthy.

Character

1. ___
2. ___
3. ___

Capacity

1. ___
2. ___
3. ___

Capital

1. ___
2. ___
3. ___

6-2 Credit Bureaus

When you get your first loan or credit card, the money you borrow and your payments will be tracked by a credit bureau. A **credit bureau** is an organization that collects information about the financial and credit transactions of consumers. It keeps track of individuals who have credit and the payments they make, including late payments. Businesses request information from credit bureaus about potential customers and their histories for paying bills. Three major credit bureaus are Equifax, Experian, and TransUnion.

✓ Check Your Understanding

What is the function of a credit bureau? What are the names of three major credit bureaus?

___

Credit Report

When you apply for credit, the lender will request a credit report from Equifax, Experian, or TransUnion before extending credit. A **credit report** is a record of a person's credit history. **Credit history** is a person's credit and financial behavior over a period of years. Lenders use your credit report when deciding whether they will extend credit to you.

The report may list employment information as well as your current and former addresses. It will show your credit cards, car loans, mortgages, or any other type of credit that has been extended to you. A credit report shows accounts you have opened or closed and any current balances. Any claims from collection agencies, late payments, or defaults are included. To **default** means failure to pay a debt or other obligation. Negative information may stay on a credit report for seven to ten years.

A copy of your credit report can be obtained online, by phone, or through a written request. You should have access to your credit report online through your bank or credit card. Even with excellent credit, it is a good idea to check your credit report periodically. Report any errors immediately.

✓ Check Your Understanding

Why should you check your credit report frequently?

> **FYI**
> Most banks and credit card companies provide access to your FICO score online. It's a good idea to check it frequently.

Credit Score

A **credit score** is a numerical measure of a person's creditworthiness. The number indicates how well a person handles credit. It is also called a *FICO score*. It was named for the Fair Isaac Corporation, the company that developed the rating system. Equifax, Experian, and TransUnion keep track of your FICO score as well as your credit history. The FICO score assembles all the information in your credit report and calculates a single number to indicate your creditworthiness.

Lenders will check your credit score when you apply for credit, so it is extremely important to keep this number high. The range of numbers used for credit scores by credit bureaus, lenders, and government agencies varies a bit. Typical scores and ratings are shown in Figure 6-1. Although ratings from different sources vary, a score above 800 is considered excellent. A good score is 670 or more. You may be given limited or no credit if your score is below 580.

The higher your score, the lower the interest rate you may be able to get on a loan. People with low credit scores may be required to pay high interest rates on loans or be denied a loan altogether. They may even be turned down for jobs or housing. Your FICO score is one of the most important numbers you will use in your adult life. It may determine whether you get a loan for a car or a house, are approved to rent an apartment, or even obtain employment.

Assume you have a FICO score of 765. You are approved to borrow money at 4.5 percent interest. If your score decreases to 500, you will have to pay 7 percent interest. How much less will you pay in simple interest in one year on a loan of $6,500 if you have the higher score?

Figure 6-1 Your credit score measures how well you handle credit. *What activities might raise a credit score? What activities might lower it?*

Credit Scores

Score	Rating
800 and above	**Excellent**—this score qualifies you for the best financing and interest rates.
740–799	**Very good**—this range qualifies you for favorable financing and interest rates.
670–739	**Good**—this score range usually qualifies you for most loans.
580–669	**Fair**—you will have trouble getting a loan.
579 and below	**Poor**—you will need to improve your score before applying for a loan.

Goodheart-Willcox Publisher

Step 1. Calculate interest at 4.5%.

Loan amount	$6,500.00
Interest rate	× .045
Annual interest amount at 4.5%	$292.50

Step 2. Calculate interest at 7%.

Loan amount	$6,500.00
Interest rate	× .07
Annual interest amount at 7%	$455.00

Step 3. Calculate the difference.

Interest at 7%	$455.00
Interest at 4.5%	− 292.50
Difference	$162.50

You Do the Math | 6-1

Your FICO score is an excellent 800. You are approved to borrow $8,000 at 3.25 percent. Your friend's score is 525, and she will have to pay 7.5 percent for the same amount. How much less will you pay in simple interest in one year with your higher score than your friend will pay?

Step 1. Calculate interest at 3.25%.

Loan amount _____

Interest rate _____

Annual interest amount at 3.25% _____

Step 2. Calculate interest at 7.5%.

Loan amount _____

Interest rate _____

Annual interest amount at 7.5% _____

Step 3. Calculate the difference.

Interest at 7.5% _____

Interest at 3.25% _____

Difference _____

To keep your FICO score high, pay on time and never make late payments. Keep your debt low and do not become overextended by buying more than you can afford. If your score is low, paying bills on time, setting up automatic payments so you're never late, applying for new credit in moderation, and keeping your balances low will significantly improve your score, sometimes within a few months. Be responsible with credit and check your FICO score often.

✓ Check Your Understanding

Why is it important to have a good credit score?

_____
_____
_____

Internet Connection

FICO Scores

1. Using the Internet, search for *what determines a FICO score*. List three things that can increase a score.

   _____
   _____
   _____

2. List three things that can decrease a FICO score.

   _____
   _____
   _____

6-3 Credit Cards

FYI: The average credit card interest rate in 2022 was 19.59%.

A **credit card** allows the holder to make purchases up to an authorized amount and pay for them later. Credit cards enable you to shop online, carry less cash, and pay for items needed in emergencies.

Credit cards are used primarily to make purchases of goods or services. Most credit card purchases are unsecured loans. An *unsecured loan* is money borrowed based on the signature of the borrower. This means you can borrow money to purchase goods and services just by signing your name. Your signature confirms an agreement to pay the debt; you are legally obligated to pay these unsecured debts.

Most businesses accept major bank credit cards such as Visa, Mastercard, and American Express. Some businesses, such as Kohl's, Target, and Shell, also offer their own credit cards. Store credit cards are called *proprietary credit cards*. They usually offer special discounts and other offers to get customers to use their cards.

In addition to making purchases with a credit card, you may obtain a cash advance when you need cash. A **cash advance** is a loan against your credit card. Cash advances allow the cardholder to request cash at a bank, at an ATM, or online. Some credit card companies send convenience checks to the cardholder that can be used to obtain a cash advance. A *convenience check* is used just like any other check, but the money is charged as a cash advance to your credit card.

Unlike credit card purchases, cash advances do not have a **grace period**, or a set number of days before you will be charged interest if your balance is not paid in full (typically 20–25 days). Interest charges begin from the moment the cash advance is taken. Even if you pay the money back in full by its due date, you will be charged interest. In addition, there is usually a transaction fee of 2 to 5 percent of the amount of the advance. If you obtain the cash advance at an ATM, any ATM fees will also apply. Although a cash advance is not recommended as a good financial choice, it may be an option in an emergency.

Suppose you obtain a cash advance of $500. The transaction fee is 3 percent of the advance. The credit card company charges an interest rate of 25 percent for cash advances. How much will it cost with simple interest to borrow the money as a cash advance for one year?

Step 1. Calculate the transaction fee.

Cash advance	$500
Transaction fee percentage	× .03
Transaction fee	$15

Step 2. Calculate the interest.

Cash advance	$500
Interest rate percentage	× .25
Interest amount	$125

Step 3. Calculate total fees.

Transaction fee	$15
Interest amount	+ $125
Total fees	$140

It will cost you $140 just to borrow the money for one year. A cash advance can be a very expensive way to borrow money.

You Do the Math | 6-2

You want a $1,000 cash advance on your credit card. The transaction fee is 2 percent of the cash advance. The credit card company charges an interest rate of 18 percent for cash advances. How much will it cost to borrow the money as a cash advance for one year?

Step 1. Calculate the transaction fee.

Cash advance _____

Transaction fee percentage _____

Transaction fee _____

Step 2. Calculate the interest.

Cash advance _____

Interest rate percentage _____

Interest amount _____

Step 3. Calculate total fees.

Transaction fee _____

Interest amount _____

Total fees _____

✓ Check Your Understanding

Explain how a credit card can be used for a cash advance.

_____

_____

_____

FYI
If you report a lost or stolen credit card before it is used, your liability is zero. If someone uses it before you report it, your liability should be $50.

6-4 Selecting a Credit Card

Many credit cards come with benefits such as earning cash back or points. However, it is important to resist the temptation to overspend when paying with credit. Is what you want today worth spending your future income? Remember, you must pay this money back. Using credit of any kind always ties up future income. When selecting a credit card, it is important to consider both the cost of using the credit card as well as the credit terms offered.

Cost of Credit

Using a credit card is not free. Some credit card companies charge an annual membership fee. This fee can be as much as $500. The type of card you have determines whether there will be a fee and its amount.

There will be a cap, or maximum, on how much you can purchase with your credit card. Based on your credit history and ability to pay, the lender will set a *credit limit*. Going over this limit could cost you a hefty fee, so it is wise to stay within the limit the lender has set. Maxing out your credit cards will also lower your FICO score. One way to be sure you do not get into a lot of debt is to keep your limit low on credit cards. Call the credit card company and request that your limit not be raised.

Available credit is the difference between your card's credit limit and the amount of credit you have already used. This is the amount you would be able to obtain as a cash advance. For example, your credit limit is $6,000 and you have already made purchases of $900 using the credit card. What is your available credit?

Credit limit	$6,000.00
Credit used	− 900.00
Available credit	$5,100.00

You Do the Math | 6-3

Your credit limit is $4,500. You charged $1,200 on the card. What is your available credit?

Credit limit	_____
Credit used	_____
Available credit	_____

Cardholders pay a finance charge for using credit card accounts if the balance is not paid in full every month. A **finance charge** is the interest paid by a credit cardholder to a lender for the use of credit. When you make a purchase with a credit card, you are charged interest on the unpaid balance of the account. The **annual percentage rate (APR)** is the annual rate a lender charges for the use of credit. For example, a credit card company might offer an APR of 17 percent or more.

In addition to membership fees and interest, lenders may charge additional fees, as well as penalties, for the use of credit cards. Examples of these charges often include:
- fees for going over your credit limit
- increased interest rate or minimum payment as a result of late payments or going over your credit limit
- penalties for a late payment, even if it is one day late
- penalties if the amount used to pay off a credit card balance does not clear the bank because there is not enough money in your checking account

When credit is not managed wisely, these extra charges add up. Assume your credit card company charges a $20 fee for going over your limit and a $25 penalty for a late payment. If you do both in the same month, how much will you pay for these fees?

Over limit fee	$20.00
Late payment penalty	+ 25.00
Total fees	$45.00

You Do the Math | 6-4

Your credit card company charges a $28 fee for going over your limit and a $27.50 late payment penalty. If you do both in the same month, how much will you pay for these fees?

Over limit fee	_____
Late payment penalty	_____
Total fees	_____

Be selective when choosing a credit card. Your goal should be to have a card with no annual fee and the lowest interest rate possible. Some lenders offer special credit cards with lower APRs for teens.

Only buy what you can afford to pay for in full each month to avoid paying interest. Avoid "prestige" cards that charge high annual membership fees just to carry their card.

Check Your Understanding

Name some of the costs associated with the use of credit.

_____
_____
_____
_____
_____

Credit Terms

Credit terms and agreements vary for credit cards. Some cards require you to pay the entire balance each month and do not charge interest. Other cards have a revolving credit agreement. **Revolving credit** is a type of credit agreement that offers a choice of paying in full each month or making payments over time. If you choose to pay only part of the charges, you will be charged interest. You should be able to receive credit card statements and make payments for credit card bills online.

If you do not pay all charges in full each month, you must make a minimum payment. The *minimum payment* required by the bank or store issuing your credit card is the least amount you are required to pay that month. Assume you have no charges on your credit card. Then, you charge $260 for back-to-school clothes. If your minimum payment is 5 percent of the balance, what will be your minimum payment?

Statement balance	$260.00
Minimum payment percentage	× .05
Minimum payment	$13.00

> **Beware of "teaser rates"** that are only good on your credit card for a few months. Another low rate might only be available if you are transferring balances from other cards. These rates will increase drastically after several months of the lower rate.

You Do the Math | 6-5

You have no charges on your credit card. Then, you charge a total of $600 on your credit card this month. Your minimum payment is 3 percent of the balance. What will be your minimum payment?

Statement balance	_____
Minimum payment percentage	_____
Minimum payment	_____

With a revolving credit account, you could be charged interest on the amounts not paid during the grace period. The interest rate could be 20 percent or more. Before you decide to buy something on credit, consider whether you can pay for that item in full when payment is due. If not, you should calculate the cost of the credit as an additional cost of the item. That "bargain" is not a good deal if you pay minimum payments and interest for the next several months or years. If you always pay off balances in full each month, you should stay out of trouble with credit card debt.

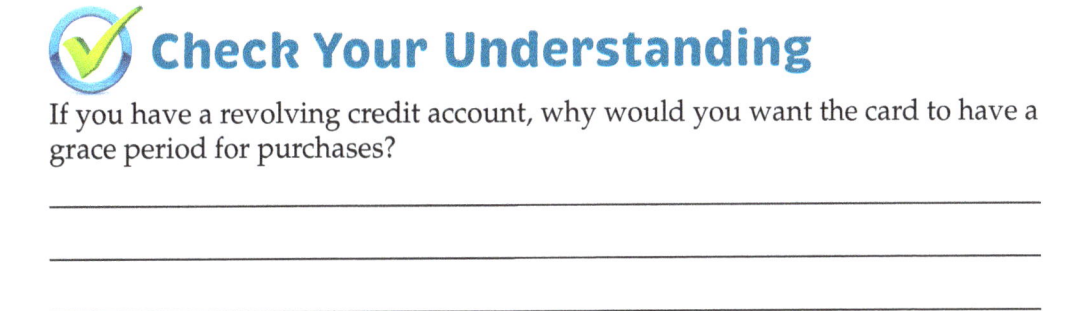

✓ Check Your Understanding

If you have a revolving credit account, why would you want the card to have a grace period for purchases?

_____
_____
_____

Are You Financially Responsible?

Handling a Credit Card: A Checklist

Having credit is a privilege and it should be taken seriously. Good credit is an asset that will help you in the future. Bad credit is a liability that may keep you from having the things that you need or want. How would you rate your "credit personality"?

	Yes	No	
1.	____	____	I want more of everything and am not satisfied with what I have.
2.	____	____	I tend to buy things because my friends have them, even when I really cannot afford them.
3.	____	____	I am strong enough to resist impulse buying.
4.	____	____	I am willing to give up future income to buy things I want but may not be able to afford now.
5.	____	____	I know I should pay my credit card statement in full each month.
6.	____	____	I think I really need a credit card. I do not want one just because my friends have them.
7.	____	____	I understand what credit history means and its importance to my future.
8.	____	____	I know what a FICO score is and its importance.
9.	____	____	I understand that I should only have one credit card at first.
10.	____	____	I will not charge anything that I know I cannot afford to pay for in full when I receive the statement.

6-5 Purchasing Decisions

You will have many choices to make about what to buy, when to buy it, and how to pay for it. Think about the purchasing decisions you typically make. Some decisions require more thought than others.

- An *impulse decision* is made without any planning or research. You see an item, you like it, and you buy it on the spot.
- A *routine decision* requires little thought because it is made often. Every Saturday, you go to a movie. This is routine and does not require much thought.
- A *limited decision* requires some amount of research and planning. You know you need to purchase a computer. You research different models, such as tablets and laptops, and you plan for the purchase in your budget.
- An *extensive decision* requires a great deal of research and planning. This type is usually made when making serious plans or when buying something with a higher price. Examples include planning how to pay for college or purchasing a car.

Impulse and routine decisions do not usually involve much thought. However, decisions that require research, planning, or a lot of money need more attention.

✓ Check Your Understanding

Name four types of decisions.

_____

_____

_____

Your Turn

Types of Financial Decisions

Some financial decisions require more thought and research than others do. Recall the last three financial decisions you recently made. Categorize each one as impulse, routine, limited, or extensive. Provide reasons for each.

Decision	Type	Reasoning

Comparison Shopping

One way to make good purchasing decisions is to comparison shop. **Comparison shopping** is gathering information about products to find the best option among similar ones. Comparison shopping means looking at the price, quality, and other information about a product that is important to you. You can learn a lot about a product by reading the label. There are also many websites that can help you compare products.

Decision-Making Process

Decision-Making Process

1. Define the decision to be made
2. Gather information
3. Choose the best option
4. Act on the decision
5. Evaluate the decision

Goodheart-Willcox Publisher

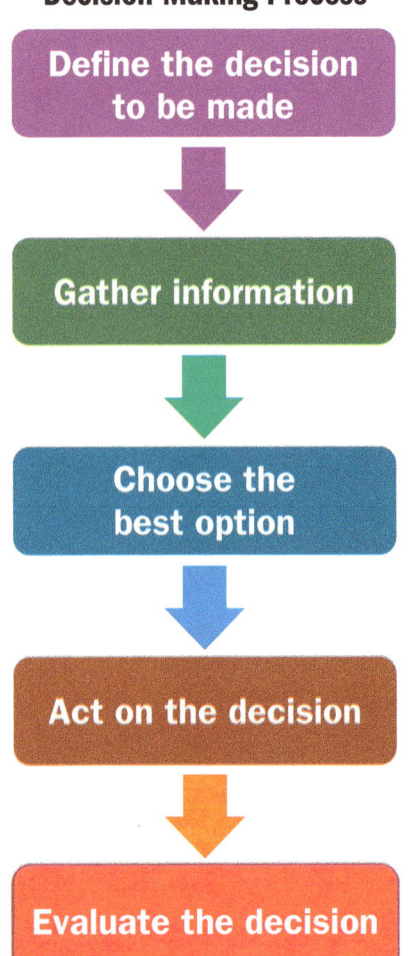

Figure 6-2 Decision-making is the process of solving a problem. *How can you use the decision-making process when deciding if you should use credit?*

A *decision-making process* can help you make wise purchases. **Decision-making** is the process of solving a problem. It includes choosing a course of action after evaluating available information and weighing the costs, benefits, and consequences of alternative actions. Figure 6-2 shows the steps in the decision-making process.

For example, assume you have $100 to spend. You want to buy a pair of boots that costs $68 and a jacket that costs $89. You only have $100 so you must make a choice.

1. **Define the decision to be made.** Identify the choices to be made. *I want to buy a pair of boots and a jacket.*
2. **Gather information.** Gather information that will help you make a choice based on facts. *I have $100 to spend. The boots cost $68 and the jacket costs $89.*
3. **Choose the best option.** After considering all potential solutions, pick the one that best fits the situation. *I need a new pair of boots, but I want a jacket.*
4. **Act on the decision.** Once a decision is made, make it happen. *I will buy the boots because they are a real need.*
5. **Evaluate the decision.** After time has passed, the solution can be analyzed to determine if it was the correct course of action. *I made the right decision because we got a lot of snow and my old boots were worn out.*

Choices must be prioritized, which means you choose one item or decision over another. You cannot have everything you want, so you must make a trade-off and give up something. A **trade-off** is what is given up when someone makes one choice over another. An **opportunity cost** is the value of the option given up. In the previous example, you made a trade-off and bought the item you needed the most. The opportunity cost, or what you gave up, was the jacket.

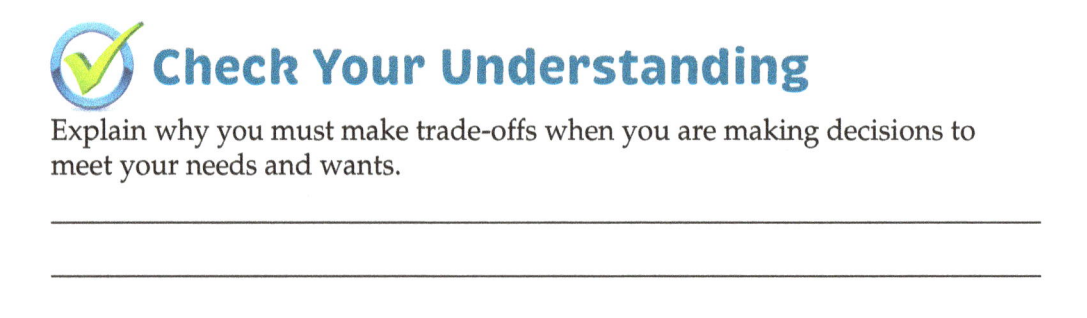

✓ Check Your Understanding

Explain why you must make trade-offs when you are making decisions to meet your needs and wants.

_____

_____

_____

Your Turn

Decision-Making Process

Applying the decision-making process can help you make smart choices when spending your money. Use the decision-making process to analyze a financial decision you need to make or have recently made.

1. Define the decision to be made:
   _____
   _____

2. Gather information:
   _____
   _____

3. Choose the best option:
   _____
   _____

4. Act on the decision:
   _____
   _____

5. Evaluate the decision:
   _____
   _____

6-6 Credit Card Debt

It is not uncommon for students to have $5,000–$10,000 or more in credit card debt by the time they leave college, in addition to student loans. What do students use credit cards to buy? Is it books and tuition or pizza, entertainment, and clothes? Do you really want to pay for that pizza for the next five years or longer? Many students do exactly that if they graduate with credit card debt.

FYI: If you pay your credit card bills on time, banks will sometimes automatically raise your credit limit. If you do not want them to do this, you can call the bank and request that your limit stay the same.

Many people overuse a credit card and create debt that takes years to pay off. *Describe what your plan will be to avoid credit card debt.*

LightField Studios/Shutterstock.com

A *credit card statement* is a summary of all the activity on a credit card. Always check to see if the charges on your statement are for purchases you have made. An example of a credit card statement is shown in Figure 6-3.

Credit card statements must state how long it will take you to pay off your balance if you make only the minimum payment. Look carefully at the credit card statement shown in Figure 6-3. Notice that with a balance of only $152.33 and an interest rate of 24.5 percent, it would take *five years* to pay off your balance and you would pay a total of $275!

Figure 6-3 A credit card statement is sent each month to summarize the activity on a credit card. *How can the information on this document help you follow your financial plan?*

Credit Card Statement

Account Statement

For the period ending Aug 9, 20-- Days in billing cycle: 31
Questions or lost/stolen card? Call Customer Service 1-800-555-1234

Account Number: XXXX-XXXX-XXXX-XXXX
Page: 1 of 4

Summary of Account Activity

Previous Balance	$0.00
Payments	$0.00
Other Credits/Adjustments	$0.00
Purchases	+$152.33
Cash Advances	$0.00
Fees Charged	$0.00
Interest Charged	$0.00
Total New Balance	**$152.33**
Past Due Amount	$0.00
Credit Limit	$3000.00
Credit Available	$2847.00

Payment Information

Total New Balance	$152.33
Minimum Payment Due	$5.00
Payment Due Date	Sep 9, 20--

Late Payment Warning: If we do not receive your minimum payment by the date listed above, you may have to pay a Late Payment Fee of up to $25.00.

Minimum Payment Warning: If you make only the minimum payment each period, you will pay more in interest and it will take you longer to pay off your balance. For example:

If you make no additional charges using this card and each month you pay...	You will pay off the balance shown on this Statement in about...	And you will end up paying an estimated total of...
Only the minimum payment	5 years	$275
$6	3 years	$217 (Savings=$58)

If you are experiencing financial difficulty and would like information about credit counseling or debt management services, you may call 1-800-123-4567.

Goodheart-Willcox Publisher

Online financial calculators can be used to see approximately how long it will take to pay off balances at various interest rates. A sample credit card payment calculator is shown in Figure 6-4. The methods used by banks to calculate credit card balances on which you pay interest charges vary. Therefore, the results shown for the online calculators may not match those for your account exactly. However, the results will give you an idea of the payments needed. For example, suppose you have a charge of $260. The APR is 18 percent. If you make a minimum payment of $15 per month, it takes 21 months to pay off the charge and the related interest. To avoid paying interest, charge only what you can pay for in full when you receive your bill.

Credit Card Payment Calculator

Credit balance	$260.00
APR	18%
Monthly payment amount	$15.00
Display results (monthly or yearly)	monthly

Calculate

Results

Number of monthly payments required to pay off the balance:	21
Interest amount:	$43.00

Goodheart-Willcox Publisher

Figure 6-4 A financial calculator can be used to estimate how long it will take to pay off credit card debt. *How might this information affect your decision to use credit?*

✓ Check Your Understanding

Why is it useful for credit card statements to show how long it will take to pay off your balance and the total interest you will pay?

_____

_____

_____

Internet Connection

Credit Card Payment Calculator

1. Find a financial calculator online. Use a search term such as *credit card payment calculator*.
2. Using the calculator, fill in the following chart to see how many months it will take to pay off these credit card balances.

Balance	Interest Rate	Monthly Payment	Months to Pay Off
$5,000	18%	$150	
350	16%	25	
12,000	12%	200	
1,650	10%	100	
3,600	8%	50	

Dollars and Sense

Are You Ready for a Credit Card?

"We accept all major credit cards." How many times have you seen this sign? The advertisement forgets to tell you that you still must pay for whatever you purchase. You might not pay today, but you must pay when you receive your statement. Do you think you will have more money in 30 days when the bill arrives than you have today? If you do not have the money to pay the bill in full, you could be charged some hefty finance charges.

Credit cards are a big responsibility that should not be taken lightly. It is very tempting to use a credit card for your immediate needs or wants. Nevertheless, you still must pay for the purchases. Overusing credit, especially credit cards, gives people the most problems financially. Don't go overboard with credit simply because it is easy to get what you want.

If you think you are responsible enough to have your own credit card, do some homework before you apply for one. Answer the following questions as you think about getting a credit card.

- Will I need a cosigner when I open an account?
- Are there any fees associated with opening an account? If so, how much are they?
- Am I required to pay the balance in full each month?
- Are there late fees if I miss the date to pay the bill?
- What is the interest rate?
- How are finance charges on unpaid balances calculated?
- Is there a monthly or annual fee charged for having the credit card?
- Is there a credit limit, and will it be raised automatically if I pay on time?
- Am I responsible enough to keep my credit limit low?
- Am I responsible enough to pay off a credit card in full each month?
- Does the bank offer any fraud insurance for the card?

If you decide you are responsible enough to manage a credit card, remember to use it wisely. Get only one credit card you can use in places where you generally shop or online. Keep the credit card in a safe place to protect your identity. Also, keep a record of the credit card number in a safe place in case the card is lost or stolen. Do not let friends borrow your credit card. Be responsible, respect the limits, and pay the balance by the due date.

If your credit card is lost or stolen, you are only liable for $50 no matter how much has been charged on it. However, there are steps you should take if that happens. Call the credit card company immediately to report a lost or stolen card. Also, contact the three major credit bureaus to let them know your card has been lost or stolen to prevent damage to your credit report.

6-7 Bankruptcy

Excessive debt can lead to bankruptcy. **Bankruptcy** is a legal situation in which the courts excuse a debtor from repaying some or all debt. In return, the debtor must give up certain assets or possessions. Declaring bankruptcy is a legal decision that a person, company, or organization is unable to pay debts owed. Filing for bankruptcy usually does not eliminate student loans or unpaid taxes. You may still be responsible for paying these debts.

Bankruptcy laws are divided into *chapters*, with two main types of personal bankruptcies. **Chapter 7 bankruptcy**, also called *straight bankruptcy*, eliminates most types of debt and stays on your credit report for ten years. You must turn over your property to be sold to pay your *creditors*, which are the people or businesses to whom you owe money. If you file for Chapter 7 bankruptcy, you may be allowed to keep your home, car, and other personal items, called *exemptions*. The laws regarding property that can be exempt vary by state.

Chapter 13 bankruptcy allows a person with regular income to pay all or some debts to a trustee, who will pay the creditors. Payments should be lower than what you are paying now. A Chapter 13 plan represents at least an effort to repay your creditors. You usually get to keep the assets you own while lowering some of your interest and penalties. A Chapter 13 bankruptcy stays on your credit report for ten years or if discharged early, seven years.

Bankruptcy should be used only as a last resort. Any type of bankruptcy lowers your credit score and stays on your credit record for years. This can make it very difficult to get credit and force you to pay higher interest rates.

> **FYI**
> If you have a large amount of debt, you can work directly with your creditors to discuss options for repayment. One option is *loan consolidation*, which is combining multiple debts into one debt with one interest rate. Another option is to renegotiate the repayment schedule.

✓ Check Your Understanding

What is the difference between Chapter 7 and Chapter 13 bankruptcies?

_____
_____
_____
_____
_____
_____

There are laws that regulate lenders and provide protection to those who use credit. Some important laws with which you should be familiar are as follows.
- The *Truth in Lending Act* requires a lender to provide truthful and complete information about the cost of using credit.
- The *Fair Credit Reporting Act* requires a person's credit report to be made available to the person and authorized third parties and that it be accurate.
- The *Equal Credit Opportunity Act* prevents creditors from discrimination and ensures creditors will only deny credit for financial reasons.
- The *Fair Debt Collection Practices Act* establishes rules for debt collectors to ensure debt collection is fair and honest.

In addition, each state establishes a maximum percentage of interest that may be charged. If you have any questions about credit or credit laws, seek advice from a professional to learn about your rights as a consumer.

✓ Check Your Understanding

List some of the laws with which all credit cardholders should be familiar.

_____
_____
_____

Internet Connection

Truth in Lending

1. Using the Internet, search for *Truth in Lending disclosure statement*. Select one of the examples you find and read the statement.
2. What does this statement mean to you as someone who may be using credit or will do so in the future?

_____
_____
_____
_____
_____

Chapter 6 Review and Assessment

Summary

6-1 Discuss earning the privilege of credit.

Credit is an agreement in which one party lends money or provides goods or services to another with the understanding that payment will be made later. Before granting credit, the lender must decide if you are creditworthy. The three Cs of credit are character, capacity, and capital.

6-2 Explain the role of credit bureaus.

A credit bureau collects information about the financial and credit transactions of consumers. Businesses request information from credit bureaus about potential customers and their histories for paying bills. Three major credit bureaus are Equifax, Experian, and TransUnion. When you apply for credit, the lender will request a credit report or FICO score from these bureaus before extending credit.

6-3 Summarize the use of credit cards.

A credit card allows the cardholder to make purchases up to an authorized amount and pay for them later. In addition to making purchases with a credit card, you may obtain a cash advance, which is a loan against the available credit on a credit card.

6-4 Summarize selecting a credit card.

When selecting a credit card, consider the cost of using the credit and the credit terms offered. Using a credit card is not free if the balance is not paid in full each month. Credit terms and agreements vary for credit cards.

6-5 Evaluate purchasing decisions.

Types of decisions related to purchasing include impulse, routine, limited, and extensive decisions. Comparison shopping can help you make good purchasing decisions, as can the *decision-making process*. The steps of this process are define the decision, gather information, choose the best option, act on the decision, and evaluate the decision.

6-6 Discuss credit card debt.

It is not uncommon for students to have credit card debt that may take several years to repay. A credit card statement is a summary of all the activity on a credit card. It states how long it will take to pay off a balance. Always check to see if the charges shown on the statement are for purchases you have made.

6-7 Define types of personal bankruptcy.

Chapter 7 bankruptcy eliminates most types of debt and stays on your credit report for ten years. Chapter 13 bankruptcy allows a person with regular income to pay all or some debts to a trustee and stays on your credit report for ten years unless discharged early.

Review Your Knowledge

Choose the correct answer for each of the following.

1. _____ A _____ is someone who signs for you to be able to get credit.
   A. character
   B. credit bureau
   C. lender
   D. cosigner

2. _____ Identify the three Cs of credit.
   A. character, capacity, capital
   B. capacity, capital, credit score
   C. capital, credit score, character
   D. capital, character, cosigner

3. _____ Assume you have $50 to spend this weekend. You want to go to an amusement park that costs $40 to enter. You also want to go to a movie, for which a ticket costs $17.50. You choose to go to the amusement park and give up seeing the movie. In this scenario, the _____ is the trade-off and _____ is the opportunity cost.
   A. amusement park; $40
   B. movie; $17.50
   C. amusement park; $17.50
   D. $40; movie

4. _____ Which document is a record of a person's credit history?
   A. credit bureau
   B. credit report
   C. credit card statement
   D. credit score

5. _____ What is a credit score?
   A. a person's ability to pay debts
   B. a person's willingness to repay debts
   C. a person's assets minus liabilities
   D. a numerical measure of a person's creditworthiness

6. _____ The amount of credit you have left before you reach your credit limit is your _____.
   A. minimum payment
   B. available credit
   C. annual percentage rate (APR)
   D. cash advance

7. _____ What is important to consider when selecting a credit card?
   A. credit terms
   B. cost of credit
   C. grace period
   D. All of the above

8. _____ What is the first step in the decision-making process?
   A. Choose the best option.
   B. Gather information.
   C. Define the decision to be made.
   D. Act on the decision.

9. ____ Which type of credit agreement offers a choice of paying in full each month or making payments over time?
    A. cash advance
    B. revolving credit
    C. proprietary credit
    D. available credit
10. ____ Which document provides a summary of all the activity on a credit card?
    A. credit application
    B. comparison-shopping statement
    C. credit card statement
    D. credit report

Build Your Vocabulary

For each word or term, write the correct definition using your own words.

11. credit

12. creditworthy

13. credit bureau

14. credit history

15. default

16. credit card

17. cash advance

18. finance charge

19. annual percentage rate (APR)

20. grace period

21. comparison shopping

22. decision-making

23. bankruptcy

24. Chapter 7 bankruptcy

25. Chapter 13 bankruptcy

Apply Your Math Skills

Calculate the answers to the following problems. Show your calculations.

26. Your FICO score of 790 enables you to borrow $6,500 at 3.5 percent interest. Your friend needs the same amount. However, because his FICO score is 600, he will have to pay 6 percent interest. How much less will you pay in simple interest in one year for the same amount of money?

27. You want to take out a cash advance on your credit card for $2,000. The transaction fee is 4.5 percent of the cash advance. The credit card company charges an interest rate of 20 percent for cash advances. How much will it cost to borrow the money as a cash advance for one year with simple interest?

28. Your credit limit is $3,500. You have charged $875 on the card. What is your available credit?

29. Your bank charges a fee of $28.50 for going over your credit limit and $23.00 for a late payment penalty. If you do both in the same month, how much will you pay for these fees?

30. You have no charges on your credit card. Then, you buy earbuds and music downloads with your credit card this month for a total of $265. Your minimum payment is 6 percent of the balance. What will be your minimum payment?

CHAPTER 7
Insurance: Protecting Your Assets

Essential Question
How can insurance help manage risk?

Learning Outcomes

When you complete Chapter 7, you will be able to:

- **7-1** Discuss insurance protection.
- **7-2** Summarize car insurance.
- **7-3** Describe homeowners insurance.
- **7-4** Summarize renters insurance.
- **7-5** List types of health insurance plans.
- **7-6** Describe disability insurance.
- **7-7** Identify types of life insurance.
- **7-8** List other types of insurance.

Key Terms

risk
insurance
premium
deductible
car insurance
collision coverage
comprehensive coverage
liability coverage
homeowners insurance
renters insurance
health insurance
disability insurance
life insurance
beneficiary
face value
term life insurance
whole life insurance
umbrella insurance policy

Reading Prep

Before reading this chapter, review the Learning Outcomes. Based on this information, write down two or three items you think will be important to note while you are reading.

What is Your Financial IQ?

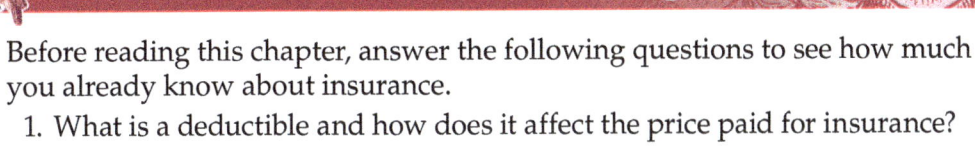

Before reading this chapter, answer the following questions to see how much you already know about insurance.

1. What is a deductible and how does it affect the price paid for insurance?

2. What determines the cost of car insurance?

3. For what does collision coverage pay?

4. What is homeowners insurance?

5. How do you think an insurance company assesses the value of your property in the event of a fire or theft?

6. Why is homeowners insurance required in order to purchase a home?

7. What is renters insurance?

8. What do you know about health insurance coverage?

9. Why might a person need life insurance?

10. What does disability insurance cover?

7-1 Insurance Protection

Life is full of risks. A **risk** is the chance an unfavorable situation could happen to you or something you own. This often results in loss, financial or otherwise. The loss could be due to damage or theft. For example, your house could be damaged in a fire or your car could be stolen. Whenever possible, you should avoid or reduce risk. For example, driving your car responsibly and within the speed limit helps you reduce the risk of an accident.

Insurance is a service purchased to protect against financial loss. An *insurance policy* is a contract that explains the kinds of losses covered by the insurance. It also states the dollar amount of the coverage you are purchasing.

There are many types of insurance you will need to buy as an adult. Insurance will be an important part of your financial plan. Purchasing it can be costly, so you must think about how much you need and can afford. Then you can include the cost in your budget.

A **premium** is an amount of money paid for insurance. Insurance companies usually allow premiums to be paid annually, semiannually, quarterly, or monthly. If you spread your payments over months or quarters, the company usually will charge an extra fee. You may have to pay more if you choose not to pay in one annual payment as a lump sum. This decision will have an impact on your budget.

Consider this example. Your insurance premium is $1,450 if you pay it annually. If you pay it semiannually, you pay $734. If you pay it quarterly, you pay $377. If you pay it monthly, you pay $130. What is the annual cost for each option? How much more will you pay if you pay monthly rather than once a year?

Step 1. Calculate semiannual premium.

Semiannual premium	$734.00
Number of payments in year	× 2
Annual premium	$1,468.00

Step 2. Calculate quarterly cost.

Quarterly premium	$377.00
Number of payments in year	× 4
Annual premium	$1,508.00

Step 3. Calculate monthly cost.

Monthly premium	$130.00
Number of payments in year	× 12
Annual premium	$1,560.00

Step 4. Calculate the difference.

Premium paid monthly	$1,560.00
Premium paid annually	− 1,450.00
Difference in cost	$110.00

You Do the Math | 7-1

Your insurance premium is $1,635 if paid annually. If paid semiannually, the premium is $835. If paid quarterly, it is $421. If paid monthly, it is $143. What is the annual cost for each option? How much more will you pay if you pay monthly?

Step 1. Calculate semiannual premium.

Semiannual premium _____

Number of payments in year _____

Annual premium _____

Step 2. Calculate quarterly cost.

Quarterly premium _____

Number of payments in year _____

Annual premium _____

Step 3. Calculate monthly cost.

Monthly premium _____

Number of payments in year _____

Annual premium _____

Step 4. Calculate the difference.

Premium paid monthly _____

Premium paid annually _____

Difference in cost _____

A risk is the chance that an unfavorable situation could happen to you or something you own. *In what ways can risks cause financial loss?*

Tinny Photo/Shutterstock.com

When a person with insurance suffers a loss, he or she makes a claim. A *claim* is the process of documenting a loss against an insurance policy. Usually, the insurance company requires you to pay a deductible when making a claim. A **deductible** is an amount of money that must be paid before the insurance company begins to pay on a claim. The higher the deductible, the lower your premium will be. You may be able to lower the cost of your insurance if you raise the deductible.

✓ Check Your Understanding

How does insurance protect you against loss?

_____
_____
_____
_____

7-2 Car Insurance

FYI: A safe-driving course may lower your car insurance premiums up to 10 percent.

Car insurance, or *auto insurance*, protects against financial loss related to a passenger car. It will protect you if your car is damaged or stolen. This type of insurance may also protect you if you cause damage to someone else's property or injure someone with your car.

You might already know that car insurance can be very expensive for those under age 25. Other factors can affect how much you pay. These include your:
- gender
- driving record
- prior insurance claims
- location
- credit record
- marital status
- type of car

You will get a better rate if you are named on the policy of a parent or guardian. Good grades and driving classes should also lower your costs.

If you are thinking about buying a car, research the cost of insurance for the one you want before you buy it. You will not be able to get a car loan without proof of insurance. Typically, the newer and sportier the car, the more insurance will be. Consider the cost of the insurance as part of the cost of the car. You may reconsider the type of car you want to buy.

When shopping for car insurance, you can pick and choose what you buy, as shown in Figure 7-1. There are many options when selecting the type of car insurance right for you. Do not spend money to buy more insurance than you actually need. Make sure you have coverage that suits you.

Collision coverage pays for damage to your car caused by a collision with another car. If you have a newer car, you will want to have this type of coverage to repair or replace your car. If you are driving a car that is 10 years old, you may not need this type of insurance.

Comprehensive coverage pays for damage unrelated to a collision. For example, your car might be stolen or damaged in a fire.

It is the law in most states to have liability coverage. **Liability coverage** protects people who suffer injuries or whose property is damaged in a car accident. Always protect yourself with liability coverage. You do not want to take a chance on legal action by a person who suffered injuries as a result of your driving.

Deductibles for car insurance can range from $250 to $1,500. You may be able to lower the cost of your insurance if you raise the deductible. For example, you could change it from $250 to $500 or more.

> **FYI**
>
> A car that is *totaled* is damaged beyond repair. The insurance company may pay the "Blue Book" value of the car. This amount might not be what you think it is worth. The term "Blue Book" refers to the *Kelley Blue Book*, a publication that lists the value of the make and model of each car. It is considered the standard guide of car values.

Types of Car Insurance Coverage

Type	Coverage
Property liability	Covers damage you cause to others' property if an accident is your fault
Bodily injury liability	Covers injury to other persons if an accident is your fault, including medical bills and lost wages
Uninsured/underinsured motorist	Covers your expenses if the person who caused the accident does not have insurance or does not have enough coverage, or if you are a victim of a hit and run
Collision	Covers your auto if it is damaged in a collision with another car regardless of which party was responsible
Comprehensive	Pays the cost of damages to a car that occur as a result of a non-collision incident
Medical	Covers medical treatment for you and your passengers if you are in an accident regardless of fault
Roadside assistance	Covers the cost if your car breaks down and needs to be towed
Rental reimbursement	Covers cost of a rental car for a short time if your vehicle is damaged or stolen

Goodheart-Willcox Publisher

Figure 7-1 You will have many choices when selecting a car insurance policy. *What does "adequate coverage" for car insurance mean to you?*

Your Turn

Car Insurance Application

Complete the following form for car insurance. This exercise will be good practice for when you are ready to apply for insurance.

Personal Auto Application				
Insured Information				
Driver's Name:				
Driver's License Number:				
Date of Birth:				
Marital Status:	Single ☐	Married ☐	Divorced ☐	
Home Address:				
City:	State:		Zip:	
Phone Number:				
Fax Number:				
E-mail Address:				
Vehicle Garaging Address:				
Prior Coverage Information				
How Long Have You Had Continuous Coverage?				
Prior Carrier Name:				
Prior Policy Number:				
Limits of Insurance				
Liability Limits for Per Vehicle/Per Accident:	25/50 ☐	50/100 ☐	100/300 ☐	250/500 ☐
Combined Single Limit:	100,000 ☐	300,000 ☐	500,000 ☐	
Property Limit (Your Vehicle):	$			
Comprehensive Deductible:	250 ☐	500 ☐	1,000 ☐	
Collision Deductible:	250 ☐	500 ☐	1,000 ☐	
Vehicle Information				
Vehicle Year:				
Vehicle Make and Model:				
Vehicle License Number:				
VIN Number:				
Odometer Reading:				
Annual Mileage:				

Goodheart-Willcox Publisher; Source: Endless Insurance Services

Check Your Understanding

What is the purpose of car insurance?

_____

_____

_____

Internet Connection

Car Insurance

1. Each state requires different types and amounts of car insurance for drivers. Search the Internet using the phrase *mandatory car insurance* plus the name of your state. List your state's requirements.

   _____

   _____

2. Has your state adopted no-fault insurance? If so, explain how it works.

   _____

   _____

3. Use the Internet to find *car insurance estimate by model*. Follow the directions provided on the website you select to find the approximate premiums for five different cars. At least one should be your "dream" car, the brand-new car you would buy if you had the money. At least one should be a very affordable used car. Determine the cost of the premium for each of the five cars if you pay semiannually, quarterly, or monthly. Assume you want full coverage and have a $500 deductible.

Premiums

Car	Annual	Semiannual	Quarterly	Monthly

continued

Internet Connection (continued)

4. Look up the *Kelley Blue Book* value for the same five cars.

Car	Blue Book Value

Dollars and Sense

Know Your Car Insurance Policy

Including money for insurance is an important part of financial planning and creating your budget. While in school, you will probably be on the car insurance policy of your parents or guardians. If you are, have your parent or guardian explain the coverage on you and your car. It is important for you to understand what is covered and your responsibilities as a driver.

Always keep the following items and information in a safe place inside the car, such as in the glove compartment:
- insurance card
- phone number of your insurance company
- car registration
- pen and paper to write down any information if an accident should happen

As you become independent and responsible for your car insurance costs, you will have to budget for insurance premiums. It is important to have proper coverage and the ability to pay the premiums on time. *Never drive a car without liability coverage.*

Talk with an experienced person who can guide you on the types of coverage needed for your car. Check your budget and see how much you can afford to spend for insurance. Then, research several insurance companies to see what rates they offer.

7-3 Homeowners Insurance

Homeowners insurance protects against damage to a house and its contents. Often, it also provides liability coverage if a person were to be injured at your home. An example of a liability that could be covered is a person who was hurt after slipping and falling on your ice-covered sidewalk.

Just as with a car loan, you will not be able to get a loan to buy a home unless you have proof of insurance on the house. The insurance must cover the cost of replacing the house. This may be a different amount than what you paid for it.

Contents in a home include furniture, appliances, electronics, and clothing. A home's contents are usually insured for at least 50 percent of the value of the house. For example, your home is insured for $285,000. You chose 65 percent coverage on the contents of your home. What is the dollar amount of coverage you will have on the contents of your home?

Value of home	$285,000.00
Percent coverage for contents	× .65
Coverage on contents	$185,250.00

You Do the Math | 7-2

Your home is insured for $345,000. You insured the contents for 60 percent of the home's value. What is the dollar amount of coverage you will have on the contents of your home?

Value of home	_____
Percent coverage for contents	_____
Coverage on contents	_____

If you own items such as high-end electronics or expensive jewelry, you may need extra coverage. Keep an updated inventory of household and personal items in a safe place. Your insurance company may provide a booklet to keep an inventory of the items.

Contents can be insured for replacement value or actual cash value. *Replacement value* is the amount you would need to pay to replace the item. *Actual cash value* is the replacement cost minus wear and tear. Replacement value coverage is usually more expensive to buy.

Your policy may also pay for the cost of temporary housing if your home is damaged. You might not be able to live in your home safely while it is being repaired after a fire, for instance. The more coverage you have, the higher your premiums will be.

✓ Check Your Understanding

Why is homeowners insurance needed?

_____
_____
_____
_____
_____
_____

7-4 Renters Insurance

When you rent a place to live, the property owner's insurance covers the building itself. However, it does not cover your possessions. You might be surprised when you total the value of your belongings. You might have furniture, electronics, jewelry, clothes, and other household items. It would be costly to replace these items if they were damaged or stolen.

Renters insurance protects against theft or damage to the contents of rented property. You may be asked to provide proof of renters insurance before renting an apartment. This type of insurance also provides liability coverage if someone were to be hurt in your apartment. For example, a person could become injured by tripping over a pet.

If you go away to college, you may be included on the homeowners or renters insurance policy of your parents or guardians. This may be the case whether you live in a dorm room or rent an apartment.

Renters insurance is much less expensive than homeowners because you are not insuring the building. Some policies pay the actual cash value of the lost items. Other policies cover replacement costs. When you buy renters insurance, a policy that pays the replacement value of your belongings may be a better choice.

Assume you live in a rented apartment. You pay premiums of $18.75 per month for renters insurance. How much is your renters insurance for one year?

Monthly premium	$18.75
Number of months	× 12
Annual cost	$225.00

You Do the Math | 7-3

You live in a rented house. You pay premiums of $25.50 per month for renters insurance. How much is your renters insurance for one year?

Monthly premium	_____
Number of months	_____
Annual cost	_____

✓ Check Your Understanding

Do you need renters insurance if the owner of your apartment building has insurance on the building? Why or why not?

_____

_____

_____

Your Turn

Inventory

Assume you will be renting your own apartment. List items you would take with you when you move. Write the approximate replacement cost for each item. Include furniture, clothes, computers, and everything you think you would bring. Total the value of all items.

Item	Replacement Cost
	$
	$
	$
	$
	$
	$
	$
	$
	$
	$
	$

7-5 Health Insurance

> **FYI**
> Currently, most young people can be covered under their parents' health insurance until age 26.

Health insurance protects against financial loss due to illness or injury. These costs can be very expensive. One hospital stay can be devastating financially. Having sufficient health insurance is essential.

Some employers pay some or all the cost of health insurance for their employees. If you obtain health insurance through your employer, you may not have a choice in the plan. Even so, you will likely pay more money for less coverage if you choose to buy it on your own.

Health insurance plans can be very confusing. Ask questions before selecting a plan. Know what your deductible and premium amounts will be. Find out if you will have copayments. A *copayment* is a flat fee you must pay when you receive medical services.

Health insurance plans may offer coverage for prescription drugs. Often, people have no clue what these medications actually cost. They simply pay a copayment of $4, $10, or $15 and do not think about the total cost. In reality, it may be hundreds of dollars for a 30-day supply. Select a plan with prescription coverage if you can.

Assume your employer deducts $75 each week from your paycheck for health insurance. Your plan requires a $15 copayment for each doctor visit and a $15 copayment for prescriptions. If you visit your doctor three times this month and fill two prescriptions, what is your total health care expense for the month?

Step 1. Calculate your health insurance premiums.

Weekly premiums	$75.00
Number of premiums per month	× 4
Monthly insurance premium	$300.00

Step 2. Calculate doctor copayments.

Doctor copayment	$15.00
Number of visits	× 3
Total doctor copayments	$45.00

Step 3. Calculate prescription copayments.

Prescription copayment	$15.00
Number of prescriptions	× 2
Total prescription copayments	$30.00

Step 4. Calculate monthly medical costs.

Monthly premiums	$300.00
Doctor copayments	45.00
Prescription copayments	+ 30.00
Total monthly cost	$375.00

You Do the Math | 7-4

You pay $163.75 semimonthly for health insurance premiums. Your plan requires a $20 copayment for a doctor visit. It requires a $15 copayment for prescriptions. You visit your doctor twice and need four prescriptions in one month. What is your total medical expense for the month?

Step 1. Calculate your monthly health insurance premiums.
- Semimonthly premiums _____
- Number of premiums per month _____
- Monthly insurance premium _____

Step 2. Calculate doctor copayments.
- Doctor copayment _____
- Number of visits _____
- Total doctor copayments _____

Step 3. Calculate prescription copayments.
- Prescription copayment _____
- Number of prescriptions _____
- Total prescription copayments _____

Step 4. Calculate monthly medical costs.
- Monthly premiums _____
- Doctor copayments _____
- Prescription copayments _____
- Total monthly cost _____

Keeping physically fit throughout your life usually will keep your health care costs lower. Make exercise and eating right a part of your life *now*. Stick with it as you get older.

The *Consolidated Omnibus Budget Reconciliation Act (COBRA)* allows you to keep the health care provided through an employer if you leave your job. You can extend your coverage for up to 18 months. You will have to pay the full premium, so it is very expensive. Still, you will be able to have health care coverage until you can be covered under another plan.

There are many types of health insurance coverage. Three main types are HMO, PPO, and POS plans.

HMO Plans

HMO stands for *health maintenance organization*. HMOs are a popular type of health insurance plan. With an HMO, you must use doctors, hospitals, and clinics in the HMO's network. HMOs are often less expensive than other types of plans. You will usually pay a copayment for a medical visit, and you may have an annual deductible.

FYI: Many health insurance providers charge higher premiums to people who use tobacco products.

Before choosing an HMO plan, look over the list of doctors carefully. You may not be covered if you receive care from a doctor that is not in the network. A referral may be needed if you must see a specialist.

PPO Plans

PPO stands for *preferred provider organization*. PPOs have a network of doctors and hospitals, so you have more freedom to choose. Typically, a referral for a specialist is not needed. You may also use other doctors and hospitals that are not in the network. You will usually have a copayment for any medical care you receive, and you may have an annual deductible.

POS Plans

POS stands for *point of service*. With a POS plan, you select a primary care physician from a list of those in the network. This person supervises your care and refers you to specialists if needed. You can also use an out-of-network provider, but it will cost more out of pocket (the amount you will have to pay). You will usually not have to pay copayments, but you may have an annual deductible.

✓ Check Your Understanding

What is the purpose of health insurance?

_____
_____
_____
_____

Internet Connection

Minimizing Health Care Costs

1. Search the Internet for ways you can stay healthy to help minimize your health care costs. Use a search phrase such as *tips for staying healthy.*
2. List at least five things you can do to stay healthy and avoid paying some of the costs of health care.

_____
_____
_____
_____

7-6 Disability Insurance

Once you begin to work and support yourself, you need to think about disability insurance. **Disability insurance** pays a portion of income to a worker who becomes injured or ill and cannot work. If you cannot work, the loss of income can cause major financial problems. You may be able to buy disability coverage through your employer. Some employers provide this type of insurance at no cost as an employee benefit.

These insurance plans typically pay approximately 60 percent of your wages or salary, with a waiting period of 30 to 60 days or more before coverage begins. This is one more reason to have that three- to six-month cash reserve!

Disability insurance is not the same as workers' compensation. *Workers' compensation insurance* helps pay for medical care and lost wages if an employee becomes injured or ill from their job. Every state requires employers to have this coverage.

> **FYI**
> Although more people buy life insurance in the event of death, you are approximately three times more likely to become disabled during your working years than you are to pass away.

✓ Check Your Understanding

Why is disability insurance important?

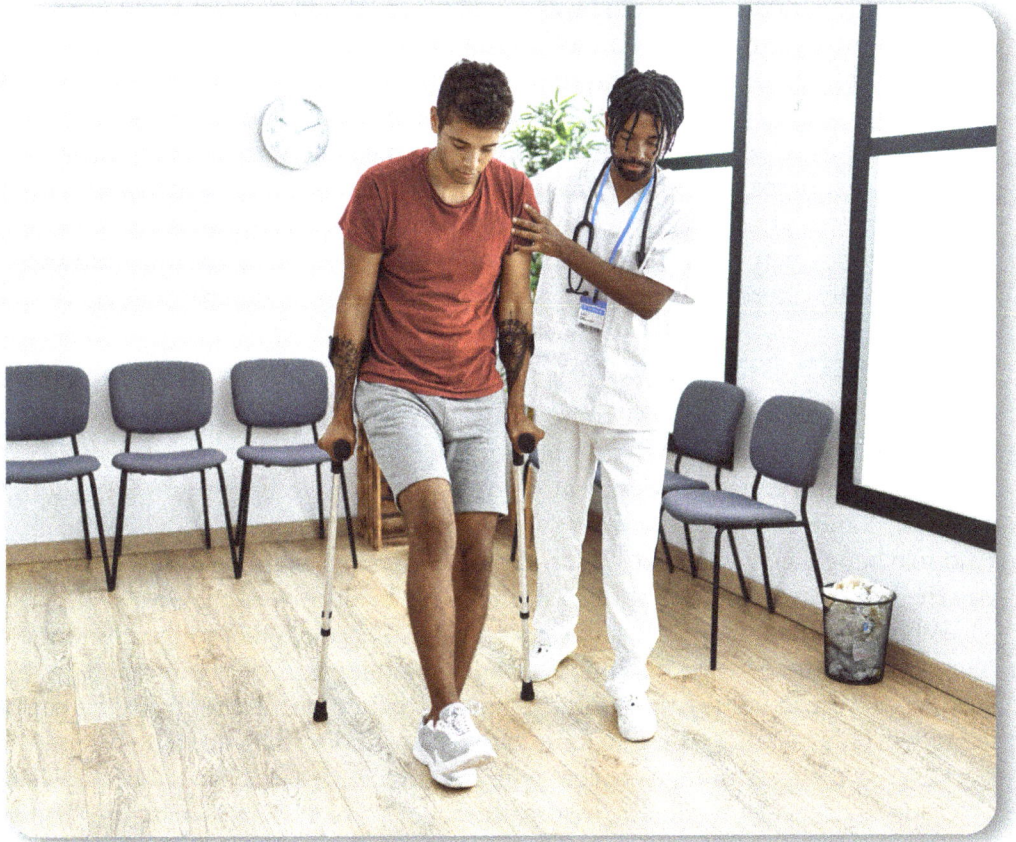

_____
_____
_____

Health insurance usually covers costs related to accidents. *Why do you think it would be a good idea to purchase health insurance?*

Krakenimages.com/Shuutterstock.com

7-7 Life Insurance

Most young people do not think about life insurance. Once you have a spouse, children, or others who depend on you, life insurance is important. **Life insurance** provides benefits after the death of the insured person to people named as beneficiaries. A **beneficiary** is a person named in the policy to receive the benefits. More than one beneficiary may be named. A young single adult might name parents or siblings. A married person might name a spouse or children.

Life insurance premiums are based on several factors. These include the age, health, occupation, and hobbies of the insured person. In other words, if your hobby is rock climbing, your premiums will be higher. Someone whose hobby is stamp collecting will not have to pay as much. The younger and healthier you are, the less costly life insurance may be.

The **face value** of a life insurance policy is the amount that will be paid out upon your death, also called a *death benefit*. These amounts are generally not taxable. It is recommended to have at least enough life insurance to cover the costs of a funeral.

There are two basic types of life insurance. They are term life insurance and whole life insurance.

Term Life Insurance

Term life insurance provides coverage only for a specific period. The term might be for five or ten years, for instance. This is the most basic form of life insurance. It is also the least expensive. How much you need will vary based on your financial responsibilities. Term insurance may be the most affordable type of life insurance for you to buy on your own. When you get a full-time job, your employer may offer low-cost group term life insurance.

The premium for term insurance is typically low when you are young. The cost may rise as you get older. The policy may terminate if you change jobs. Some policies have a clause that guarantees renewal of the policy, usually at a higher rate. Term insurance is often used as protection when taking out a loan such as a home mortgage. This is to guarantee the debt will be repaid if the borrower dies.

Your policy may have the option of being converted to whole life insurance. This is usually offered within the first several years you have the policy.

Whole Life Insurance

Whole life insurance is insurance that is in effect for the life of the insured person if you continue to pay premiums. Other names for it are *permanent life, universal life,* and *variable life*. Typically, you will pay a fixed premium for as long as you live and have the policy. The value of the policy, or the death benefit, is paid to a beneficiary when the insured person dies. You will be covered if you pay the premiums. It does not matter what your health status may be.

Whole life insurance grows in cash value. *Cash value* refers to the amount of money the insured person would receive if the policy was paid out before he or she dies. The cash value may build up enough to pay for the premiums as you get older. This means you will continue to be covered with little or no out-of-pocket cost; a big advantage of whole life insurance.

You may cancel a whole life insurance policy to receive its cash value. The amount depends on how long you have had the policy and its terms.

You also may be able to withdraw part of the cash value or request a portion as a loan. The death benefit will be reduced by the amount you withdraw or borrow. The death benefit is restored when a loan is repaid in full. The company will charge you interest to borrow against your policy. However, the loan may provide needed cash in an emergency. The interest rate should be lower than credit card interest.

Whole life insurance may give you the option of receiving a monthly income. This is called an *annuity*. If you choose this option, one lump sum will not be paid to a beneficiary when you die. Instead, you will receive the money paid into the policy plus interest in small monthly payments. This can help you pay expenses during your retirement. Some policies also may provide for long-term care for older adults.

Although term insurance is cheaper and good to have while you're working, it's a good idea to have a mixture of both term and whole-life insurance.

Check Your Understanding

Explain the purpose of life insurance and the various types that are available.

_____
_____
_____
_____

Internet Connection

Insurance Plan

1. What is your insurance plan for the next several years? In the table that follows, list types of insurance you think you might need. Then, estimate what you think each one will cost.
2. Next, conduct Internet research to determine the actual cost of each type. You might begin by entering the type of insurance listed along with the word *cost* as a search term. For example, *life insurance cost*.

Type of Insurance	Estimated Cost	Actual Cost
	$	$
	$	$
	$	$
	$	$
	$	$

7-8 Other Types of Insurance

There are many more types of insurance you may want to buy. Remember that you want to be insured, but not *over*insured. It's impossible to cover every imaginable setback—that's why you need your emergency fund. The premiums must fit into your budget. Here are some other types of insurance you may want to review in the future.

- Disease coverage pays if you develop a specific disease, such as cancer. This type of insurance is not needed if you have adequate health insurance.
- Dental and vision insurance cover costs related to your teeth and eyes. These are good to have if they fit in your budget.
- Warranty insurance on appliances, cars, and other purchases extends the manufacturer's warranty on the product. Think carefully before you purchase this type of insurance. Its cost may be more than the value of the item you are buying.
- Flood insurance is required if your home is in a designated flood plain.
- Long-term care insurance pays if you need to stay in a nursing home or an assisted-living facility or need in-home care.
- Travel insurance covers losses if you must cancel a trip and are not able to get your money back. Flight insurance may be included free if you charge airline tickets on a specific credit card.
- Pet insurance covers veterinary expenses for pets.

Some families choose to buy an umbrella policy. An **umbrella insurance policy** is liability insurance that protects against losses not covered by other policies. It is called this because it shields you more broadly than your primary coverage. This type of policy often goes into effect only when all other policies have paid their full amounts.

Think about how much insurance you really need. Consider the premiums you can afford. Then, select the plans that are right for you.

✓ Check Your Understanding

List examples of other types of insurance you may need to purchase throughout your life.

_____
_____
_____
_____

Are You Financially Responsible?

Looking to Buy Insurance: A Checklist

Young adults need to begin thinking about insurance. There are many kinds of insurance available. It is sometimes challenging to decide what is most important. Use this checklist to help you consider your insurance needs.

	Yes	No	
1.	_____	_____	Do I understand what *risk* means and why it is important to have insurance?
2.	_____	_____	Do I know how much car insurance costs and how often I must pay it?
3.	_____	_____	Do I know what car insurance covers?
4.	_____	_____	If I move into an apartment, do I know how much renters insurance will cost?
5.	_____	_____	Do I have an inventory of my personal items that would need to be replaced in the event of a theft or fire?
6.	_____	_____	Will I be covered by someone's health insurance until I am 26?
7.	_____	_____	Do I have dental insurance?
8.	_____	_____	Do I have vision insurance?
9.	_____	_____	Do I have a life insurance policy?
10.	_____	_____	Do I have a plan for paying for insurance that I purchase?

Chapter 7 Review and Assessment

Summary

7-1 Discuss insurance protection.

Insurance is a service that is purchased to protect against financial loss. A premium is an amount paid for insurance. A deductible is the amount that must be paid before the insurance company pays a claim. The higher the deductible, the lower your premium will be.

7-2 Summarize car insurance.

Car insurance provides protection against financial loss related to a passenger car. Collision coverage pays for damage to your car caused by a collision with another car. Comprehensive coverage pays for damage unrelated to a collision. Liability coverage protects people who suffer injuries or whose property is damaged in an accident. You will not be able to obtain a loan to buy a car without proof of insurance.

7-3 Describe homeowners insurance.

Homeowners insurance protects against damage to a house and its contents. Typically, it also provides liability coverage if someone were to be injured at your home. You will not be able to obtain a loan to buy a home without proof of insurance.

7-4 Summarize renters insurance.

Renters insurance protects against theft or damage to the contents of rented property. This type of insurance also provides liability coverage if someone were to be hurt in your apartment.

7-5 List types of health insurance plans.

There are three main types of health insurance plans. They are HMO, PPO, and POS plans.

7-6 Describe disability insurance.

Disability insurance pays a portion of your income if you are ill and cannot work. You may be able to buy disability coverage through your employer.

7-7 Identify types of life insurance.

Two basic types of life insurance are term life insurance and whole life insurance. Term life insurance is a policy that provides coverage only for a specific period. Whole life insurance is a policy that is in effect for the life of the individual if you continue to pay premiums.

7-8 List other types of insurance.

Other types of insurance include disease coverage; dental and vision insurance; warranty insurance; flood insurance; long-term care insurance; travel insurance; and pet insurance. An umbrella policy covers losses above the limits of your other policies.

Review Your Knowledge

Choose the correct answer for each of the following.

1. ____ Which of the following is *not* a type of property insurance?
   A. homeowners insurance
   B. health insurance
   C. renters insurance
   D. car insurance

2. ____ The amount you must pay for a loss before your insurance pays is a ____.
   A. deductible
   B. liability
   C. premium
   D. comprehensive

3. ____ Car insurance that pays for damage to your car in an accident is called ____ coverage.
   A. liability
   B. collision
   C. comprehensive
   D. premium

4. ____ Car insurance that pays for damage if your car is stolen is called ____ coverage.
   A. liability coverage
   B. collision
   C. comprehensive
   D. premium

5. ____ If you damage someone's fence while driving, which type of insurance covers you?
   A. homeowners insurance
   B. collision coverage
   C. comprehensive coverage
   D. liability coverage

6. ____ Insurance that pays benefits to replace part of your income if you are unable to work because of illness or accident is ____ insurance.
   A. health
   B. disability
   C. comprehensive
   D. liability

7. ____ The face value of a life insurance policy is the same as the ____.
   A. death benefit
   B. premiums
   C. beneficiary
   D. cash value

8. ____ Which type of life insurance covers you for a set period of time?
   A. whole life insurance
   B. variable life insurance
   C. term life insurance
   D. universal life insurance

9. ____ In a life insurance policy, more than one ____ may be named.
   A. beneficiary
   B. risk
   C. face value
   D. term
10. ____ Which type of insurance can help defray the costs of living in a nursing home?
    A. term life
    B. renters
    C. disease
    D. long-term care

Build Your Vocabulary

For each word or term, write the correct definition using your own words.

11. risk

12. insurance

13. premium

14. car insurance

15. homeowners insurance

16. renters insurance

17. health insurance

18. life insurance

19. whole life insurance

20. umbrella insurance policy

Apply Your Math Skills

Calculate the answers to the following problems. Show your calculations.

21. Your car insurance premium is $2,236 if paid annually. If you pay semiannually, you pay $1,130; quarterly, $575; monthly, $195. What is the annual cost for each option? How much more will you pay if you pay monthly rather than once a year?

22. Your home is insured for $323,000. You want to insure the contents for 55 percent of the home's value. What is the dollar amount of the coverage you will have on the contents?

23. You live in a rented apartment. You pay premiums of $14.25 per month for renters insurance. How much does your renters insurance cost for one year?

24. You pay $147.25 semimonthly for health insurance premiums. Your plan requires a $15 copayment for each doctor visit, and a $20 copayment for prescription medicines. If you visit your doctor three times this month and require five prescriptions, what is your total medical expense for the month?

25. You pay $138.60 semimonthly for health insurance premiums. Your plan requires a $30 copayment for each doctor visit, and a $5 copayment for prescription medicines. If you visit your doctor once this month and require two prescriptions, what is your total medical expense for the month?

_____
_____
_____
_____

CHAPTER 8
Education: Funding Your Future

Essential Question
Why is education important to your future?

Learning Outcomes
When you complete Chapter 8, you will be able to:
- 8-1 Summarize the importance of researching a career.
- 8-2 Name options for postsecondary education.
- 8-3 List ways to fund postsecondary education.
- 8-4 Define lifelong learning.

Key Terms
career plan
postsecondary education
academic degree
community college
proprietary school
trade school
Reserve Officers' Training Corps (ROTC)
529 plan
student loan
lifelong learning
professional development
mentor
seminar

Reading Prep
College and Career Readiness

Before reading this chapter, examine the illustrations in the chapter. Write down any questions you have about them. Try to answer the questions as you read.

What is Your Financial IQ?

Before reading this chapter, answer the following questions to see how much you already know about continuing your education after high school.

1. How long does it typically take to earn an associate degree? A bachelor degree? A master degree?

2. What is the difference between a university and a community college?

3. Why would someone attend a trade school?

4. Explain the difference between a community college and a trade school.

5. List ways a student can earn a scholarship.

6. Can you get an education by enrolling in the military?

7. Name several ways to pay for a college education.

8. Explain the difference between a scholarship and a grant.

9. How does a student qualify for financial aid?

10. What is meant by *lifelong learning*?

8-1 Your Career

Have you thought about what you will do when you finish high school? The choices you make will have a huge impact on your life. You probably have been thinking about "what I want to be when I grow up" for most of your life. Now, you will be making decisions as to what that career will be.

Choosing the right career is not only about how much money you might make. It is also about determining your values and what will make you happy in life. Your guidance counselor may help you research careers that match your interests, or you may voluntarily take aptitude or career assessment tests to help match your skills and interests to a career.

As you research careers, learn about opportunities for employment in the careers that interest you. What are the employment trends in your occupations of interest? Will the need expand or decline in the future? What education or training is required? How much can you expect to earn? You want to find answers to these questions in your research. This is an exciting time of your life. The opportunities are endless!

✓ Check Your Understanding

What are two questions you should research about careers that interest you?

_____
_____
_____
_____
_____

Internet Connection

Career Choices

1. Using the Internet, access the US Bureau of Labor Statistics' *Occupational Outlook Handbook*. Choose five career options that interest you. List the careers you researched.

_____
_____
_____
_____

continued

Internet Connection (continued)

2. Search the *Occupational Outlook Handbook* using the term *fastest growing occupations.* Read about careers that are projected to grow quickly in the United States during the next few years. List five of those careers that you might be interested in pursuing.

_____
_____
_____
_____
_____

3. Choose the career in which you are most interested. On a separate sheet of paper, write a short report about the career. In the report, include the following items:
   - the career name
   - the employment outlook
   - training and education necessary
   - any certifications needed
   - salary or wages for the career

FYI
Most people will change careers several times during their working years for a variety of reasons.

A **career plan** is a list of steps needed to reach a career goal. There is no set format for writing a career plan. Many free templates can be found on the Internet. However, your plan should include education and other activities that can help you meet your career goal. It should also address job opportunities.

✓ Check Your Understanding

What information is contained in a career plan?

_____
_____
_____
_____

Career planning begins with exploring careers. The career clusters can help you identify various jobs and the levels of education that are required. The *career clusters*, shown in Figure 8-1, are 16 groups of occupational and career specialties. Each cluster has careers that range from entry-level jobs to positions that require years of education and experience.

The careers in a cluster are grouped together based on the knowledge and skills needed for each career. For example, the occupations *teacher, librarian,* and *school principal* are in the Education and Training career cluster. If you are interested in one career, you may be interested in other careers in the same cluster.

The 16 Career Clusters

Careers involving the production, processing, marketing, distribution, financing, and development of agricultural commodities and resources. **Agriculture, Food & Natural Resources Career Cluster**	Careers involving management, marketing, and operations of foodservice, lodging, and recreational businesses. **Hospitality & Tourism Career Cluster**
Careers involving the design, planning, managing, building, and maintaining of buildings and structures. **Architecture & Construction Career Cluster**	Careers involving family and human needs. **Human Services Career Cluster**
Careers involving the design, production, exhibition, performance, writing, and publishing of visual and performing arts. **Arts, A/V Technology & Communications Career Cluster**	Careers involving the design, development, support, and management of software, hardware, and other technology-related materials. **Information Technology Career Cluster**
Careers involving the planning, organizing, directing, and evaluation of functions essential to business operations. **Business Management & Administration Career Cluster**	Careers involving the planning, management, and providing of legal services, public safety, protective services, and homeland security. **Law, Public Safety, Corrections & Security Career Cluster**
Careers involving the planning, management, and providing of training services. **Education & Training Career Cluster**	Careers involving the planning, management, and processing of materials to create completed products. **Manufacturing Career Cluster**
Careers involving the planning and providing of banking, insurance, and other financial-business services. **Finance Career Cluster**	Careers involving the planning, management, and performance of marketing and sales activities. **Marketing Career Cluster**
Careers involving governance, national security, foreign service, revenue and taxation, regulation, and management and administration. **Government & Public Administration Career Cluster**	Careers involving the planning, management, and providing of scientific research and technical services. **Science, Technology, Engineering & Mathematics Career Cluster**
Careers involving planning, managing, and providing health services, health information, and research and development. **Health Science Career Cluster**	Careers involving the planning, management, and movement of people, materials, and goods. **Transportation, Distribution & Logistics Career Cluster**

States' Career Clusters Initiative 2008; Goodheart-Willcox Publisher

Figure 8-1 The career clusters connect students to careers and the knowledge and skills needed to achieve them. *How can you use the career clusters to help you begin thinking about your future career?*

Your Turn

Career Planning

The following chart can help you begin thinking about what you can do now and over the next several years to prepare for a career that interests you. Consider what you can do at school, such as taking certain classes or joining a club or team. Also consider what you can do outside of school, such as volunteer work, hobbies, and potential part-time jobs.

Career Planning

Career that interests me:
Steps I can take before I enter high school to prepare for this career:
1.
2.
3.
Steps I can take while I am in high school to prepare for this career:
1.
2.
3.
What will I need to do after I graduate from high school to prepare for this career?

8-2 Postsecondary Education

The value of education beyond high school cannot be underestimated. It is measured in terms of both personal as well as financial benefits. Achieving an education enables you to become a well-rounded person and should help increase your wealth potential and advancement in your career.

Postsecondary education is any education after high school. There are many ways to earn postsecondary education and prepare for a career. Some options include four-year colleges or universities, two-year schools, trade schools, and the military.

College or University

There are many colleges and universities from which to choose. At college, you may meet people from your state or from around the world. Whether you go

Achieving an education enables you to become a well-rounded person and can increase your wealth potential. *In what ways might a postsecondary education help you reach your career goals?*

Daniel M Ernst/Shutterstock.com

to a local college or one across the country, you will become more aware of the diversities throughout our nation.

Many degrees can be earned at a college or university. You can choose from many areas of interest when selecting a program of study. An **academic degree** is an award given by a college or university indicating the person has successfully completed a course of study. The following shows the approximate length of time necessary for various degrees; however, many students take longer to complete the requirements.

- An *associate degree* is earned upon completion of a two-year program.
- A *bachelor degree* is earned upon completion of a four-year program.
- A *master degree* typically requires one or two years of education after earning a bachelor degree.

According to the US Census Bureau, earnings potential greatly increases with academic degrees. For example, a typical college graduate earns much more per year than a high school graduate, as shown in Figure 8-2. These are average figures and depend on the state of the economy and where you live. A college graduate may expect to earn twice as much as a high school graduate over a lifetime. The more advanced your degree, the more your earnings should be.

As a college graduate, you earn $23,000 more each year than a high school graduate. If you work for a total of 45 years, how much more will you earn than a high school graduate who worked for the same number of years?

Amount per year	$23,000
Number of years worked	× 45
Difference in earnings	$1,035,000

The additional earnings seem like a pretty good reason to pursue higher education.

Figure 8-2 Annual and lifetime earnings generally increase as a person continues his or her education. *How can increased lifetime earnings affect your ability to meet your financial goals?*

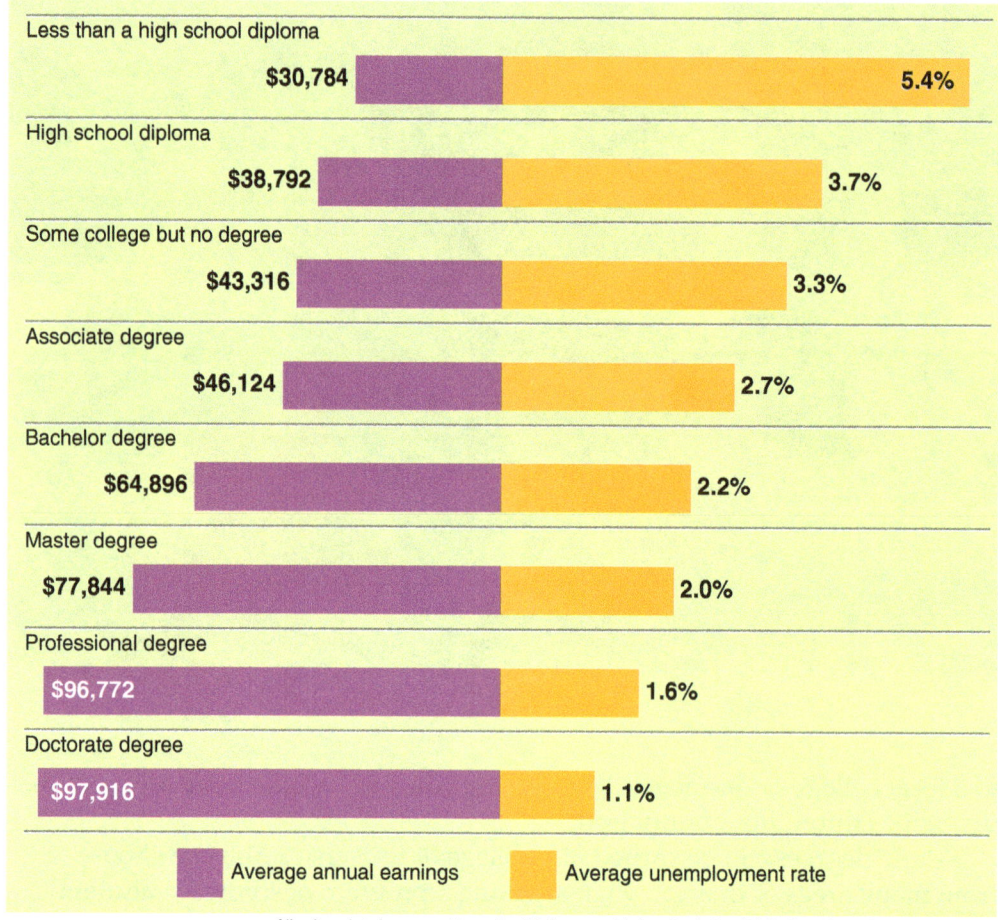

Education Level	Average annual earnings	Average unemployment rate
Less than a high school diploma	$30,784	5.4%
High school diploma	$38,792	3.7%
Some college but no degree	$43,316	3.3%
Associate degree	$46,124	2.7%
Bachelor degree	$64,896	2.2%
Master degree	$77,844	2.0%
Professional degree	$96,772	1.6%
Doctorate degree	$97,916	1.1%

All salary data is sourced from the US Bureau of Labor Statistics (BLS). Goodheart-Willcox Publisher.

You Do the Math | 8-1

Over your lifetime, your earnings as a college graduate are $27,500 more each year than your friend who is a high school graduate. If you both work a total of 43 years, how much more will you earn?

Amount per year _____
Number of years worked _____
Difference in earnings _____

✓ Check Your Understanding

According to the numbers in Figure 8-2, how much more does a person with a bachelor degree typically earn per year than a high school graduate?

_____
_____
_____
_____

Internet Connection

Wages

1. Visit the US Bureau of Labor Statistics (BLS) website. Using the search bar, conduct a search for *state wage estimates*. Find the most recent data for your state.
2. In the table that follows, list five careers. Record the average annual earnings in your state for each career.

Career Title	Average Annual Earnings

Two-Year Schools

A **community college** is a two-year college supported by the government that offers associate degrees. Some students choose to attend a local community college to earn an associate degree. Others may attend community college for a year or two and continue on to a four-year college to complete a bachelor degree. Credits earned from a two-year state college usually can be transferred to a four-year school.

A **proprietary school** is a privately owned educational institution that offers vocational or occupational skills but may not be under the authority of the Department of Education. The school may offer certification or licensing rather than degrees. Programs at a proprietary school usually take two years or less to complete. Examples of programs at these schools may include courses in business, paramedical training, and computer science. Self-improvement classes are also often offered.

Before you attend a proprietary school, find out if the school is accredited. *Accredited* means the school and its programs have been proven to meet educational standards and are approved by a governing organization. Also, verify the credits you earn will transfer to a four-year school. If not, you will have to retake those classes if you go to a four-year college or university.

FYI
Most schools offer classes online. Always research the school to ensure that it is legitimate. The United States Distance Learning Association (USDLA) is a good source of information.

Trade School

A **trade school** is a school that teaches a skilled trade. These schools focus more on skills than academics. They are sometimes called *vocational schools* or *career and technical colleges*. Trade schools can prepare you for careers that involve manual or technical skills, such as plumber, electrician, or auto mechanic. Many of these schools have smaller classes and better teacher-to-student ratios than bigger colleges. Sometimes the programs at these schools cost much less than attending a four-year college or university.

The demand for skilled workers is high and earnings may be more than you make with a four-year degree. Trade schools definitely may be a good option for those who do not want to spend four years in school or may not have the funding for college. Credits from a trade school, however, may not transfer to a college should you decide to continue your education there.

Military

Joining the military also provides opportunities for education and training. If you join the military, you will be required to serve active or reserve duty. You will receive a salary, housing, and health care. The military can also provide opportunities to see the world.

Military training can be considered equal to college credit or professional training. Also, most branches of the military offer the chance to earn a tuition-free college degree.

Reserve Officers' Training Corps (ROTC) is a military program offered on many college campuses that provides leadership training for commissioned officers. Graduates of ROTC programs become officers in a branch of the military, such as the US Army or the US Air Force. ROTC offers a wide variety of education and training programs with little or no cost to you. Many high schools offer *Junior ROTC* programs.

✓ Check Your Understanding

What choices will you have for furthering your education after you graduate?

_____
_____
_____
_____

Internet Connection

Costs of Education

1. Research at least three colleges, universities, or trade schools that you would consider attending. Then, complete the table that follows by listing the costs for one semester.

Name of School	Tuition for One Semester	Books for One Semester	Dorm Expenses for One Semester	Total for One Semester	Total for One Year (Two Semesters)

2. If costs remained the same, how much would you spend over a two-year period?

3. If costs remained the same, how much would you spend over a four-year period?

8-3 Funding Your Education

As you are making decisions about your education, you will need to create a financial plan for funding. Whether you attend a trade school or university, someone must pay for the cost of the education. Funding your education should be a big part of your overall financial plan. Figure 8-3 shows potential sources of funding for postsecondary education. There are many college calculators online that can help you estimate how much money you will need. It is a good idea to start making these plans now.

The most common planning for higher education involves a 529 plan. A **529 plan** is a savings plan for education operated by a state or educational institution. These plans encourage parents or guardians to set aside money for their children's educational expenses. Many plans offer tax advantages for doing so. Money put into a 529 plan may be used to pay for expenses at qualified postsecondary institutions across the nation. However, there are restrictions on how this money can be used. There are penalties if the money is used for anything other than educational expenses. Details of individual plans vary.

Figure 8-3 There are many options for funding a college education. *Explain which of these options might work well for you and your educational plan.*

Sources of Funding for Postsecondary Education

Source	Description
529 plan	All states have 529 saving plans; some offer more than one. Money put into the plan must be spent on educational expenses.
Scholarship	Students may qualify for scholarships in academics, sports, music, dance, or other areas, and they may be based on ACT or SAT scores. Scholarships do not have to be repaid.
Grant	Grants are issued by governmental agencies, corporations, states, and other organizations. Grants do not have to be repaid.
Work-study program	Part-time jobs on a college campus are given to students who show financial need to help finance their education. These jobs are often funded by the school or government.
Need-based award	For need-based awards, students must show financial need. Funding for these awards comes from governments, schools, and other groups.
Governmental education loan	These loans have interest rates that are lower than those on regular bank loans. Money loaned by the government must be repaid, but repayment may be postponed until you begin working.
Private education loan	These loans have interest rates that are higher than those for governmental education loans. Money loaned by a private institution must be repaid.
Military benefits	Enlisting in the US military can provide education, training, and opportunities to see the world. ROTC programs and military service academies are other options to consider.

Goodheart-Willcox Publisher

Financial aid is available from the federal government and other sources. The Federal Student Aid program provides more than $120 billion to students each year. A few states may offer money for good grades in high school. Pell grants are also available to students with low family incomes and may be used at almost all colleges. The maximum amount per year in 2023 was $6,895. Pell grants are not loans, and do not have to be repaid. Information and applications are available online. If you are already working, some companies will reimburse you for college courses as long as you make good grades; a great way for someone else to fund your education!

Many scholarships, grants, and other sources of financial aid go unused because no one has applied for them. Do not fail to apply for help just because you don't want to write an essay or fill out an application. Talk to your school counselor to learn whether you might qualify for these types of aid and meet all deadlines for applying.

Your Turn

Financial Aid Application

Completing applications to take entrance tests, apply for financial aid, and other forms requires a lot of information. For practice, complete the sample application for financial aid that follows.

Date: _____

APPLICATION FOR FINANCIAL ASSISTANCE

STUDENT INFORMATION:

Applying for: Fall 20 ____ Spring 20 ____ Summer 20 ____

Student Status: ☐ Prospective Student ☐ Current Student ☐ Undergraduate Student ☐ Graduate Student

1. Name: _____
            Last   First   Middle   Maiden

2. Permanent Mailing Address: _____
            Number   Street   Apartment/Box #   Home Phone Number

   _____
       City   State   Zip Code   Cell Phone Number

3. E-mail Address: _____
4. Will you complete the Free Application for Federal Student Aid (FAFSA)?   ☐ Yes ☐ No
5. Where do you plan to live during the academic year?   ☐ On-campus ☐ Off-campus ☐ With parents
6. Are you the beneficiary of a 529 prepaid tuition or 529 college tuition savings plan?   ☐ Yes ☐ No
7. Are you currently employed?   ☐ Yes ☐ No ☐ Full-time ☐ Part-time
8. Do you plan to work while in school?   ☐ Yes ☐ No ☐ Full-time ☐ Part-time

ELIGIBILITY FOR SCHOLARSHIPS:

9. You may be eligible for a scholarship based on ethnicity or major. Providing the following allows you to be considered for these.

   Ethnic Background: _____ Anticipated Major: _____

10. Please indicate if you will be applying for any of the following types of aid/scholarships:

    ☐ Art ☐ Debate ☐ Music ☐ Theatre ☐ Work-Study ☐ Loans

FINANCING YOUR EDUCATION:

11. Please indicate other sources of financial help (by amount) that you will draw upon for assistance this academic year:

    ☐ Personal Savings   ☐ Educational Loans

    ☐ Family Assistance   ☐ Personal Loans

    ☐ Earnings from Work during School Year ☐ Government Benefits

    ☐ Educational Grants   ☐ Tuition Assistance from Employer

    ☐ Private Scholarships   ☐ Other

UNUSUAL CIRCUMSTANCES:

12. Families occasionally experience unusual expenses/circumstances beyond their control. If you believe such circumstances should be considered in determining your financial aid award, contact the Financial Aid Office for the appropriate forms.

Student Signature _____ Date _____

A **student loan** is money borrowed to pay college-related expenses, such as tuition and books. Student loans are offered by banks and other financial institutions and subsidized by the government. The loans usually have low interest rates and do not have to be repaid until the student has completed his or her education.

A strong word of caution: many students leave college with huge student loans that take a lifetime to repay. If you borrow money for school, use the money to pay for actual college expenses. This might be tuition, books, and room and board. Do not use borrowed money for other things such as cars and entertainment. You do not want to be still paying off your student loans when you are considering retirement or are trying to fund your children's educations!

Consider all your options when planning how to fund your education. For example, the cost to attend a private school can be much higher than state universities or local colleges but may not be worth it financially. There are some benefits of attending a prestigious college or private school, but it may not be the best choice in every situation. Research state or local colleges where tuition costs may be lower. You can still earn a degree whether you live on campus or stay at home so you can save money. On the other hand, the experience of living away from home may give you a taste of freedom and responsibility.

You want to attend a private college in another state to obtain a bachelor degree. Your family wants you to attend a local four-year college to save money. The private college costs $42,500 per year. The local college costs $9,575 per year if you live at home and commute to the school daily. Assume that no help is available in scholarships or grants for either school. Calculate the difference in cost of attending the private college for four years rather than the local college.

Step 1. Calculate the cost of private college.

Private college cost per year	$42,500
Number of years	× 4
Total cost for private college	$170,000

Step 2. Calculate the cost of local college.

Local college cost per year	$9,575
Number of years	× 4
Total cost for local college	$38,300

Step 3. Calculate the difference in cost.

Total private college cost	$170,000
Total local college cost	− 38,300
Difference in cost	$131,700

You Do the Math | 8-2

You want to attend a private college away from home to earn your bachelor degree. Your friend is going to live at home and commute to a local four-year college. The private college costs $46,250 each year. The local college costs $8,950 per year. No help is available in scholarships or grants for either college. Calculate the difference in cost of attending the private college rather than the local college.

Step 1. Calculate the cost of private college.

Private college cost per year _____

Number of years _____

Total cost for private college _____

Step 2. Calculate the cost of local college.

Local college cost per year _____

Number of years _____

Total cost for local college _____

Step 3. Calculate the difference in cost.

Total private college cost _____

Total local college cost _____

Difference in cost _____

Some students are fortunate to have their families or guardians help pay for college. These families may use savings, current income, and loans. Parents, other family members, and students often work together to cover the cost of college. You might contribute money you have saved or earned, and money received through loans you will have to repay. More than half of students attending college get some form of financial aid.

Check Your Understanding

What choices will you have for funding your education?

_____
_____
_____
_____

Your Turn

College Budget

When you get ready to go to college, you will need to create a new budget. Remember that fixed expenses are those that occur regularly, and variable expenses are those that may change from day to day.

1. Based on your own spending experiences, estimate the amount you think your living expenses would be for the first month of college. Enter the amounts in the table that follows. Indicate if each expense is fixed or variable. This will not include tuition, housing, or books.

Living Expenses for College

Expense	Amount	Fixed	Variable
Car insurance			
Clothes			
Entertainment			
Food			
Gas for car			
Gifts			
Haircuts			
Personal care items			
Cell phone			
Sports equipment			
Miscellaneous (list)			
Monthly Total			

Your Turn (continued)

2. What will be the total expenses for one semester (1 month × 4)?

   _____

   _____

3. What will be the total expenses for one year (1 semester × 2)?

   _____

   _____

4. If your expenses remained the same, how much would you spend over a two-year period?

   _____

   _____

5. If your expenses remained the same, how much would you spend over a four-year period?

   _____

   _____

Dollars and Sense

College Access

College access refers to building awareness about college opportunities, providing guidance regarding college admissions, and identifying ways to pay for college. Preparing to go to college presents many challenges to students and families. Earning good grades and finding the money to pay for college are two of them.

Going to college is a big step for your future and an important part of your financial plan. The sooner you begin planning, the better. It is never too early. As you plan for your education, research as much as possible to find out how to prepare academically as well as financially.

Make the most of your remaining years in school by doing the very best you can. Become involved in organizations at your school or in your community. Colleges look for well-rounded individuals who take part in a variety of activities.

Many websites provide information to help you from the time you are in grade school until you apply for college. Each state offers resources. Do a search on *college access* in your state to find information. If you have already been thinking about a specific college, check its website to see if you will qualify for enrollment with your grades and test scores. In addition, find out what financial aid might be available to you.

- The College.gov website discusses why to go, what to do, and how to pay for college.
- The College Board offers a financial calculator to help project the cost of an education.
- The National College Access Network is dedicated to increasing college access and success.
- The website CollegeData lists information on specific colleges, including scholarship information and four-year graduation rates.

If you have not already done so, talk to your family, friends, and counselors for information to begin planning for college today.

8-4 Lifelong Learning

Lifelong learning is acquiring new skills and knowledge throughout a person's life. It typically refers to adults who are learning in a variety of situations. Lifelong learning often relates to hobbies and interests, including cooking, foreign languages, and physical fitness or for professional development.

Professional Development

Improving or gaining new skills related to work is called **professional development**. It is also called *continuing education*. When you graduate from college or a technical school, you should have the skills you need to begin your career. However, technology and methods of completing work change rapidly. As your career progresses, you may need to take classes to update your skills or learn new ones.

Some employers pay for the cost of this training, which may be provided on the job or as a class. Careers in nursing, teaching, accounting, auto repair, computer systems, and many other areas require workers to have the latest training to stay employed. This training teaches workers to use new equipment or procedures.

You can learn new skills and knowledge in other ways, too. You may learn from a mentor at work or in a professional association. A **mentor** is someone who has knowledge and skills and shares them informally with an individual. Seminars are another good source of information. A **seminar** is a meeting or conference for exchanging ideas or learning new things. Some are free or cost less than formal classes at a school.

After your formal education is complete, you will continue to learn new skills or attend classes for additional training throughout your lifetime. *Based on your career choice or interests, what type of continuing education might you need?*

Personal Interests

As an adult, you may want to learn more about your personal interests. You might choose to read books or articles, watch documentaries, or attend classes or seminars. Personal enrichment classes are generally designed for your enjoyment. They help you learn something new or improve skills. For example, suppose you will be traveling to a foreign country and do not know how to speak their language, so you may take a language class before your trip. Maybe you always wanted to play the piano or guitar, so you take lessons. Whatever your interests are, there are ways to learn more about them.

Check Your Understanding

Explain lifelong learning.

_____
_____
_____

Are You Financially Responsible?

Preparing for Your Education: A Checklist

As you start planning for your education after high school graduation, you need to complete some specific tasks. This checklist is only a starting point, and you should expand it as your research progresses. It is never too early to start planning for life after graduation.

	Yes	No	
1.	____	____	I generally focus on getting good grades. Doing so can help me earn scholarships and be accepted into the school of my choice.
2.	____	____	I have checked with my counselor to make sure I have taken or am taking the courses necessary to be accepted into a postsecondary institution.
3.	____	____	I will take the PSAT, SAT, ACT, and AP exams when applicable.
4.	____	____	I have practiced completing college entrance applications and financial aid applications. These forms require time and information, so practice is necessary.
5.	____	____	I have created a file to keep certificates of awards, grades, and other items that show my accomplishments so that I can include these when I apply for college.
6.	____	____	I participate in school and community activities. Most colleges expect students to have participated in a variety of school activities as well as volunteer work.
7.	____	____	I have taken an aptitude or career assessment test to see how my skills and talents may influence my career choice.
8.	____	____	I have researched various schools to see which one is suitable for my needs.
9.	____	____	I have visited campuses to see what each school offers and how specific programs match up to my interests and needs.
10.	____	____	I have created a plan to pay for my education. A plan may include loans, financial aid, employment, or other resources.

Chapter 8 Review and Assessment

Summary

8-1 **Summarize the importance of researching a career.**

Choosing the right career involves considering your future income potential as well as your values in life. When researching careers of interest, learn about opportunities for employment, trends, education or training required, and how much you can expect to earn.

8-2 **Name options for postsecondary education.**

Postsecondary education options include four-year colleges or universities, two-year schools, trade schools, and the military.

8-3 **List ways to fund postsecondary education.**

One way to fund a postsecondary education is savings in the form of a 529 plan. Financial aid options include scholarships, grants, work-study programs, and need-based awards. Student loans offered by financial institutions or the federal government are another option.

8-4 **Define lifelong learning.**

Lifelong learning is acquiring new skills and knowledge throughout a person's life. Learning may be for professional development or personal interests.

Review Your Knowledge

Choose the correct answer for each of the following.

1. ____ What can you do to help match your skills and interests with a career?
   A. Take an aptitude test.
   B. Take a career assessment test.
   C. Talk with a counselor.
   D. All the above.

2. ____ Which academic degree typically takes four years to complete?
   A. associate degree
   B. bachelor degree
   C. master degree
   D. vocational degree

3. ____ Which type of postsecondary institution is supported by the government and offers associate degrees?
   A. trade school
   B. vocational school
   C. community college
   D. proprietary school

4. ____ Schools that focus more on skills than academics are called ____.
   A. trade schools
   B. vocational schools
   C. technical colleges
   D. All the above.
5. ____ Which of the following statements is true of ROTC?
   A. The program is offered at many high schools.
   B. The program provides leadership training for commissioned officers.
   C. The program is not available at colleges.
   D. The program does not offer education or training.
6. ____ Which of the following is *not* important in choosing a career?
   A. educational requirements
   B. your interests
   C. employment trends
   D. friends' career choices
7. ____ A savings plan for educational expenses operated by the state is called a ____.
   A. 529 plan
   B. Pell grant
   C. student loan
   D. federal student aid program
8. ____ What is an advantage of a trade school?
   A. skilled worker demand
   B. less cost than four-year university
   C. comparable earnings to four-year degrees
   D. All of the above.
9. ____ Money borrowed to pay for postsecondary educational expenses with a rate of interest subsidized by the government is a ____.
   A. student loan
   B. federal student aid program
   C. 529 plan
   D. Pell grant
10. ____ What is professional development?
    A. learning new skills related to your personal interests
    B. improving or gaining new skills related to work
    C. any education received after high school
    D. part-time jobs on a college campus held by students to finance their education

Build Your Vocabulary

For each word or term, write the correct definition using your own words.

11. career plan

_____

_____

12. postsecondary education

13. academic degree

14. proprietary school

15. 529 plan

16. community college

17. professional development

18. lifelong learning

19. mentor

20. seminar

Apply Your Math Skills

Calculate the answers to the following problems. Show your calculations.

21. Your earnings are $26,250 more each year as a college graduate than your friend who is a high school graduate. You both work 46 years. What is the difference in your earnings?

22. A worker's total earnings for 35 years are $422,750 more with a master degree than with a bachelor degree. What is the difference in earnings per year between a master degree and a bachelor degree for this worker?

23. In your lifetime, your earnings would be $620,000 more with a master degree than they would be with a bachelor degree. If you worked a total of 45 years, what would be the difference in your earnings per year?

24. You want to attend a private school away from home for your bachelor degree. However, your family wants you to attend a local college. The private school costs $47,800 each year for 4 years. The local college costs $7,865 each year for 4 years. No help is available in scholarships or grants for either school. How much could you save by attending the local college for 4 years?

25. You want to consider attending the local college for the first 2 years and then transferring to the private college for the last 2 years. No help is available in scholarships or grants for either school. How much would it cost to attend the local college for 2 years before transferring to the private college for the remaining 2 years? How much would you save by attending the local college for the first 2 years? Use the tuition costs given in the previous question.

CHAPTER 9

Loans and Leases: Paying for Cars and Housing

? **Essential Question**

Why might a person need a loan to purchase a car or home?

Learning Outcomes

When you complete Chapter 9, you will be able to:
- **9-1** Discuss buying a car.
- **9-2** Explain leasing a car.
- **9-3** Summarize renting a living space.
- **9-4** Discuss home mortgages.
- **9-5** Explain buying a condominium.

Key Terms

depreciation
collateral
repossession
installment loan
car lease
lessee
lessor
security deposit

apartment lease
mortgage
equity
foreclosure
private mortgage insurance (PMI)
escrow account
fixed-rate mortgage

amortization
adjustable-rate mortgage (ARM)
homeowners association (HOA) fee
assessment

College and Career Readiness

Reading Prep

Before reading this chapter, review the key terms. Note any words you do not know that you would like to discuss in class.

What is Your Financial IQ?

Before reading this chapter, answer the following questions to see how much you already know about paying for a car and housing.

1. Do you think a car is an investment? Why or why not?

2. How do the price and type of car affect the cost of car insurance?

3. What is a secured debt?

4. Describe an installment loan and its purpose.

5. What is an *upside-down* or *underwater* loan?

6. Why would a person lease a car instead of buying a car?

7. Who pays the insurance on a leased car?

8. What is a security deposit?

9. Why would a person get a mortgage?

10. What does it mean when a lender forecloses on property?

9-1 Buying a Car

Car ownership is a huge financial responsibility; not only for the cost of the car itself, but also for insurance, tires, and other maintenance costs to keep the car running. When you buy a car, you will also pay sales tax, a title fee, and a registration fee. You should be prepared for these expenses as well as the monthly payments if you need a loan to purchase your car.

A car is not an investment that will increase in value over time. As soon as you drive a new car off the lot, it starts losing value. A decrease in the value of an asset is known as **depreciation**. Think carefully about the kind of car you want. In some cases, it may make more sense to buy a used car rather than a new one. You may even want to lease a car rather than buy one.

As you create your financial plans, loan payments may be a part of your expenses each month if you have not saved enough money to pay cash. This is known as *financing* the purchase. Two types of loans available for consumers are unsecured and secured loans.

An *unsecured loan* is money borrowed based on a signature by the borrower. No collateral is required for the loan if the borrower is creditworthy. **Collateral** is property a borrower promises to give up in case of default. Credit card debt is unsecured. You can borrow money or purchase goods or services by just signing your name. You are, however, legally obligated to pay these unsecured debts.

A *secured loan* is money borrowed with collateral, such as a car or house. If the borrower fails to repay the loan, the collateral is taken. The lender gets the property if you do not repay the loan. For example, suppose you get a loan for your car. You sign an agreement saying that if you do not make your payments, the lender can take your car. **Repossession** is taking collateral when a borrower fails to repay a loan. Secured debt is usually available at lower interest rates than unsecured debt because the bank can take something of value if you do not repay the loan.

A car loan is a type of installment loan. An **installment loan** is a purchase that is paid for in equal monthly payments for a specific amount of time. When you apply for an installment loan, the process will be very similar to the process of getting a credit card. You will complete an application and the lender will review your credit history to see if you are a good risk. The loan application will ask you to authorize the lender to request your credit report.

When you apply for a car loan, there will be options as to how long the loan will extend. Many car loans are for two to five years, which is 24 to 60 months. Some dealers offer loans for six years, which is 72 months, to finance a new car. The longer the term of the loan, the lower the monthly payments will be; but you will also pay more interest.

Make sure you read the contract carefully before signing for an installment loan. A contract should indicate the total amount of interest you will pay over the loan period. The contract should state there is no prepayment penalty. A *prepayment penalty* requires you to pay extra fees if you pay off the loan before the end of its term. Not having this penalty allows you to pay off the loan at any time without paying extra fees. The contract should also allow you to pay extra money each month. The extra amount should reduce the principal so you can pay off the loan early.

> **FYI**
> Repossession means the lender can reclaim the car if you fail to make your payments. The car is not legally yours until the loan is completely paid.

Check Your Understanding

Why might a lender require collateral?

_____
_____
_____

Your Turn

Car Loan Application

Completing application forms takes a lot of information and practice to get them right. For practice, complete the following application for a car loan.

CAR LOAN APPLICATION FORM

Name: _____
            First   Middle   Last

Address: _____
      Street   Apt #   City   State and Zip

Phone: _____
     Daytime   Evening   Cell

Date of Birth: __ __ / __ __ / __ __ __ __   E-mail: _____

Employer: _____   Title: _____   Phone: _____

Length of time at job: _____   Salary (hourly wage): _____   Monthly gross income: _____

Own or rent home: ☐ Own ☐ Rent   Monthly payment: _____   Total monthly expenses: _____

Loan Type: ☐ Used car ☐ New car   Loan amount: $ _____   Term _____ years

Down payment amount: $ _____   Do you have a cosigner available? ☐ Yes ☐ No

Have you filed for bankruptcy in the past seven years? ☐ Yes ☐ No   Please explain: _____

Marital Status: ☐ Single ☐ Married ☐ Separated ☐ Divorced

Permission for electronic fund transfer: ☐ Yes ☐ No

Financial References

	Bank/Institution	Account Number
Checking Account		
Savings Account		

Permission to Obtain Consumer Credit Report

By signing this application form, I hereby give the company the right to obtain a consumer credit report regarding me for this application and the loan should the application be approved.

I certify that the above information is correct to the best of my knowledge.

Applicant Signature _____   Date _____

Contracts for some installment loans (for furniture or appliances, for example) may state "90 days same as cash" or "12 months same as cash." This means there will be no interest due *IF* you pay the loan within the time frame. If the loan is not paid during this time, interest will be due on the full amount of the loan, not just the remaining balance. Make sure these loans are paid in full during the specified time frame!

In addition to the price of the car, you will pay tax and fees when you buy a new car, as well as a destination fee of $1,000–$1,800. The car dealer pays this fee to have the car delivered to the dealership site and passes this cost to you. There should be no destination charge on a used car. You will pay sales tax at the rate set for your state on the purchase price including any options you select. You may also have to pay sales tax on the destination fee. You will pay Department of Motor Vehicles (DMV) fees to license and register your new car. These fees vary by state. They may be about 1 to 1.5 percent of the price of the car. Consider the following example.

You purchased a car for $18,750, which includes a destination fee of $1,000. The state sales tax rate is 6 percent. The DMV fees are 1.2 percent of the price of the car. What is the total you must pay?

Step 1. Calculate the sales tax.

Price of the car	$18,750.00
Sales tax percentage	× .06
Sales tax amount	$1,125.00

Step 2. Calculate the DMV fee.

Price of the car	$18,750.00
DMV fees percentage	× .012
DMV fees amount	$225.00

Step 3. Total the amounts.

Price of the car	$18,750.00
Sales tax amount	1,125.00
DMV fees amount	+ 225.00
Total amount	$20,100.00

You Do the Math | 9-1

You purchased a car for $25,890, which includes a destination fee of $1,250. The state sales tax rate is 7 percent. The DMV fees are 1 percent of the price of the car. What is the total you must pay?

Step 1. Calculate the sales tax.

    Price of the car   _____

    Sales tax percentage   _____

    Sales tax amount   _____

Step 2. Calculate the DMV fee.

    Price of the car   _____

    DMV fees percentage   _____

    DMV fees amount   _____

Step 3. Total the amounts.

    Price of the car   _____

    Sales tax amount   _____

    DMV fees amount   _____

    Total amount   _____

Now that you have calculated the total cost of the car, can you afford the car? Will you need a car loan to pay part of the cost? You can search online for a car-loan calculator to help you determine monthly payments by entering the amount of the loan and number of months into the calculator. Using the previous example, if you financed the entire amount of $20,100, the monthly payment would be $465.63, as shown in Figure 9-1. Your car loan payment will be an important part of your budget. Before you get a car loan, make sure you can afford the monthly payments. Four years is a long time to make payments on a car.

Car Loan Calculator

Car loan amount:	$ 20,100			
Car loan term:	4	years or	48	months
Interest rate:	5.3	% per year		
Monthly car loan payments:	$ 465.63			

Goodheart-Willcox Publisher

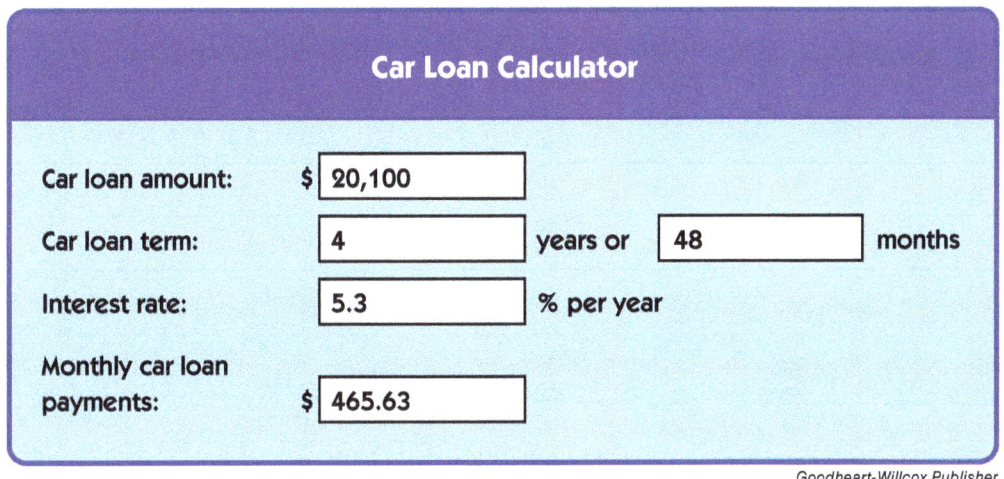

Figure 9-1 A car-loan calculator can help you decide whether you can afford to purchase a car. *How might the monthly payment of a car loan affect someone's budget?*

There may be an opportunity to trade your current car for another. For example, you want to trade in your car that is valued at $2,750 for a new one. You look at a new car with a sticker price of $21,300. The dealership will take your car as a trade and give you a loan of $18,700. How much are you paying for the new car? Note that this amount is $150 *more* than the sticker price of the new car.

Loan amount	$18,700.00
Value of old car	+ 2,750.00
Cost of new car	$21,450.00

You Do the Math | 9-2

You want to purchase a new truck with a sticker price of $24,200. Your car is valued at $4,850. The dealer says he will take your car in trade and give you a loan of $19,900. How much are you paying for the new truck?

Loan amount	_____
Value of old car	_____
Cost of new truck	_____

Sometimes trading in a current car is a good deal, but sometimes it is not. A better option might be to sell the car yourself.

The longer you finance a car, the more you will pay in interest, but there is another factor to consider. If you finance a car for five or six years, you might owe more than the car is worth before you finish paying off the loan. Owing more than the value of any asset is called being *underwater* or *upside down* on the loan. If you have an accident and total the car, the insurance company will reimburse you for the *Kelley Blue Book* value of the car and **not** what you still owe on it. You may be without a car and still must make payments—a terrible situation! If you think you need more than three years to pay off a car loan, you should probably look for a less expensive car.

Check Your Understanding

Why should you calculate the total cost of a car before purchasing the car?

_____
_____
_____
_____

Internet Connection

Car Values

1. In the table that follows, write the makes and models of five cars owned by people you know, such as family members or neighbors. The term *make* refers to the brand name of the car, such as Chevy or Honda. The term *model* refers to the name of the particular car, such as Malibu or Civic.
2. Visit the *Kelley Blue Book* website. Use this website to find the value of each car. Write the amounts in the table.

Year	Make	Model	Blue Book Value

9-2 Leasing a Car

You may decide to lease a car rather than purchase one. A **car lease** is a contract that allows a person to use a car in exchange for payment. The person who leases a car is the **lessee**. The dealership is the **lessor**. The important thing to remember about leasing is that you are not making payments toward ownership. When leasing, you are making payments to use the car for a specific amount of time, usually two or three years. When you lease, you are responsible for insurance and maintenance, just as if you owned the car. You will also pay for the title and registration, as well as the sales tax.

There may be a required down payment to lease a car, and you may have to pay a security deposit. A **security deposit** is an amount paid to protect the dealer against financial loss if the lessee damages the car or fails to make payments. It is required by the dealer for assurance that the car will be in good condition when you return it. If you return the car in good condition, you should get the security deposit back. You will not get the down payment back. When the lease is up, you may have the option to purchase the car. However, the cost to do so may be higher than the value of the car. You might need a loan to finance the purchase unless you have enough money saved to buy it without a loan.

Artist1/Shutterstock.com

Car ownership brings with it huge financial responsibility. *What types of personal responsibility do you anticipate having when you buy your first car?*

Copyright Goodheart-Willcox Co., Inc.
May not be reproduced or posted to a publicly accessible website.

FYI

If you turn in a leased car before the lease is up, you will probably be charged an *early termination fee*. Such a fee would be stated in the lease contract.

The dealer should be able to offer you different monthly payments depending on your down payment amount. Typically, the larger the down payment you make, the lower your monthly payments will be.

Suppose you lease a car for three years. The lease requires a down payment of $1,200 plus a security deposit of $500. You make monthly payments of $400 for three years. What is the total cost to lease the car for three years?

Monthly payments	$400.00
Number of months	× 36
Payments for lease	$14,400.00
Down payment	1,200.00
Security deposit	+ 500.00
Total cost	$16,100.00

Remember that you may receive your security deposit of $500 back at the end of the lease.

You Do the Math | 9-3

You lease a truck for two years. The lease requires a down payment of $500 plus a security deposit of $550. You will make monthly payments of $485 for two years. What is the total cost to lease the truck for two years?

Monthly payments	_____
Number of months	_____
Payments for lease	_____
Down payment	_____
Security deposit	_____
Total cost	_____

Lease agreements usually have a mileage limit, such as 12,000 miles annually. If you put more miles on the car, you may be charged extra for each mile over the limit. If you drive a lot for work or travel, leasing may not be a wise option.

Should you buy or lease? Your age, job situation, and other factors will determine the better solution for you when it is time to decide. Unless it is essential to have a new car every two or three years, purchasing a car is usually a better option. Figure 9-2 shows a comparison of factors related to buying or leasing a car.

✓ Check Your Understanding

Explain what it means to lease a car.

_____
_____
_____

Buy or Lease Comparison

Factor	Buy	Lease
Ownership of car	Buyer has ownership	Lessor has ownership
Car license and title	Buyer pays	Lessee pays
Sales tax (most states)	Buyer pays	Lessee pays
Mileage limit	Buyer owns, so no limit	Lessor sets yearly limit plus extra cost per mile over the limit
Insurance premiums	Buyer's responsibility	Lessee's responsibility
Maintenance	Buyer's responsibility	Lessee's responsibility
Monthly payments	May be higher than lease payments	May be lower than loan payments
End of term	Buyer owns the car (when loan is repaid)	Lessee returns car and has no ownership
Excessive wear and tear	Decreases the value of the car	Lessee may be charged a fee

Goodheart-Willcox Publisher

Figure 9-2 Multiple factors can help you determine whether you should buy or lease a car. *Explain whether you think buying or leasing a car would be better for you.*

Are You Financially Responsible?

Buying a Car: A Checklist

Getting a loan for your first car may be your first installment loan, and it will affect your credit rating. Treat the process with respect. Make sure the loan is one you can afford. If this is your first loan, you may be required to have a cosigner. How would you rate your "car personality"?

Yes   No
1. ___ ___ I will look for dependability in a car instead of a new or sporty car.
2. ___ ___ I will make sure I can make the payments before getting a loan.
3. ___ ___ I will do all the calculations on the cost of borrowing money to make sure I am getting the deal that works best for me.
4. ___ ___ I will have a cosigner available to sign with me for the loan, if needed.
5. ___ ___ I will shop around for the best interest rates for a car loan.
6. ___ ___ I will practice completing an application for a loan so I am prepared when I apply.
7. ___ ___ I will calculate the cost of insurance before buying a car.
8. ___ ___ I will calculate the costs of car maintenance before buying a car.
9. ___ ___ I will calculate the cost of gas before buying a car.
10. ___ ___ I will read the contract for the loan and make sure I understand each point.

FYI Many people spend 35% or more of their net pay on housing.

9-3 Renting a Living Space

Housing will play a major part in your financial plan. As a young person, you will probably rent your first living space rather than purchase a home. It is very exciting to be out on your own and rent your first apartment.

When you rent a living space, you will be required to sign a lease. An **apartment lease** is a contract that outlines the conditions of the agreement to rent the apartment for a certain length of time, usually a year. The renter is the lessee, and the property owner is the lessor in an apartment lease. The lease will probably state specifics such as those in the following list.

- The term of the lease states the length of time for which you will rent the apartment, usually for one year with renewal options.
- The monthly rent amount, the day of the month rent is due, and any penalties for late payment should be listed.
- The lease states that you will be responsible for the property and not cause any damages. If you do cause damages, you will have to pay to make repairs.
- The amount of the security deposit and when it is due is stated in the lease. A *security deposit* is an amount paid to protect the property owner against financial loss if the renter damages the property or fails to make payments. A typical security deposit is equal to the amount of the first month's rent, but it may be more. The deposit is usually due when the lease is signed. If the property is left in good condition when the lease is up, the deposit should be refunded.

When you are in college or working at your first job, it may make sense to live with a roommate in an apartment to share expenses. *What are some potential advantages and disadvantages of having a roommate?*

Zinkevych/Shutterstock.com

- The lease should state whether you are responsible for utilities such as water and electricity.
- The lease should state whether pets are allowed as well as any restrictions on them, such as a weight limit.

When you apply to rent an apartment, the property owner will check your credit rating to determine if you are a good risk.

When you are in college or working at your first job, it may make sense to have a roommate to share your expenses. Remember to include renters insurance when planning for that first apartment.

Check Your Understanding

Provide examples of information that may be included in an apartment lease.

_____
_____
_____
_____
_____
_____

Your Turn

Renting an Apartment

Renting your first apartment will take a lot of research. You will need to determine if you have enough money to rent an apartment. You will also have to decide where to live. Make a list of ten items to consider before you start an apartment search.

1. _____
2. _____
3. _____
4. _____
5. _____
6. _____
7. _____
8. _____
9. _____
10. _____

Dollars and Sense

Renting Your First Place

Even though it now seems a long time away, before you know it, you will be renting your first apartment. You may rent an apartment because you are going to college in another town. Maybe you have landed your first job and now you are ready to live on your own. In either case, renting your first place will be fun if you do a lot of planning in preparation.

The first thing you need to do is to create a budget. You created a budget in Chapter 3. It will be a good idea to create an "apartment budget" to guide you in what you can afford. You will list your fixed and variable expenses. Then, you will determine how much money you have each month for apartment rent. This will take some time. Start working on your budget before you are ready to start looking for an apartment.

Remember that renting an apartment involves paying for utilities, renters insurance, and other expenses that you have not had before. Make sure you do your homework and know exactly how much money you will need.

Once your budget has been prepared, the apartment hunt can begin! After you have decided how much you can afford each month, the next important factor will be location. You will want to find a place that is close to school or work. The price must fit within your budget.

After you select a location, you can use the Internet and other resources to find places available for rent. Select four or five possible apartments and set up appointments to look at them. If you have a roommate, it is important that you agree on a place that you both like and how expenses will be split.

You may need to look at several apartments to find one you want to rent. Then you will need to fill out an application. The property owner will probably check your credit and ability to make monthly payments. Then, you will hear whether your application to rent has been accepted. Read carefully and make sure you understand the lease before you sign it.

FYI
Mortgage interest may be listed on your income tax return as an itemized deduction if your deductions total more than the standard deduction. Interest on car loans, credit cards, and most other loans is not tax deductible.

9-4 Buying a House

The biggest investment for many people is a house. There are many reasons to buy a house. Financially, it is usually a wise decision. Unlike a car, the value of a house normally goes up over a period of years, while the amount you owe on a mortgage goes down. A **mortgage** is a type of secured loan used for buying property. The difference between what you owe on your house and its current market value is called **equity**.

With a home mortgage, your home is the collateral for the loan. If you do not make the payments, the lender can repossess it. **Foreclosure** is a process in which the lender takes possession of the house if you fail to make the mortgage payments.

Depending on where you live, the average cost of a small "starter" home could be well over $100,000. Prices vary depending on the area of the country. Traditionally, lenders require 20 percent of the price as a down payment on a house. That would be $20,000 for a very modest $100,000 house.

It is possible to borrow more than 80 percent of the home's value. Some loans are available with only 5 percent down. However, with a down payment of less than 20 percent, you may be required by the lender to buy private mortgage insurance. **Private mortgage insurance (PMI)** insures payment if the borrower defaults on the loan. PMI can add as much as $50–$100 or more to your monthly payment, depending on the amount borrowed. To discontinue the PMI, the loan must be paid down to 80 percent of the home's purchase price and a current appraisal, or valuation, obtained.

When you buy a home, you will pay taxes on the home and property insurance premiums. Rather than pay each of these expenses once a year, you may choose to set up an escrow account. An **escrow account** is an account for holding money in trust for others. In this case, an account is set up by the lender for you. You pay part of your insurance premium and taxes each month along with your mortgage payment. That way, you save gradually for the cost of taxes and insurance instead of making a lump-sum payment. The lender will then take this money and pay your taxes and insurance premium when they are due.

Do a lot of research before buying a house. Look at not only the house, but also the neighborhood, community, schools, businesses, and the general area. You may be there a long time. Hopefully, the value of the house will increase, and you will build equity. Just as with car loans, *never* owe more on a house than its current value.

There are laws that protect the consumer from lender and seller abuse. If you have questions about loans, seek advice from a professional to learn about the laws that protect you as a consumer.

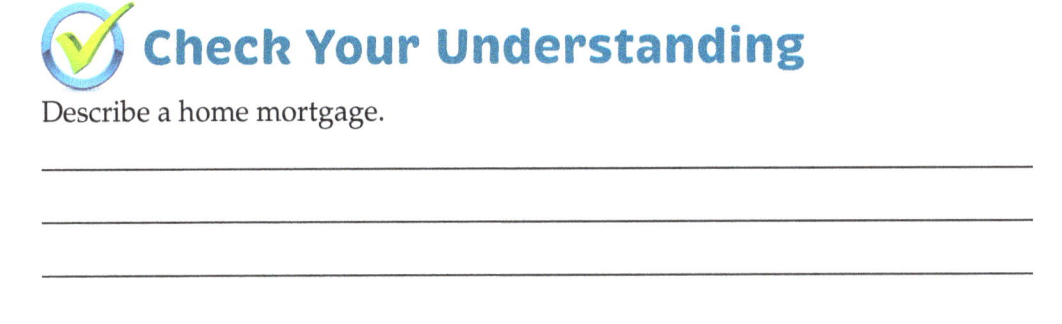

✓ Check Your Understanding

Describe a home mortgage.

_____

_____

_____

_____

Fixed-Rate Mortgage

When you borrow money to buy a home, you may get a fixed-rate mortgage. A **fixed-rate mortgage** is a secured loan with an interest rate that does not change. The term of the mortgage is usually either 15 or 30 years but may be for other terms. Your monthly payments will stay the same until the loan is paid in full. Typically, you can pay off the loan early or make additional payments with no penalty. The amount of your required payment will not go up.

Buying a house takes a lot of money. Your mortgage payment will consist of principal and interest. At the beginning of your mortgage loan, your payments will mostly go toward interest. Very little of the payment will reduce the principal. Even though your payment remains the same, the amount you pay toward the principal will gradually increase as the interest slowly decreases. The process of making equal payments on a loan while reducing the principal is **amortization**. You can find mortgage calculators online. These calculators will help you determine what your payments will be and how much interest you will pay over the life of the loan.

> **FYI**
>
> Amounts in the example are basic loan payments and do not include PMI, taxes, or insurance.

Consider the following example. The principal paid over the first year of a mortgage of $150,000 has an interest rate of 6 percent. Monthly payments are $900. Note that the payment is fixed, but the amount of the interest and principal changes each month.

Step 1. Calculate the amount of interest for the first month.

Amount of loan	$150,000.00
Interest rate	× .06
Annual interest	$9,000.00
Number of months	÷ 12
First month's interest	$750.00

Step 2. Calculate the amount applied toward principal.

Monthly payment	$900.00
Interest payment	− 750.00
Amount applied toward principal	$150.00

Step 3. Calculate the new principal balance for the second month.

Amount of loan	$150,000.00
Amount applied toward principal	− 150.00
Principal for the second month	$149,850.00

Month	Beginning Balance	Yearly Interest	Monthly Interest Amount	Principal Reduction Amount	New Balance
1	$150,000.00	$9,000.00	$750.00	$150.00	$149,850.00
2	149,850.00	8,991.00	749.25	150.75	149,699.25
3	149,699.25	8,981.96	748.50	151.50	149,547.75
4	149,547.75	8,972.87	747.74	152.26	149,395.49
5	149,395.49	8,963.73	746.98	153.02	149,242.47
6	149,242.47	8,954.55	746.21	153.79	149,088.68
7	149,088.68	8,945.32	745.44	154.56	148,934.12
8	148,934.12	8,936.05	744.67	155.33	148,778.79
9	148,778.79	8,926.73	743.89	156.11	148,622.68
10	148,622.68	8,917.36	743.11	156.89	148,465.79
11	148,465.79	8,907.95	742.33	157.67	148,308.12
12	148,308.12	8,898.48	741.54	158.46	148,149.66
Totals			$8,949.66	$1,850.34	

You Do the Math | 9-4

Calculate the principal paid for the first year on a mortgage of $135,000 with an interest rate of 5.75 percent. Monthly payments are $795.

Month	Beginning Balance	Yearly Interest	Monthly Interest Amount	Principal Reduction Amount	New Balance
1					
2					
3					
4					
5					
6					
7					
8					
9					
10					
11					
12					
Totals					

Adjustable-Rate Mortgage

An **adjustable-rate mortgage (ARM)** is a secured loan with an interest rate that can change periodically. The interest rate can go lower or higher based on market conditions. There may be a cap on the rate, known as a *maximum interest rate*. The interest rate for this type of mortgage can increase several percentage points over the life of the loan. This means your monthly payment could increase to a payment you cannot afford to pay.

In most cases, a mortgage with a fixed rate is preferable over an adjustable rate. With a fixed-rate mortgage, your interest rate and payments are guaranteed not to increase. If interest rates decrease, you should be able to refinance at a lower rate.

FYI
In the early 2000s, many people got ARMs with very low initial interest rates. When rates went up, they were unable to continue making payments. As a result, they lost their homes to foreclosure.

✓ Check Your Understanding

Why is a fixed-rate mortgage less risky for the borrower than an adjustable-rate mortgage?

_____

_____

_____

Your Turn

Mortgage Payments

You want to purchase a house for $285,000 with a 20 percent down payment of $57,000. Set up a spreadsheet to calculate principal and interest payments for the first year of a 30-year, $228,000 mortgage with an interest rate of 5.25 percent. The monthly payment is $1,259. Write the answers for the first year of payments. Keep in mind that these payments will not include taxes or insurance.

Month	Beginning Balance	Yearly Interest	Monthly Interest Amount	Principal Reduction Amount	New Balance
1					
2					
3					
4					
5					
6					
7					
8					
9					
10					
11					
12					
Totals					

Internet Connection

Mortgage Calculator

1. You are a first-time home buyer. You want to purchase a house in your area that costs $185,000 and make a $20,000 down payment. Assume you have good credit and are not including taxes and insurance in your monthly payments. You want a fixed-rate mortgage with a term of 15 or 30 years.
2. Find an easy-to-use mortgage calculator online. Then, fill in the following table to compare payments with different interest rates.

Interest Rate	Monthly Payments Term 15 Years	Monthly Payments Term 30 Years
5%		
5.5%		
6%		
6.5%		
7%		

9-5 Buying a Condo

If you choose not to rent an apartment or buy a house, buying a condominium may be a good choice for you. A *condominium*, or *condo*, is a form of property ownership. The buyer purchases a part of a structure rather than all of it. Think of a condo as an apartment that you buy rather than rent. You will pay your mortgage, taxes, insurance, and other expenses that are a part of home ownership.

Other people also own parts of the condo building or complex. As a group, all the owners make up the homeowners association. Each owner (member) is required to pay a fee. A **homeowners association (HOA) fee** is a monthly or yearly fee for insurance on the building, upkeep of the buildings and common areas, landscaping, snow removal, pool, and other amenities. Fees are typically set by the HOA board of directors who are elected by the members. If the number of members is small, the entire group may vote on fees and other issues. Consider these fees when determining whether you can afford your monthly payments.

There could also be additional costs if the HOA needs money for large expenses. An **assessment** is an amount required by the HOA to pay for major expenses. A new parking lot or a new roof might be needed. Ask to see the records for the past several years to see if assessments are regularly imposed on members.

FYI
Some neighborhoods of single-family homes also have homeowners associations. If you buy a home in a neighborhood with an HOA, you will also have to pay HOA fees on top of your mortgage, taxes, and insurance.

The additional fees a condo owner must pay will increase monthly fixed expenses for housing. Assume you purchase a condo and your mortgage is $735.00 per month. In addition, you pay $85.50 for PMI and $125.00 for HOA fees each month. What are your monthly fixed condo expenses?

Mortgage payment	$735.00
PMI	85.50
HOA fees	+ 125.00
Total monthly fixed condo expenses	$945.50

Keep in mind, this amount does not include monthly expenses such as utilities, cable, Internet, and other items related to your home.

You Do the Math | 9-5

Your condo mortgage payments are $833.45 monthly. You pay $92.25 for PMI and $130.00 for HOA fees each month. What are your monthly fixed condo expenses?

Mortgage payment	_____
PMI	_____
HOA fees	_____
Total monthly fixed condo expenses	_____

Check Your Understanding

Describe the role of a homeowners association (HOA).

_____
_____
_____
_____
_____

Chapter 9 Review and Assessment

Summary

9-1 Discuss buying a car.

Many people get a car loan to finance the purchase of a car. A car loan is a secured loan in which the car you are buying serves as the collateral. A car loan is also an installment loan. In addition to the sales price, taxes and fees are added when you buy a car. Once you have calculated the total cost of the purchase, consider whether you can afford it.

9-2 Explain leasing a car.

A car lease is a contract that allows a person to use a car in exchange for payment. The person who leases a car is the lessee. The dealership is the lessor. There is usually a required down payment and security deposit. When the lease is up, you may decide to purchase the car.

9-3 Summarize renting a living space.

When you rent a living space, you will be required to sign a lease. When you are in college or working at your first job, it may make sense to have a roommate to share your expenses.

9-4 Discuss home mortgages.

A mortgage is a type of secured loan in which your home is the collateral for the loan. A fixed-rate mortgage is a secured loan with an interest rate that does not change. An adjustable-rate mortgage (ARM) is a secured loan with an interest rate that can change periodically based on market conditions.

9-5 Explain buying a condominium.

A condominium is a form of property ownership in which the buyer purchases a part of a structure rather than all of it. Each owner is required to pay a homeowners association (HOA) fee for building insurance, upkeep of the buildings and common areas, landscaping, snow removal, pool, and other amenities. An assessment is an amount required by the HOA to pay for major expenses.

Review Your Knowledge

Choose the correct answer for each of the following.

1. _____ _____ is the gradual decrease in the value of an asset.
    A. Repossession
    B. Foreclosure
    C. Appreciation
    D. Depreciation

2. _____ Which type of loan is backed by something of value?
   A. PMI loan
   B. unsecured loan
   C. secured loan
   D. underwater loan
3. _____ A car loan is an example of a(n) _____.
   A. unsecured loan
   B. mortgage
   C. lease
   D. installment loan
4. _____ Owing more on an asset than it is worth is called being _____.
   A. underwater
   B. in equity
   C. in assessment
   D. in foreclosure
5. _____ When you lease a car, you are the _____ and the car dealer is the _____.
   A. renter; cosigner
   B. lessor; lessee
   C. lessee; lessor
   D. cosigner; lessee
6. _____ A loan obtained when you purchase a home and use the home as collateral is a(n) _____.
   A. unsecured loan
   B. foreclosure
   C. mortgage
   D. assessment
7. _____ What is the difference between what you owe on your home and its current market value?
   A. equity
   B. assessment
   C. collateral
   D. escrow
8. _____ When a bank takes possession of a home because the borrower has failed to make loan payments, it is called _____.
   A. being underwater
   B. a mortgage
   C. an assessment
   D. a foreclosure
9. _____ A(n) _____ account is used for holding money in a trust for others.
   A. mortgage
   B. assessment
   C. escrow
   D. foreclosure
10. _____ Which type of mortgage allows the interest rate to change?
    A. fixed-rate mortgage
    B. adjustable-rate mortgage
    C. underwater mortgage
    D. collateral mortgage

Build Your Vocabulary

For each word or term, write the correct definition using your own words.

11. collateral

12. repossession

13. car lease

14. security deposit

15. apartment lease

16. private mortgage insurance (PMI)

17. fixed-rate mortgage

18. amortization

19. homeowners association (HOA) fee

20. assessment

Apply Your Math Skills

Calculate the answers to the following problems. Show your calculations.

21. You purchase a car for $24,400, which includes a destination fee of $850. Your state sales tax is 5 percent. The DMV fees are 1.5 percent of the price of the car. What is the total you must pay?

    _____
    _____
    _____
    _____

22. Your old car has a value of $1,850. You want to buy a new car with a sticker price of $19,750. The dealer will take your old car in trade and give you a loan of $17,900. How much are you actually paying for the new car?

    _____
    _____
    _____
    _____

23. You decide to lease a car for three years. You will make payments of $535 for the three years. The lease requires a down payment of $1,500 plus a security deposit of $950. What is the total cost to lease the car for three years?

    _____
    _____
    _____
    _____

24. Calculate the principal paid over the first year on a mortgage of $143,500 with an interest rate of 5.5 percent. Monthly payments are $815. What is the total amount of interest paid for the year? What is the total principal paid for the year? What is the ending balance? Use a separate sheet of paper for your calculations.

    _____
    _____
    _____
    _____

25. Your condominium mortgage payments are $736.90 per month. You pay $85.80 for PMI and $175.00 for HOA fees each month. What are your monthly fixed condominium expenses?

    _____
    _____
    _____
    _____

CHAPTER 10
Investing: Making Your Money Work for You

Essential Question

How can investing help create wealth?

Learning Outcomes

When you complete Chapter 10, you will be able to:
- **10-1** Discuss investing basics.
- **10-2** Define investment portfolio.
- **10-3** Summarize stocks as an investment.
- **10-4** Summarize bonds as an investment.
- **10-5** Summarize mutual funds as an investment.
- **10-6** Explain the meaning of financial independence.

Key Terms

investing	dividend	corporate bond
entrepreneur	recession	municipal bond
growth	expansion	government bond
average rate of return	bull market	mutual fund
investment portfolio	bear market	financial independence
diversification	stock split	dollar-cost averaging
stock	bond	fiscal responsibility
trading	coupon rate	

Reading Prep

Before reading this chapter, write the main heading for each section, leaving space under each. Under each heading, list any key terms that appear in that section. Use this list to create an outline for taking notes during reading and class discussion.

What is Your Financial IQ?

Before reading this chapter, answer the following questions to see how much you already know about investing.

1. What is investing?

2. Why is it a risk to invest?

3. What is an investment portfolio?

4. Why is diversification important when investing?

5. Explain what it means to own stock in a company.

6. How can a stock split benefit an investor?

7. What are bonds?

8. How do mutual funds spread risk?

9. Explain the meaning of financial independence.

10. Why should you live below your means?

10-1 Investing Basics

When creating a financial plan, many people decide to invest some of their money. Investments are an important part of an overall financial plan. **Investing** is purchasing an item of value with the hope that it will increase in value over time. Buying stocks, bonds, and mutual funds are examples of investments. In addition, there are other ways to invest your money. Some common investment options include:
- real estate used for rental property to generate profit
- collectibles, such as sports memorabilia or stamp collections
- precious metals, such as gold and silver
- gemstones, such as diamonds and emeralds

You should research these options carefully before you decide whether they are right for you.

Investments generally offer better returns than savings accounts. However, investing involves risk. A *risk* is the possibility that an unfavorable situation could happen. When you invest money, you are taking the risk that you may lose all or part of the money you invested. There is no guarantee that you will not lose your principal when you invest. No government insurance will cover your losses if an investment goes down in value.

As you grow in your career, you may decide to invest and start a business of your own. An **entrepreneur** is a person who organizes and operates a business. Being your own boss may be a worthy goal. However, you should realize that an entrepreneur is responsible for *everything* in the business. To start a business, you must be persistent, have financial backing, and do your homework. New businesses rarely make a profit for several years. The risks can be large, but so can the rewards.

> **FYI**
> More than 10 percent of all businesses are franchises licensed to sell a company's products or services, such as Great Clips, UPS Stores, and some fitness centers. The entrepreneur pays a franchise fee for the right to use the company's name.

✓ Check Your Understanding

Why does investing involve risk?

_____
_____
_____

Growth

Most people invest for **growth**, which is an increase in the value of an investment over time. Investing for growth is not a "get rich quick" scheme but is a plan for building wealth over a long term.

When creating a financial plan, most people want to know how long it will take their investments to grow. You can apply the *Rule of 72* to estimate how long it will take to double an investment with a fixed annual interest rate.

For example, you made an investment in which the annual interest rate is 3 percent. How many years will it take to double your investment?

Start with	72
Divide by the interest rate	÷ 3
Number of years to double	24 years

You Do the Math | 10-1

The annual interest rate on your investment is 8 percent. How many years will it take to double your investment?

Start with	_____
Divide by the interest rate	_____
Number of years to double	_____

Remember that this is just an estimate. However, it is useful for quick calculations. Naturally, the higher the interest rate on your investment, the fewer number of years it will take to double your money.

✓ Check Your Understanding

What does *growth* mean as it relates to investing?

_____
_____
_____

Average Rate of Return

An investment does not normally earn the same rate of return each year over a long period of time. One year it may earn 5 percent, while the next year it may lose 2 percent. The **average rate of return** is the average percentage of gain or loss of an investment over a specific period of time.

To find the average rate of return, total the amount of increase or decrease in value for each year of the investment. Divide the total amount by the number of years of the investment for the average return amount. Then, divide the average return amount by the number of years for the average rate of return.

total amount earned ÷ number of years = average return amount

average return amount ÷ initial investment amount = average rate of return

There is no guaranteed rate of return on most investments because interest rates and growth *fluctuate* (go up and down in value). When investing over a period of 30 to 35 years, an average rate of return of 7 to 9 percent is not unrealistic. When making an investment, look at the rate of return for the past several years if possible. Doing so is a better indication of how the investment is likely to grow than just looking at the rate of return for the previous year or two.

The following is an example of a 10-year investment. The initial investment amount was $1,500. Negative numbers are shown in parentheses to represent losses for those years. What is the average rate of return on this investment?

Year	Interest Earned
1	$75.00
2	50.00
3	100.00
4	100.00
5	75.00
6	50.00
7	(50.00)
8	(25.00)
9	25.00
10	+ 50.00
Total amount	$450.00
Number of years	÷ 10
Average return amount	$45.00
Initial investment	÷ $1,500
Average rate of return	3%

You Do the Math | 10-2

The following is a seven-year investment. The initial investment amount was $1,000. What is the average rate of return on this investment?

Year	Interest Earned
1	$100.00
2	(75.00)
3	85.00
4	100.00
5	75.00
6	(35.00)
7	+ 70.00
Total amount	_____
Number of years	_____
Average return amount	_____
Initial investment	_____
Average rate of return	_____

Check Your Understanding

Why is average rate of return an important concept to understand?

_____
_____
_____

10-2 Investment Portfolio

An **investment portfolio** is a collection of the investments a person has made. Stocks, bonds, mutual funds, and other investments you own make up your investment portfolio. The *investment pyramid* in Figure 10-1 shows various investment options and their levels of risk.

You will need to research and investigate investments before buying them. Do not invest blindly. Examine companies and organizations whose products and services you and your friends use. Study those that have been around a long time and have a history of profits. In addition, there may be costs associated with buying some investments. Consider these in your plans to purchase.

Figure 10-1 Different investment options come with different levels of risk. *Explain why you would want to purchase investments in the top, middle, or bottom of the pyramid.*

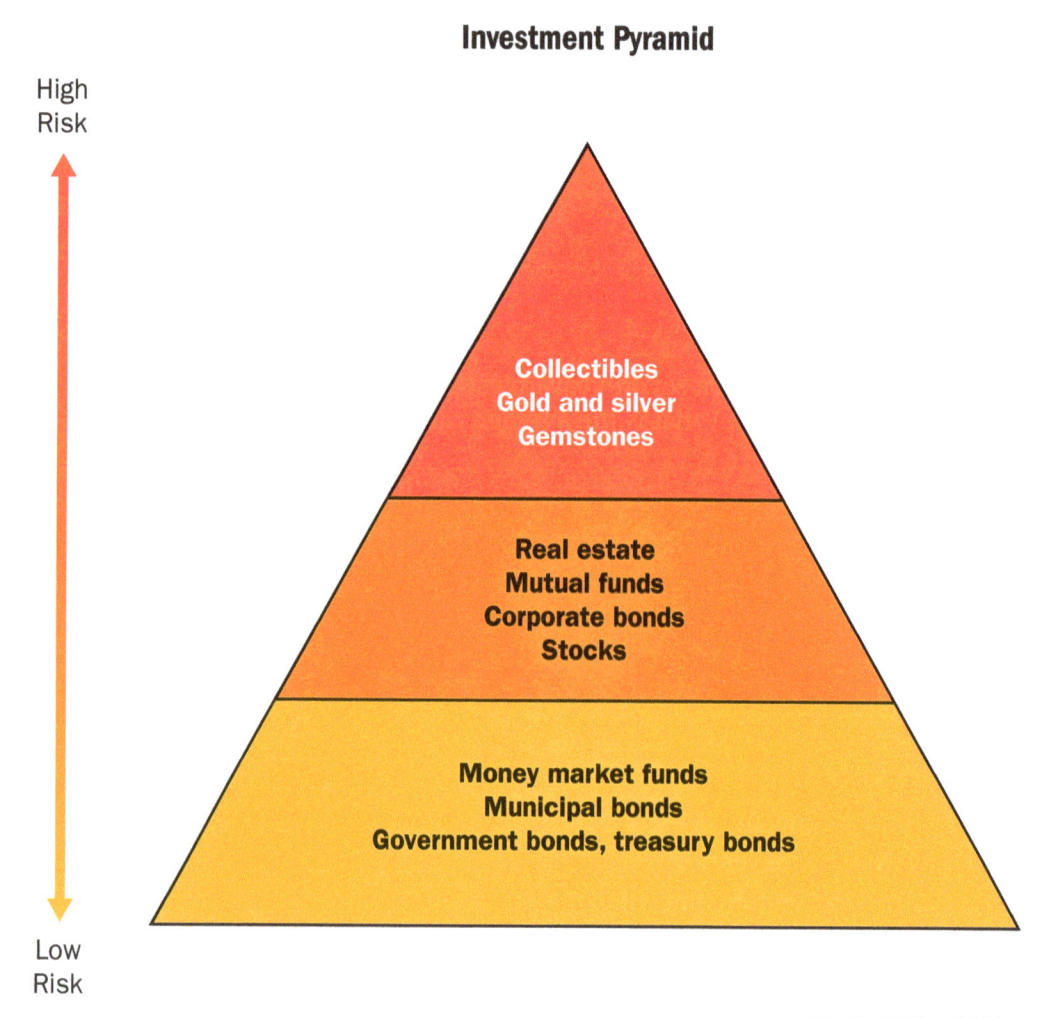

Investment Pyramid

High Risk ↑ ↓ Low Risk

- Collectibles
- Gold and silver
- Gemstones

- Real estate
- Mutual funds
- Corporate bonds
- Stocks

- Money market funds
- Municipal bonds
- Government bonds, treasury bonds

Goodheart-Willcox Publisher

The most important thing to remember when investing is to diversify. **Diversification** means spreading risk by putting money in different types of investments. No matter how good the opportunity looks for a single investment, something could happen and you could lose everything.

If you have any questions about investments, seek advice from a professional to learn about laws that protect you as a consumer. A *financial advisor* is a person who helps people make decisions about their financial plans. A person in this role can help you understand how to make good decisions when buying stock or other investments.

Most people invest hoping the value of their investments will grow over a period of years. *Why would it be beneficial for you to start investing now?*

Check Your Understanding

What is the most important thing to remember when building an investment portfolio?

___

10-3 Stocks

As a part of an investment plan, many people choose to invest in stocks. **Stock** is a share of ownership in a corporation. The ownership entitles the purchaser to share in the company's profits. Most experts suggest that young people own more stocks than bonds. When you purchase stock, you will receive a stock registration statement that includes a trade confirmation. A sample stock registration statement is shown in Figure 10-2.

```
Adam Smith                    TRADE CONFIRMATION
100 Main Street         RETAIN FOR YOUR PERMANENT TAX RECORDS
Anytown, USA

    WE ARE PLEASED TO CONFIRM THE FOLLOWING TRANSACTIONS SUBJECT TO THE INFORMATION,
        DISCLOSURES, AND TERMS ON THE FRONT AND REVERSE SIDES OF THIS DOCUMENT:

                    IN YOUR CASH ACCOUNT
     On Trade Date    05/31/20--        For Settlement Date    06/04/20--

       You Bought    463.822 SHARES              Price         $5.3900

                                        Principal Amount     $2,500.00
    DESCRIPTION:
    PRUDENTIAL HIGH YIELD FUND
    CL Q
    SOLICITED
    AS OF 05/31/20--
                                                 TOTAL       $2,500.00
```

Figure 10-2 A stock registration statement is issued when stock is purchased. *Why might it be a good idea to check the math on this document?*

Stock Market Report

107.54 −0.12 (−0.11%) (Cost per share at the end of the day and its percentage of decrease)

Nasdaq Real Time Price

Open	High	Low	Prev. Close	52 Wk. High	52 Wk. Low	P/E	Mkt. Cap	NYSE
106.82	108.43	105.82	107.66	156.73	84.07	60.42	196.46B	Price in USD
↑	↑	↑	↑	↑	↑	↑	↑	
Earliest price for the day	Highest price for the day	Lowest price for the day	Price at closing previous day	High for the last 12 months	Low for the last 12 months	Price/Earnings ratio: Price ÷ Earnings per share for previous year	Total value of all the company's stock, found by multiplying individual stock value × number of shares outstanding. This is $196.46 billion.	

Figure 10-3 Stock market reports are commonly published online. *Why do you think investors frequently check the performance of their stocks?*

FYI

One of the world's largest stock exchanges is the New York Stock Exchange (NYSE) located on Wall Street in New York City. Wall Street has become known as the financial center of the United States.

When you buy stock in a company, you can follow its progress by checking the company's website. A sample of a stock market report for one company is shown in Figure 10-3.

Stocks are bought and sold on a *stock market*, also called a *stock exchange*. Companies sell stock to raise money for the operation or expansion of the company. Buying and selling stocks is commonly known as **trading**. Many large companies are publicly traded corporations. These companies sell their stock to the public. However, some companies are privately held corporations. The stock of these companies is not available for sale to the public.

In the United States, stock trading is regulated by the federal government. The *Securities and Exchange Commission (SEC)* is the federal agency that regulates financial markets in the United States. The mission of the SEC is to protect investors and make sure markets operate with fairness and efficiency.

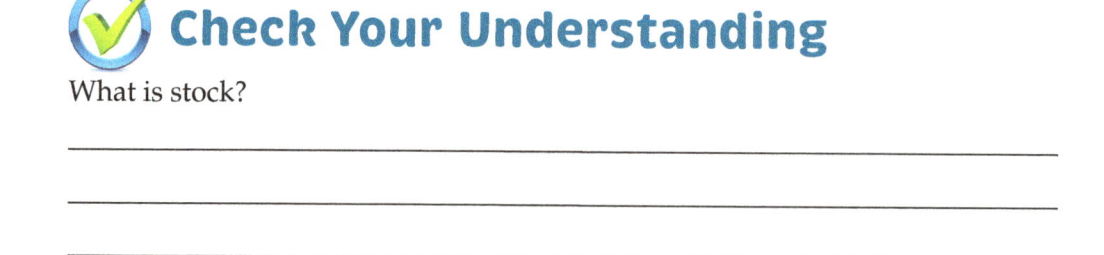

✅ **Check Your Understanding**

What is stock?

_____
_____
_____

Your Turn

Stock Market Report

Review the following stock market report and answer the questions that follow.

STOCK	DIV	LAST	CHG	YTD %CHG	STOCK	DIV	LAST	CHG	YTD %CHG
BkofAm	.88	35.72	−.78	+7.9	Disney	—	110.36	−1.42	+27.0
BerkHa A	—	466020	−1979	−0.6	DukeEngy	4.00f	97.55	−1.63	−5.3
BerkHa B	—	307	−1	−0.5	Elevance	5.92f	485.60	+2.06	−5.3
BroadCInc	14.40	599.41	−2.30	+7.2	EliLilly	4.52f	341.79	+1.06	−6.6
CecoEnv	0.30	14.38	−.20	+23.1	ExxonMbl	3.64	114.35	+.43	+3.7
Chemed	1.52f	493.18	−3.75	−3.4	FifthThird	1.32f	37.26	−.42	+13.6
Chevron	6.04f	168.44	−1.56	−6.2	FFnclOH	0.92	25.66	−.28	+5.9
CinnFin	3.00f	126.25	−1.44	+23.3	GenElec	0.32	80.79	−1.17	+24.1
Cintas	3.8	438.09	−1.64	−3.0	HomeDp	7.60f	315.55	−5.24	−0.1
Cisco	1.52f	46.73	−.23	−1.9	JPMorgCh	4.00f	140.42	−2.22	+4.7
CocaCola	1.76f	59.62	−.10	−6.3	JohnJn	4.40f	161.40	−2.21	−8.6
Costco	3.60	500.63	−3.18	+9.7	Kroger	1.04	44.09	−.18	−1.1
Danaher	1.00f	255.11	−6.83	−3.9	LSI Ind It	0.20	13.71	−.17	+12.0

1. From the market report above, list 3 to 5 companies that you are familiar with.

   _____

2. Which company has the highest YTD percentage of increase?

   _____

3. Which company has the largest YTD percentage of decrease?

   _____

4. Which company paid the highest dividend?

   _____

5. List the companies that did not pay dividends.

   _____

6. Which company paid the lowest dividend?

   _____

continued

Your Turn (continued)

7. List the companies that paid less than one dollar in dividends.
   _____

8. What was the last value of CocaCola?
   _____

9. How many companies had a decrease in percentage YTD?
   _____

10. How many companies had an increase in percentage YTD?
    _____

Internet Connection

Stock Quotes

1. In the first column of the table that follows, list five companies with which you are familiar. These can be clothing stores, restaurants, gyms, online retailers, or other companies.
2. Then, visit each company's website to check its current stock price. Type the company name/stock price for an easy search.
3. Write the current price of that company's stock in the second column of the table.

Name of Company	Price of Stock

Types of Stock

Two basic types of stock are common stock and preferred stock. *Common stock* is stock that has voting rights and earns dividends when they are declared by the company. A **dividend** is a share of the company's profits received by its stockholders. Common stockholders can vote on company policies and elect directors at shareholder meetings. Holders of *preferred stock* are paid dividends before common stockholders and have first claim on assets if the company fails, but they have no voting privileges.

✓ Check Your Understanding

Name two types of stock.

_____

_____

_____

Market Conditions

Your goal should be to buy stock at a low price and sell stock when its price is high. But resist the urge to sell when stock values go down. You could lose half of your investment just by missing the 10 best days in the market! Remember, owning stock is an investment designed to build value over a long time.

You are young and should have many working years ahead of you. Be prepared to ride out the fluctuations of the stock market. A **recession** is a period of slow or no economic growth. During a recession, stock prices fall and unemployment rises. Traditionally, the market has always recovered from downturns and recessions, even from the Great Depression of the 1930s, the Great Recession of the early 2000s, and early in the COVID-19 pandemic. An **expansion** is an upward trend in the stock market. Historically, expansions have lasted a lot longer than recessions.

Market fluctuations are discussed in terms of bull markets and bear markets. A **bull market** means stock prices are rising. A **bear market** means stock prices are falling or staying at a low level. The term *market correction* is sometimes used to describe a sudden change in the market. For example, stock prices may steadily increase for a period of time and then drop suddenly.

> **FYI**
> How can you remember a bull market versus a bear market? The bull walks with his horns up, which means prices are going upward. A bear walks with his paws down, which means prices are heading downward.

✓ Check Your Understanding

Explain the difference between a recession and an expansion in the stock market.

_____

_____

_____

_____

Internet Connection

Current Market Conditions

1. Using the Internet, conduct research on the current state of the stock market. Enter a search term such as *bull or bear stock market* or *current state of the stock market*. Is the stock market currently a bear or bull market? Provide facts to support your opinion.

   _____
   _____
   _____

2. Would you want to invest in any of the companies you researched in the Stock Quotes activity given the current state of the stock market? Why or why not?

   _____
   _____
   _____

FYI

Blue chip stocks are the most consistently profitable type of stock and the most expensive. These are stocks of successful, established companies. They get their name from the blue chips in poker, which are the most valuable.

Reasons to Buy Stock

Investors buy stock for many reasons. Some investors look for growth in the stocks they purchase. Other investors want a regular income from the stocks in the form of dividends.

Growth

The main reason investors buy stocks is that they are looking for growth. Hopefully, the value of stock you purchase will grow over the years of ownership. When the time comes that you want to sell it, your financial goal should be to sell it for more than you paid.

For example, you purchased 30 shares of stock in XYZ Company for $27.60 each. Your stock's rate of return varies each year over the 10 years that you keep the stock, as shown in the table that follows. How much profit will you earn if you sell after 10 years?

number of shares × price per share = total amount of purchase

Step 1. Calculate the purchase price of the stock.

Price per share	$27.60
Number of shares	× 30
Total price of stock purchase	$828.00

Step 2. Calculate yearly earnings.

Year	Beginning Balance	Rate of Return	Amount of Return	Ending Balance
1	$828.00	6.00%	$49.68	$877.68
2	877.68	5.00%	43.88	921.56
3	921.56	5.50%	50.69	972.25
4	972.25	8.00%	77.78	1,050.03
5	1,050.03	9.00%	94.50	1,144.53
6	1,144.53	7.25%	82.98	1,227.51
7	1,227.51	5.00%	61.38	1,288.89
8	1,288.89	2.50%	32.22	1,321.11
9	1,321.11	4.00%	52.84	1,373.95
10	1,373.95	3.00%	41.22	1,415.17

Step 3. Calculate your total earnings.

Ending balance	$1,415.17
Cost of original purchase	− 828.00
Total profit	$587.17

You Do the Math | 10-3

You purchased 55 shares of stock in ABC, Inc. for $32.75 each. Your stock's rate of return varies each year over the 12 years that you keep the stock, as shown in the following table. How much profit will you earn if you sell after 12 years?

Step 1. Calculate the purchase price of the stock.

Price per share _____

Number of shares _____

Total price of stock purchase _____

continued

You Do the Math | 10-3 (continued)

Step 2. Calculate yearly earnings.

Year	Beginning Balance	Rate of Return	Amount of Return	Ending Balance
1		9.00%		
2		6.00%		
3		5.50%		
4		8.00%		
5		9.00%		
6		7.25%		
7		5.00%		
8		3.50%		
9		4.00%		
10		3.00%		
11		6.00%		
12		9.00%		

Step 3. Calculate your total earnings.

Ending balance _____

Cost of original purchase _____

Total profit _____

Your Turn

Track Stocks

1. Choose five stocks from familiar companies to track over a one-month period. List the stocks in the table that follows.
2. Locate the stock quotes on each company's website to obtain the selling price of the five stocks. Assume you are buying 100 shares of each stock. Record the total cost of those shares in column two.
3. At the end of one month, check the prices again. Using these prices, record the total price of 100 shares in column three.

Your Turn (continued)

4. If you sold your 100 shares after one month, what would your gain or loss be on each stock? Write your total gain or loss for each company in column four.

Company Name/Symbol	Purchase Price of 100 Shares	Sale Price of 100 Shares	Gain or Loss
Totals			

Dividends

Another important reason to buy stock is to earn dividends. A dividend is a share of the company's profits received by stockholders. Dividends may be issued quarterly, semiannually, or annually. The company gives you part of the earnings for being an owner of the company. Many people accumulate bigger returns by leaving dividends in their portfolios.

number of shares × dividend per share = total dividend

For example, Company A issued a semiannual dividend on its profits. For the current year, each share of stock earned 75 cents semiannually. If you own 1,200 shares of Company A, what are your total dividends for the year?

Step 1. Calculate semiannual dividend.

Number of shares owned	1,200
Dividend per share	× .75
Semiannual dividend	$900.00

Step 2. Calculate annual dividends.

Semiannual dividend	$900.00
Number of times paid	× 2
Annual dividend	$1,800.00

You Do the Math | 10-4

Company B issued quarterly dividends. For the current year, each share of stock earned 35 cents each quarter. If you own 1,450 shares of Company B, what are your total dividends for the year?

Step 1. Calculate quarterly dividend.

Number of shares owned _____

Dividend per share _____

Quarterly dividend _____

Step 2. Calculate annual dividends.

Quarterly dividend _____

Number of times paid _____

Annual dividend _____

FYI

In 1919, the price of one single share of The Coca-Cola Company was $40, which is about $530 today. As a result of stock splits and reinvested dividends, this one share would now be more than 9,200 shares and worth more than $10 million.

Stock Splits

Some investors buy stock hoping that it becomes more valuable through a stock split, which increases the number of shares they own. A **stock split** occurs when a company divides its existing shares of stocks into multiple shares without changing the total value of the stock. A stock split lowers the price of the individual shares of stock, but increases the number of shares that are owned. The stock can be divided into as many shares as the company chooses. For example, it may be two-for-one or three-for-one.

Assume you own 25 shares of stock in a company. If the company splits stock shares two-for-one, you now own 50 shares. In other words, you own more shares than you originally purchased without having to buy more. After the split, your individual shares will be worth less per share. However, if the price per share increases, you will profit from the stock split. Stock splits are usually a sign the company is growing.

Suppose you purchased 100 shares of Z Company stock at $36 per share. The company is doing well and decides to have a two-for-one stock split. How many shares will you have, and how much are they worth? Has the total value of your stock changed?

Step 1. Calculate the original value.

Price per share	$36.00
Number of shares purchased	× 100
Original value of 100 shares	$3,600.00

Step 2. Calculate the value after stock split.

Price per share	$18.00
Number of shares owned	× 200
Total value of shares	$3,600.00
Has the total value changed?	No

You Do the Math | 10-5

You purchased 175 shares of Beta Company stock at $52 per share. The company decides to have a two-for-one stock split. How many shares will you now have, and how much are they worth? Has the total value of your stock changed?

Step 1. Calculate the original value.

Price per share _____

Number of shares purchased _____

Original value of 175 shares _____

Step 2. Calculate the value after stock split.

Price per share _____

Number of shares owned _____

Total value of shares _____

Has the total value changed? _____

✓ Check Your Understanding

Explain why investors buy stocks.

_____
_____
_____
_____

10-4 Bonds

Bonds, unlike stocks, do not make you a part owner of the company. A **bond** is a certificate of debt issued by a government or company. It is essentially a loan for a set period of time.

The buyer of a bond is paid interest on the money invested, typically once or twice a year. The percentage of interest earned on a bond is called a **coupon rate**. When the bond matures, usually in 10 to 20 years, the buyer is repaid the amount invested.

For example, you purchased 50 bonds from Ace Manufacturing Co. at $250 each. You earn a 5 percent coupon rate annually on your bonds until they mature in 10 years. At that time, you will be repaid the amount you invested. How much interest will you earn over the 10 years?

Step 1. Calculate total amount of bonds.

Amount per bond	$250.00
Number of bonds purchased	× 50
Total amount of bonds	$12,500.00

Step 2. Calculate interest.

Total amount of bonds	$12,500.00
Coupon rate	× .05
Annual interest earned	$625.00
Number of years until maturity	× 10
Total interest earned	$6,250.00

You Do the Math | 10-6

You purchased 60 bonds from Perez, Inc. at $75 each. You will earn a 6.75 percent coupon rate on your bonds each year until they mature in 15 years. At that time, you will be repaid the amount you invested. How much interest will you earn over the 15 years?

Step 1. Calculate total amount of bonds.

Amount per bond	_____
Number of bonds purchased	_____
Total amount of bonds	_____

Step 2. Calculate interest.

Total amount of bonds	_____
Coupon rate	_____
Annual interest earned	_____
Number of years until maturity	_____
Total interest earned	_____

There are three major bond categories. These categories are corporate, municipal, and US government bonds.

Corporate Bonds

A **corporate bond** is a bond issued by a business to raise money for operating expenses or expansion. Some corporate bonds can be a safer investment than stocks. However, they may have lower earnings than stocks over the long run.

Municipal Bonds

A **municipal bond** is a bond issued by a state, county, or city government. Parks and other recreational areas in your city or town may have been funded by municipal bonds. Interest earned from municipal bonds is exempt from federal income tax and may also be exempt from state and local taxes.

Government Bonds

A **government bond** is a bond issued by the US Treasury Department. They are the safest bonds available since they are backed by the US government. However, they do not pay a very high return. Government bonds are exempt from state and local taxes. Federal taxes are only paid when the bond is redeemed. Seek professional advice if the proceeds are to be used for tuition expenses to determine if federal tax is required.

A *Series EE savings bond* is one of the most common types of US government bond. You may have one that you received as a gift at some point in your life. There are other types of government bonds that are good short-term or long-term investments. Talk to a financial advisor for more information when you are ready to make this type of investment.

✓ Check Your Understanding

What is a bond? Name three types of bonds.

___

10-5 Mutual Funds

Because there is a risk in buying stocks, some investors purchase mutual funds. A **mutual fund** is a collection of professionally managed investments. A mutual fund uses the money of many individuals pooled together. The pooled money is invested in a variety of stocks and bonds. There may be as many as 50 to 100 companies or organizations in one mutual fund.

Mutual funds are managed by professionals who study the market and know what is going on with the companies in the fund. These people can make informed decisions about buying and selling shares in the fund.

Investing in a mutual fund helps spread out your risk. If 1, 2, or 10 companies in the fund go bankrupt, you still have ownership of many other companies. These investments offer diversification because a variety of stocks and bonds are included in the mutual fund. They also offer liquidity because they can be easily turned into cash. For these reasons, some people feel more comfortable buying mutual funds than buying individual stocks when beginning to invest.

Mutual funds may be purchased at investment companies, brokerage houses, and some banks. Some mutual funds require large amounts of money to get started in the investment. However, there are some that require as little as $250 to $500. Some will even allow you to open a savings account until you build up enough to buy into the mutual fund. A mutual fund is one way a young person can begin investing in the stock market with small amounts of money.

> **FYI**
> Some investors want to support specific causes with their investment dollars. Certain mutual funds are socially responsible funds, which only contain the stock of corporations that have proven to care about ethical and environmental issues.

Investment Comparison Over 25 Years

Single Investment		Multiple Investments	
Amount Invested	**Current Value**	**Amounts Invested**	**Current Value**
$100,000 earns 8% avg. return	$684,848	$20,000 becomes worthless	$0
		$20,000 earns 0%	$20,000
		$20,000 earns 5% avg. return	$67,727
		$20,000 earns 10% avg. return	$216,694
		$20,000 earns 15% avg. return	$658,848
Total Value	**$684,848**	**Total Value**	**$963,221**

Goodheart-Willcox Publisher

Figure 10-4 Multiple investments may outperform a single investment over a long period of time. *Why is it important to diversify investments?*

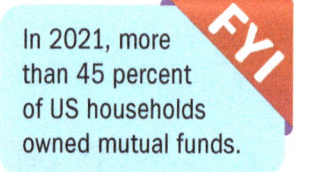

FYI
In 2021, more than 45 percent of US households owned mutual funds.

Figure 10-4 shows a comparison of investments for a period of 25 years in which a single stock is compared to multiple stocks. The value of the stocks after 25 years will vary greatly depending on the average rate of return for each one. If you invest in only one stock and it does poorly, you could gain very little or even lose your original investment. When you invest in several different stocks, you may earn a good rate of return overall. This is true even if some stocks do poorly or become worthless. Mutual funds work in a similar way. Even when some stocks in the fund don't earn much, the overall result may be good.

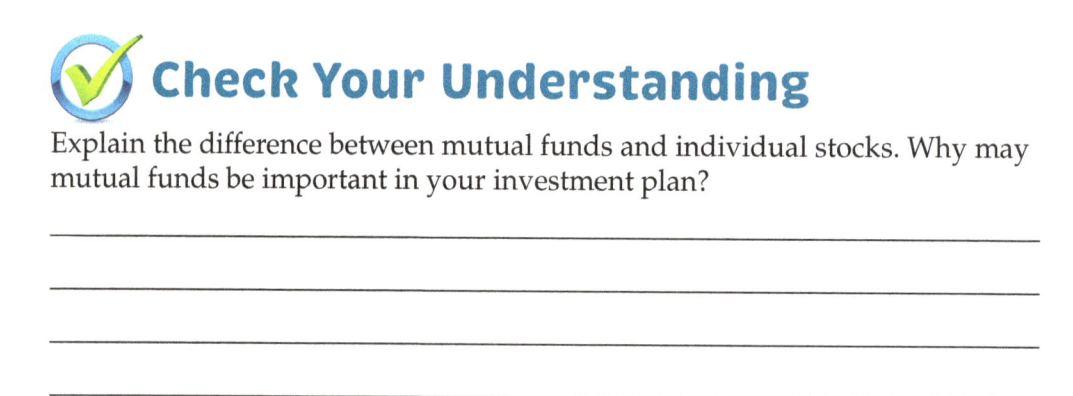

✓ Check Your Understanding

Explain the difference between mutual funds and individual stocks. Why may mutual funds be important in your investment plan?

_____
_____
_____
_____

Your Turn

Investment Portfolio

1. Many people have a variety of investments that make up their portfolios. What investments do you own or do your parents, guardians, grandparents, or other relatives own, or have owned in the past? Complete the following chart with assets that are considered investments owned by you or other members of your family.

Type of Investment	Name/Company	Value
Stocks		
Bonds		
Mutual funds		
Real estate		
Business ownership		
Collectibles		
Jewelry or gemstones		
Precious metals or coins		
Vintage cars		
Other		

2. What investments might you acquire as you get older?

_____

_____

Dollars and Sense

Your First Investment

Making investments is sometimes easier said than done. If you do not have a job, you may think you cannot start a portfolio and make an investment. However, the truth is that even if you have $100, you can make an investment and start a portfolio. How can you do that? There are several investments you can make to get started.

- **Stocks.** Technically, there is no minimum number of shares you must purchase from a publicly traded company. Before you buy, however, you need advice from a broker or financial advisor who can help you set up a plan to buy stocks on a regular schedule.
- **Bonds.** Bonds are loans to companies or governments on which interest is paid to the buyer. The interest is called the *coupon rate*. When the bond matures, the buyer is repaid the amount invested. There are three types of bonds: corporate, municipal, and government. Government bonds may be US savings bonds or treasury bonds.
- **Mutual Funds.** Mutual funds are a great way to create retirement funds or educational funds. Many banks sell mutual funds. You can ask a reliable financial advisor for help to get started.

Think big, start small. Before you know it, you will be on your way to creating an investment portfolio that will get you started on a solid financial plan.

10-6 Financial Independence

You can begin to invest at an early age and start to build wealth for your financial security in later years. If your investments are successful, you may achieve financial independence. **Financial independence** is having enough money for your basic needs and modest wants without work being a necessity. Money does not make you a better person—it just gives you choices. To reach the point where you can live on your investments, start preparing now while you are young. Time is a *powerful* factor in building wealth.

Your financial goals will change as you become established in your career and make life choices. Your income will depend on decisions you make about your career, your education, and the skills you develop. The sooner you create a financial plan, the better your chances are of attaining your goals. It does not take a lot of money to achieve wealth when you begin early. A little money and a lot of time work very well to help you achieve wealth.

MPH Photos/Shutterstock.com

You can begin to invest at an early age and start to build wealth for your financial security in later years. *What steps can you plan to take at your age to begin investing?*

Although it is never too late to start planning for financial independence, teen years are an ideal time to begin investing. Figure 10-5 shows two examples of the financial benefits that come with investing at an early age.

In example A, you begin at age 19 by investing $2,000 per year for 10 years and then stop. The money grows at a rate of 10 percent per year for 46 years. At age 65, you will have $1,083,959. That is more than $1 million from your investment of only $20,000. WOW!

In example B, assume you begin 10 years later at age 29 and invest $2,000 per year until age 65—a total of 36 years. At the same growth rate of 10 percent, you will have $658,091 from an investment of $72,000. This isn't bad, but check the math. You invest $52,000 more and end up with $425,868 less. Because of compounding, the additional early years made a *huge* difference in the amount achieved!

A great way to begin investing is to set aside a specific amount of money each month to put into your investments. **Dollar-cost averaging** is investing a fixed dollar amount at regular intervals without regard to the price at the time of the investment. When buying stocks, for example, if prices are high, you get fewer shares. However, when prices are low, you get more shares. Dollar-cost averaging is a disciplined approach to investing. It prevents you from investing a large lump sum when it may not be the best time to buy.

The ideal time to begin investing is when you are working part-time and living with your family without many expenses of your own. You can start a custodial brokerage account with a parent or guardian before you are 18. When you turn 18, you will no longer need your custodian's name on the account.

When you get a full-time job, adjust your contributions accordingly. In addition, always set aside more for investing each time you get a raise in salary. A good rule of thumb is to put a minimum of 10 percent of your salary aside for investing. However, if you cannot start there, then begin with 3 percent or 5 percent and work your way up. It is better to set a percentage rather than a dollar amount. That way, when you get a raise, you will be investing more as well as having more for expenses.

Investment Examples

Example A		Example B	
Annual investment for 10 years age 19 to age 29	$2,000	Annual investment for 36 years age 29 to age 65	$2,000
Total investment	$20,000	Total investment	$72,000
Investment period	48 Years	Investment period	36 Years
Annual earnings rate	10%	Annual earnings rate	10%
Final amount	$1,083,959	Final amount	$658,091

Goodheart-Willcox Publisher

Figure 10-5 Teen years are an ideal time to begin investing because many financial benefits come with investing at an early age. *Why is it important to begin investing as early as possible?*

How will you have the discipline to invest money each month? When your pay is directly deposited, have your bank automatically transfer part of it to an account to be used for investments. This way, you will be less likely to spend it. You won't miss it because you never get your hands on it.

To benefit from your investments later in life, start investing at a young age. Keep investing as much as you can even when doing so is difficult. You will be glad you did!

Regular investing is important, as well as the amount of the investments. Get in the habit of investing early and automatically. Pay yourself first! In other words, don't promise yourself you will invest what you have "left over" at the end of the month. It will not happen! Include money for investing in your monthly budget. Paying yourself first is an excellent lifelong habit to establish while young.

As you begin working toward financial independence by making regular investments and building a diverse portfolio, it is also important to develop fiscal responsibility. **Fiscal responsibility** is spending less than you make or *living below your means*. Make sure you never borrow more money than you are able to repay. Save enough to cover expenses for three to six months even if you lose your job. Treat saving and investing as monthly expenses. Look for opportunities to make the most of your current income and make certain you are adequately covered by insurance. These are keys to building wealth. Begin now to achieve your own "financial independence day."

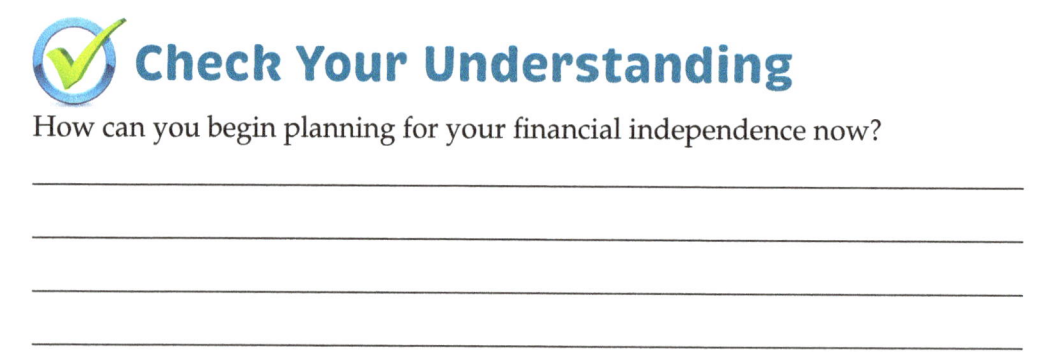

✓ Check Your Understanding

How can you begin planning for your financial independence now?

_____
_____
_____
_____

Your Turn

Saving for Investments

Keep track of every cent you spend for two weeks, similar to the exercise in Chapter 3. You may be amazed at how much money you spend. How many snacks do you consume daily? How many video games or music downloads have you purchased in the last month? Remember to record every penny spent. Then, answer the questions that follow.

Day	Amount Spent	Items Purchased
Monday	$	
Tuesday	$	
Wednesday	$	
Thursday	$	
Friday	$	
Saturday	$	
Sunday	$	
Monday	$	
Tuesday	$	
Wednesday	$	
Thursday	$	
Friday	$	
Saturday	$	
Sunday	$	

1. How much did you spend in two weeks?
   _____
   _____

2. How much of this amount could you have saved and put toward an investment?
   _____
   _____

Are You Financially Responsible?

Looking for the Right Investment: A Checklist

As a financially responsible person, you should always be looking at the status of your plan as you go through the different stages of your life. This is the time to start thinking about your investments. Use this checklist to help you as you think about your financial plan.

Yes	No	
1. ____	____	Am I currently saving anything toward my short-term or long-term financial goals?
2. ____	____	Will I have enough money to meet my long-term or short-term financial goals?
3. ____	____	Do I have enough time to reach my financial goals?
4. ____	____	Do I make enough each month from my job to meet my financial goals?
5. ____	____	Could I reduce my expenses each month?
6. ____	____	Am I willing to give up some things I now spend money for in order to have money for investing?
7. ____	____	Do I currently have any investments?
8. ____	____	If I do have investments, are they diversified?
9. ____	____	Am I willing to take risks?
10. ____	____	Do I have a mentor who will help me get started?

Chapter 10 Review and Assessment

Summary

10-1 **Discuss investing basics.**

Investing is purchasing an item of value with the hope that it will increase in value over time. When you invest, you are taking the risk that you may lose all or part of the money invested. Most people invest hoping for growth and anticipate earning a high average rate of return.

10-2 **Define *investment portfolio*.**

An investment portfolio is a collection of the investments a person has made. Stocks, bonds, mutual funds, and other investments you own make up your investment portfolio. The most important thing to remember when investing is to diversify.

10-3 **Summarize stocks as an investment.**

Stock is a share of ownership in a corporation. Two basic types of stock are common stock and preferred stock. Your goal should be to buy stock at a low price and sell stock when its price is high. Be prepared to ride out the fluctuations of stock market conditions. Investors buy stock for many reasons, which include growth, dividends, and stock splits.

10-4 **Summarize bonds as an investment.**

A bond is a certificate of debt issued by a government or company. The percentage of interest earned on a bond is called a coupon rate. Three major bond categories are corporate, municipal, and US government bonds.

10-5 **Summarize mutual funds as an investment.**

A mutual fund is a collection of investments that is managed by professionals who study the market. These investments offer diversification and liquidity.

10-6 **Explain the meaning of financial independence.**

Financial independence is having enough money for basic needs and modest wants without work being a necessity. To reach this point, start preparing now while you are young. Practice fiscal responsibility by spending less than you make. Get in the habit of investing at an early age and pay yourself first.

Review Your Knowledge

Choose the correct answer for each of the following.

1. _____ What is investing?
   A. buying a financial product or valuable item with the goal of increasing your wealth over time
   B. receiving a share of a company's profits
   C. spreading risk by putting money in different types of accounts
   D. depositing a fixed dollar amount at regular intervals without regard to the price at the time of the investment

2. _____ Spreading out risk in your investments is called _____.
   A. fluctuation
   B. investing
   C. dollar-cost averaging
   D. diversification

3. _____ A share of the ownership of a company is a _____.
   A. principal
   B. dividend
   C. stock
   D. bond

4. _____ Stock that does not have voting privileges is called _____.
   A. bull stock
   B. bear stock
   C. common stock
   D. preferred stock

5. _____ A(n) _____ is an upward trend in the stock market.
   A. fluctuation
   B. bear market
   C. recession
   D. expansion

6. _____ A company that issues a _____ divides its existing shares of stocks into multiple shares without changing the total value of the stock.
   A. dividend
   B. rate of return
   C. stock split
   D. diversification

7. _____ A period of slow economic growth is called a(n) _____.
   A. recession
   B. bull market
   C. expansion
   D. diversification

8. _____ Which type of bond is sold by cities or towns?
   A. US savings bond
   B. corporate bond
   C. coupon bond
   D. municipal bond

9. _____ What is a mutual fund?
   A. a type of US government bond that earns a fixed rate of interest
   B. a collection of investments that is professionally managed
   C. a certificate of debt issued by a government or company
   D. a collection of investments a person has made
10. _____ When is an ideal time to begin investing?
    A. after you retire
    B. during your teen years
    C. when you have a lot of money "left over" at the end of the month
    D. when you begin your career

Build Your Vocabulary

For each word or term, write the correct definition using your own words.

11. entrepreneur
    _____
    _____

12. growth
    _____
    _____

13. average rate of return
    _____
    _____

14. investment portfolio
    _____
    _____

15. trading
    _____
    _____

16. dividend
    _____
    _____

17. recession
    _____
    _____

18. bull market
    _____
    _____

19. bear market
    _____
    _____

20. coupon rate
_____
_____

21. corporate bond
_____
_____

22. government bond
_____
_____

23. financial independence
_____
_____

24. dollar-cost averaging
_____
_____

25. fiscal responsibility
_____
_____

Apply Your Math Skills

Calculate the answers to the following problems. Show your calculations.

26. Using the Rule of 72, how many years will it take to double your investment at an interest rate of 9 percent?
_____
_____

27. The following is a five-year investment. The initial investment amount was $750. Negative numbers are shown in parentheses to represent losses for those years. What is the average rate of return on this investment?

Year	Interest Earned
1	$41.00
2	48.00
3	37.00
4	(18.00)
5	43.00

_____
_____

28. The following is an eight-year investment. The initial investment amount was $500. Negative numbers are shown in parentheses to represent losses for those years. What is the average rate of return on this investment?

Year	Interest Earned
1	$25.00
2	28.00
3	(15.50)
4	29.00
5	32.00
6	34.00
7	29.00
8	26.00

_____
_____
_____
_____

29. You purchased 60 shares of a clothing company. The company's stock is priced at $33.76 per share. What was the total amount of your stock purchase?

_____
_____

30. You purchased 50 shares of stock in GWP, Inc. for $38.90 each. Your stock's rate of return varies each year over the five years you keep the stock, as shown in the table that follows. How much will you earn if you sell after five years? What are the average yearly earnings over the five-year period?

Year	Beginning Balance	Rate of Return	Amount of Return	Ending Balance
1		6.00%		
2		5.00%		
3		4.50%		
4		5.00%		
5		5.50%		

_____
_____
_____
_____
_____

31. Company Y issues dividends quarterly. For the current year, each share of stock earned $0.35 per quarter. What are your total dividends for the year if you own 375 shares of Company Y?

32. Company Z issues dividends monthly. For the current year, each share of stock earned $0.12 each month. What are your total dividends for the year if you own 260 shares of Company Z?

33. You purchased 165 shares of Alpha Company stock at $49.50 per share. The company decided to have a two-for-one stock split. How many shares will you have after the split and how much are they worth? Has the total value of your stock changed?

34. You purchased 45 corporate bonds from Baltic Manufacturing at $235 each. You will earn 4.35 percent interest on your bonds each year until they mature in 10 years. At that time, you will be repaid the amount you invested plus the interest you earned. How much interest will you earn over the 10 years?

35. You purchased 25 municipal bonds issued by your county to build a park at $145 each. You will earn 4.9 percent interest on your bonds each year for 15 years. At that time, you will receive your loan repayment plus the interest that you earned. How much interest will you earn on your bonds?

CHAPTER 11
Retirement and Estate Planning: Looking Toward Your Future

❓ Essential Question
What does the term *retirement* mean to you?

Learning Outcomes

When you complete Chapter 11, you will be able to:

11-1 Explain retirement planning.
11-2 Discuss Social Security as a supplement for retirement.
11-3 Identify common retirement accounts.
11-4 Summarize estate planning.

Key Terms

retirement account	earned income	estate planning
contribution	Roth IRA	will
distribution	401(k)	executor
individual retirement account (IRA)	rollover	intestate
traditional IRA	403(b)	trust
	estate	

Reading Prep

Before reading this chapter, write the main heading for each section. Leave space under each one. As you read the chapter, write two main points related to each heading.

What is Your Financial IQ?

Before reading this chapter, answer the following questions to see how much you already know about retirement and estate planning.

1. What is retirement?

2. What does it mean to plan for retirement?

3. At what age should you start thinking about retirement?

4. Where does money to live on come from after you have retired?

5. What Social Security benefits are available for people who are retired?

6. What is an IRA?

7. What is a Roth IRA?

8. What is a 401(k)?

9. What is estate planning?

10. Name an advantage of having a will.

If you start saving for retirement in your late teens or early adult years, you can do so by saving small amounts over a long period of time. How can paying yourself first help you begin saving for retirement?

FYI
Almost half of Americans will not be able to maintain their current standard of living when they retire.

11-1 Retirement Planning

An essential part of financial planning is looking ahead to your retirement. Although retirement is probably the last thing on your mind right now, this is exactly the time to start saving for it. If you start saving for retirement in your late teens or early adult years, you can save small amounts over a long time. Remember, time is important when planning for retirement, and you have lots of time!

There was a time when people thought they would need less money in their retirement years than they did while they were working. To some extent, that idea makes sense. For example, during retirement, you may no longer be paying for a home mortgage. Your children's college expenses may be paid. You may have lower costs for things such as clothing and cars than when you were working.

Most people now realize they want to keep or even increase their levels of income as they get older so they can keep or improve their lifestyle. New expenses may replace expenses during your working years. You may want to travel, purchase a vacation home, or save money for your grandchildren's education. You may be faced with increased health-care expenses in your later years. Everyone wants enough money to live comfortably in retirement.

Your retirement planning will involve many factors. For example, when you are ready to retire, you may decide it is time to sell some of your stocks and bonds or downsize to a smaller house or condo. You may sell assets or withdraw money from savings accounts. During retirement, you will need to balance your available income with expenses. Your income may be from investments, Social Security, and retirement accounts. Plan to have enough retirement savings to replace 80 percent of your annual working income.

Americans today are living longer and healthier lives. They are traveling and doing things they did not have time to do when they were younger, *if* they are financially secure. No matter what choices you make to start saving for retirement, the very best decision is to start *now*. Remember, *time is on your side*. You can start saving small amounts of money now rather than much larger amounts if you wait.

✓ Check Your Understanding

Why should young people think about retirement now instead of waiting until they are older?

_____
_____
_____
_____

Internet Connection

Retirement Planning for Teens

1. Using the Internet, research *retirement planning for teens*. Find and read at least two articles about retirement planning for teens.
2. List the title and complete source information for each article. Use an additional sheet of paper if needed.

   Article 1:
   _____
   _____

   Article 2:
   _____
   _____

3. On a separate sheet of paper, write a paragraph or bulleted list that summarizes the information contained in the articles about retirement planning for teens.

11-2 Social Security

Social Security will be a part of your financial plan and retirement. As you learned in Chapter 2, *Social Security* is a social insurance program run by the US government providing benefits for retired workers, disabled individuals, and other qualified persons. It is funded by taxes paid by workers and their employers. You begin contributing to the Social Security program by paying taxes when you begin working at most jobs, even part-time. Your employer matches the amount of taxes you pay. When you retire, you may be able to collect Social Security benefits. The amount of money you will receive will depend on how long you worked as well as how much you earned.

For persons born after 1960, full retirement age is 67, although it may increase in the future. This means you will be eligible to receive full Social Security payments when you turn 67. Benefits should increase the longer you wait to collect, up to age 70. You can elect to receive benefits as early as 62, but the monthly amount will be greatly reduced because you will receive payments for a longer time. If you become disabled, you may be able to collect benefits before retirement. If you should die, your family may be able to collect your Social Security benefits.

After you start working, you are eligible to obtain a yearly Social Security statement online that shows how much you have paid into Social Security each year that you worked. You will need this information to update your retirement plan. When you turn 60, the Social Security administration may send you a paper copy in the mail.

The statement will have information similar to Figure 11-1. The information will include an estimate of how much you will be able to collect when you retire.

Your Earnings Record

Years You Worked	Your Taxed Social Security Earnings	Your Taxed Medicare Earnings
2023	$580	$580
2024	1,380	1,380
2025	2,455	2,455
2026	3,507	3,507

Goodheart-Willcox Publisher

Figure 11-1 Your earnings record shows how much you have paid into Social Security each year that you worked. *How could this information help you plan for retirement?*

Your Estimated Benefits

Retirement You have earned enough credits to qualify for benefits. At your current earnings rate, if you continue working until…

your full retirement age (67 years),
your payment would be about .... $ 1,478 a month
age 70, your payment would be about .... $ 1,867 a month
age 62, your payment would be about .... $ 1,088 a month

Goodheart-Willcox Publisher. Source: Social Security Administration

Figure 11-2 This document shows an estimation of how much you will be able to collect when you retire. *Explain how this information can be used to help you make financial plans for retirement.*

Part of a sample estimate is shown in Figure 11-2. This yearly statement from Social Security will help you plan for retirement.

Think of Social Security as a *supplement*, or extra amount, to what you have invested and saved for your retirement. Do not count on it as the main source of your retirement income. There is little doubt that changes will be made to the Social Security system in coming years, even possible reductions in benefits.

✓ Check Your Understanding

Explain how Social Security provides benefits in retirement.

_____
_____
_____
_____
_____

Internet Connection

Social Security Benefits

1. Visit the website of the Social Security Administration (ssa.gov) to learn about retirement benefits. Select the Retirement link. Use the information you find to answer the following questions.
2. You become eligible for Social Security benefits by working and earning "credits" each year you work. What are credits based on? Search the site using the term *credits* to find information and list the current annual required amounts to earn credits.

_____

_____

3. At what age can you retire and receive full Social Security benefits?

_____

_____

4. Approximately what percent will your Social Security be reduced if you retire early at age 62?

_____

_____

5. Will your benefits be taxable?

_____

_____

_____

_____

11-3 Retirement Accounts

Part of your financial planning should include retirement accounts. A **retirement account** is a personal investment account set up to provide income in retirement. The money put into a retirement account is called a **contribution**.

Many retirement accounts are tax-deferred. Deferred means *delayed*. This means you do not have to pay taxes on the money you contribute to the account or the earnings. You will have to pay taxes when you take money out of the account, however. The money taken out of a retirement account is called a **distribution**.

All retirement accounts have rules that must be followed. Most charge penalties if you withdraw money before you turn 59 1/2 and require withdrawals when you turn 73, but that age is scheduled to jump to 75 in 2033. This is called the *required minimum distribution (RMD)*. Retirement accounts have limits on how much money may be contributed each year.

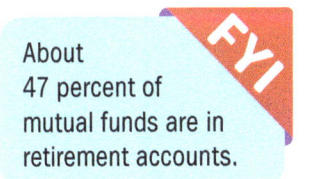

FYI
About 47 percent of mutual funds are in retirement accounts.

There are some exceptions to these rules. Check the tax laws to find current rules regarding the types of accounts you want to open when you are ready to begin saving for retirement.

Several retirement account options are available. Four common types are traditional IRAs, Roth IRAs, 401(k) plans, and 403(b) plans.

Check Your Understanding

What does *tax-deferred* mean?

_____

_____

_____

_____

Individual Retirement Accounts

FYI

Parents and grandparents cannot start IRAs for young children because the children do not have earned income. However, these accounts can be opened (with their help) as soon as you begin working.

An **individual retirement account (IRA)** is a personal savings plan that offers tax advantages for setting aside money for retirement. A **traditional IRA** is a tax-deferred personal retirement account. You can open an IRA if you have taxable compensation; there are no age limits. *Taxable compensation* is sometimes called earned income. **Earned income** is money you receive from wages, salaries, tips, commissions, and other types of income. Annual contribution limits change periodically, but the maximum annual amount a person may contribute to an IRA in 2023 is $6,500.

Withdrawals can be made from a traditional IRA at any age. However, if money is withdrawn before age 59 1/2, a 10 percent penalty is charged and income taxes paid on the money withdrawn. Mandatory withdrawals begin at age 73 (75 in 2033).

Assume you need $5,000 for an emergency. You decided to withdraw it from your traditional IRA but you are younger than 59 1/2. You are in a 25 percent tax bracket. How much will you receive as a net amount?

Step 1. Calculate 10% penalty.

Amount withdrawn	$5,000.00
Penalty rate	× .10
Amount of penalty	$500.00

Step 2. Calculate tax paid.

Amount withdrawn	$5,000.00
Tax rate	× .25
Amount of tax owed	$1,250.00

Step 3. Calculate total deductions.

Penalty	$500.00
Tax	+ 1,250.00
Total amount of reduction	$1,750.00

Step 4. Calculate net amount received.

Amount withdrawn	$5,000.00
Deductions	− 1,750.00
Amount received	$3,250.00

You would have to withdraw much more than the $5,000 you need from your account. Look at other options before you withdraw money early from any retirement account.

You Do the Math | 11-1

Assume you decide to withdraw $7,500 from your traditional IRA for a down payment on a new car. You are younger than 59 1/2. If you are in a 28 percent tax bracket, how much will you receive as a net amount?

Step 1. Calculate 10% penalty.

Amount withdrawn _____

Penalty rate _____

Amount of penalty _____

Step 2. Calculate tax paid.

Amount withdrawn _____

Tax rate _____

Amount of tax owed _____

Step 3. Calculate total deductions.

Penalty _____

Tax _____

Total amount of deduction _____

Step 4. Calculate net amount received.

Amount withdrawn _____

Deductions _____

Amount received _____

✓ Check Your Understanding

What is a traditional IRA?

_____

_____

_____

_____

Your Turn

Withdrawing Money from an IRA

If you withdraw money early from a traditional IRA, you may have to pay a 10 percent penalty in addition to the regular income taxes on the money. For example, if you are in a 28 percent tax bracket, this means you will have to pay income taxes of 28 percent plus the 10 percent penalty. You will receive only 62 percent of the money you withdraw. The other 38 percent will go to taxes and the penalty.

You decide to take an early withdrawal from your IRA to cover an emergency expense. You need $5,000. How much money do you need to withdraw from the IRA to receive $5,000 after paying the penalty and taxes? (Hint: Divide the amount of money you want to receive by the percentage of the total you will receive.)

_____

_____

FYI

One family encouraged their 16-year-old to save $1,000 annually from part-time earnings, and those contributions were matched by the parents each year for 3 years. Upon graduation from high school, $6,000 had accumulated in a Roth IRA. If the money remains in the account with an average rate of return of 10 percent, it will grow to more than half a million dollars at age 65 even if no more is added, all tax-free. This would be achieved with only $6,000 invested, and only $3,000 of personal money!

A **Roth IRA** is an individual retirement account to which after-tax dollars are contributed. It differs from a traditional IRA because the money contributed has *already* been taxed. For this reason, you may withdraw the *contributions* you have made at any age without paying a penalty or taxes. You may not withdraw the *earnings* from the account without incurring a penalty before age 59 1/2.

A Roth IRA is similar to a traditional IRA in that you must have taxable compensation. You must have earned income before you can contribute to the account. The amount you contribute cannot be more than you earned. It also cannot be more than the maximum annual limit set by the government, which is $6,500 for 2023. For example, if you earned $4,000 in one year, you could only contribute $4,000 to a Roth account during that year. If you earned more than $6,500, you could only contribute $6,500 in 2023.

It does not matter who the contributions come from as long as you have personally *earned* at least that amount contributed. However, contributions still may not go over the annual contribution limit. In other words, *anyone* can contribute money for you! If your parents or grandparents are financially secure, talk to them about matching funds that you contribute.

As with traditional IRAs, there are no age limits for contributions if you have earned income. But an extremely important difference is that you do not have to take required minimum distributions from a Roth IRA when you turn 73. If the money is not needed, it may be left tax-free to your heirs. What a great option!

It is important to note there are also income limitations for contributing to IRA accounts. If you earn over a specified amount, you may not continue contributing to your IRA. These limits change frequently, so check with your IRA provider. If your income becomes too high to contribute to your IRA, you can still leave the money to grow tax free while you contribute to other types of retirement plans!

Minors under the age of 18 who have earned income can open a Roth IRA with a parent or guardian on the account. When the minor turns 18, the guardian's name can be removed from the account. This is one way to begin saving while you are in school working part-time.

You want to open a Roth IRA and contribute as much as possible. You earned $2,240 working part-time at the library during the school year. You also earned $2,700 working full-time at a higher-paying job over the summer. What is the maximum you would be able to contribute to your Roth IRA?

Earnings	
Part-time job	$2,240
Summer job	+ 2,700
Total earnings	$4,940
Maximum contribution amount	$4,940

You would have to earn $1,560 more to contribute the maximum amount in 2023.

You Do the Math | 11-2

You already have a Roth IRA and plan to contribute as much as possible. The maximum amount allowed per person per year is $6,500. You earned $2,295 at your part-time job during the school year. You also earned $3,500 working as a camp counselor over the summer. What is the maximum you could contribute to your Roth IRA?

Earnings	
Part-time job	_____
Summer job	_____
Total earnings	_____
Contribution amount	_____

✓ Check Your Understanding

How do contributions to a Roth IRA differ from contributions to a traditional IRA?

_____

_____

_____

Dollars and Sense

Opening a Roth IRA

You are a young person with plenty of time for saving and investing. Opening a Roth IRA is a very good first step. When you begin earning money, consider opening this kind of account as soon as possible.

Starting an account is as easy as filling out an application to open a checking account. You may need to provide information such as:
- two forms of identification
- your Social Security number
- name and contact information for your employer
- names of your beneficiaries for the account
- amount of your initial contribution to start the account

If you are under age 18, you will have to open an account with a parent or guardian. You may be able to open the account with as little as $100. Verify this amount with the investment company. Some investment companies will let you set up an automatic withdrawal from your bank account. This lets you invest regularly and can help you budget your money.

The financial adviser will give you information on the options available to you for investing in a Roth IRA. Mutual funds are an excellent choice for diversification when you open a Roth IRA. Be sure to ask if there are fees for the service.

Internet Connection

How to Open a Roth IRA

1. Conduct an Internet search for information on Roth IRAs. Use *how to open a Roth IRA* as the search phrase. What did you learn?

   _____
   _____
   _____

2. Locate a local company that offers Roth IRAs. List the steps necessary to open this type of account.

   _____
   _____
   _____

401(k) and 403(b) Plans

As an employee benefit, many companies offer plans for employees to help them save for retirement. A **401(k)** is an employer-sponsored tax-deferred retirement plan. The employer contributes to the plan as well as the employee. Many times, the employer will match what the employee contributes up to a certain amount, such as 5 percent. For example, your employer might put in a dollar for every dollar you contribute up to 5 percent of your gross salary. The money you contribute is deducted from your gross wages, which reduces your taxable income.

For example, you contributed 10 percent of your $37,500 salary to a 401(k) last year. How much did you contribute? Your employer matched 100 percent of your contributions up to $6,000. What was the total contribution to your retirement fund?

Step 1. Calculate your contribution.

Your salary	$37,500.00
Contribution rate	× .10
Your 401(k) contribution	$3,750.00

Step 2. Calculate employer's contribution.

Your contribution	$3,750.00
Employer's matching rate	× 1.00
Employer's contribution	$3,750.00

Step 3. Calculate total contributions.

Your contribution	$3,750.00
Employer's contribution	+ 3,750.00
Total 401(k) contribution	$7,500.00

> **FYI**
> Many people who could open a retirement account choose not to. Even when employers offer matching funds, they do not participate. They are giving up *free* money! If an employer offers matching contributions to a retirement plan, it is a 100 percent return on your money. It is hard to beat that kind of return! When you can, take advantage of this opportunity and contribute at least the amount your employer will match each year.

You Do the Math | 11-3

You contributed 8 percent of your $28,750 salary to a 401(k) account last year. How much did you contribute? Your employer matched 50 percent of your contributions, up to $5,000. What was the total contribution to your retirement fund?

Step 1. Calculate your contribution.

Your salary _____

Contribution rate _____

Your 401(k) contribution _____

Step 2. Calculate employer's contribution.

Your contribution _____

Employer's matching rate _____

Employer's contribution _____

Step 3. Calculate total contributions.

Your contribution _____

Employer's contribution _____

Total 401(k) contribution _____

A Roth IRA is an individual retirement account in which after-tax dollars are contributed. *What would be the pros and cons of starting a Roth IRA at your age?*

Money withdrawn from a 401(k) before age 59 1/2 is subject to a 10 percent penalty plus taxes. Although there is no penalty after age 59 1/2, income tax must be paid.

If you leave a company where you have established a 401(k), you may have the option to leave your 401(k) in the account to keep growing or you may transfer it to a 401(k) provided by a new employer. The process of transferring retirement savings from one qualified account to another without incurring penalties and taxes is called a **rollover**. Some companies require you to work a minimum number of years at the company for a rollover. Strict regulations must be followed for rollovers; be sure to obtain professional advice before you act.

✓ Check Your Understanding

Describe a 401(k) plan.

_____
_____
_____
_____

FYI

Another retirement account option that may be available to you is a Roth 401(k). With this type of account, the employer may still match funds and the contribution limits are much higher than Roth IRA accounts ($22,500 in 2023). There are no income limitations on a Roth 401(k) and beginning in 2024, no required minimum distributions. However, your employer must provide this option as a benefit.

A **403(b)** is a tax-deferred retirement plan available to employees of nonprofit organizations, such as public schools, similar to a 401(k) plan. Some 403(b) plans are set up and managed by the employer. These plans often have guidelines to be followed. Contributions to a 403(b) plan are typically deducted from the employee's paycheck. Some employers may match contributions by employees up to a specified amount.

Contribution limits are generally much higher for 401(k) and 403(b) plans than they are for IRAs. The limit was $22,500 for each of these retirement plans in 2023.

✓ Check Your Understanding

Who is eligible for a 403(b) plan?

_____
_____
_____

Are You Financially Responsible?

Planning for Retirement

Many young people think retirement is too far away to worry about now. However, it is never too early to start thinking about saving money for this phase in your life. Keep in mind, not all people retire at age 65. Those who are financially secure may retire at an earlier age. Start planning today! Complete the following statements to help you consider your earnings and retirement needs.

1. I was born in the year _____. I will be able to collect full Social Security benefits at age _____ in the year _____.
2. I hope to earn _____ each year for at least five years when I begin my career.
3. I plan to invest or save _____ percent of my income each year.
4. I estimate (desire) that my average yearly salary will be $_____.
5. As soon as I get my first job, I will be able to set up a(n) _____ account that will be my first retirement account.
6. In my lifetime, I plan to work approximately _____ years.
7. If I work approximately _____ years, I should earn approximately $_____ in my lifetime. (Hint: number of working years × yearly average salary)
8. When I retire, I think I will need $_____ in savings and investments.
9. I hope to retire at age _____.
10. I hope to have investments when I retire, such as, _____.

11-4 Estate Planning

Later in life, you may have a family and will want to plan for their financial welfare through estate planning.

An **estate** is the value of a person's assets minus his or her debts. **Estate planning** is the process of arranging financial affairs so a person's wishes will be followed now and after death. Part of estate planning should include life insurance and Roth IRAs because those proceeds are tax-free. Other investments and assets left to your heirs may be taxable.

Estate planning takes into consideration many factors. One major consideration is the writing of a will. Another is whether setting up a trust is appropriate for your estate planning needs.

Wills

A **will** is a legal document that states who is to receive a person's assets when that person dies. It should identify the beneficiaries and the property or money each is to receive. If the person writing the will has minor children, a guardian should be named. Many wills also appoint a guardian for pets. A will must be signed in the presence of witnesses.

In a will, an executor is designated. An **executor** is a person who will manage the estate and be sure the deceased person's wishes are carried out. The executor is usually a trusted family member or friend. However, it may be an officer of a bank or other financial organization. In this case, the executor would be entitled to a fee.

Many people think that because they are not wealthy, they have no need for a will. **Intestate** is the legal term for not having a will. If you die intestate, the state will decide who gets your property. Inheritance laws vary by state. For example, some states give everything to a spouse while others split the estate evenly between a person's spouse and children. The state will also decide who gets custody of dependent children under 18 years of age. Do not leave such important decisions to the state or the courts. To determine the laws where you live, you can ask an estate-planning professional or check online.

The cost of creating a will can vary, but one generally can be drawn up inexpensively. There are online programs you can use to create your own will. If you create a will online, your signature must be witnessed for the will to be official.

Trusts

A trust can be created in addition to a will to help manage your assets. A **trust** is a legal document that authorizes a trustee to manage a person's estate on their behalf. A *trustee* is the person who oversees the trust. A trust is useful if you have young children or children who are disabled or unable to manage money. You can declare that all your children must reach a certain age, such as 25, before the trustee divides your estate among them. This can prevent the money from being squandered. Trusts are especially useful when there is a large estate or when property is held in more than one state.

> **FYI**
> A "living will" is a health-care directive for later in life. It is a legal document stating your wishes for medical care if you are unable to make those decisions yourself.

✓ Check Your Understanding

Explain estate planning and the importance of wills and trusts.

_____
_____
_____
_____

Are You Financially Responsible?

Financial Goals: A Checklist

Follow these simple steps to begin achieving your financial goals:

1. Get started! Start saving money today. Remember, *time is on your side*.
2. Create a financial plan early. Get in the habit of planning how you will spend and save your money.
3. Make the most of your earnings, no matter what the size of your paycheck. Make sure your paycheck is calculated correctly and that you understand all deductions.
4. Use budgets to control your spending and savings. Realize that budgets are a work in progress and will change frequently.
5. Shop around for banking services that best fit your needs. Develop a relationship with a bank so you have a dependable resource for information.
6. Protect yourself and your dependents with auto, health, and life insurance. Make sure you have renters insurance when renting an apartment or homeowners insurance when you buy a house. Research other types of insurance as you need it.
7. Ask questions and become money smart about financial matters. Take advantage of educational opportunities. Read books and financial information online. Talk to adults you trust about their challenges and successes with money.
8. Credit always ties up future income. Avoid using credit to buy what you do not need. Pay off credit cards in full each month. Know what your credit score is and how to keep it high. Practice discipline in using credit of any kind.
9. Do not sign up for car loans for longer than four years. Try to make extra payments to pay the loan off early if you are able.
10. Build equity in a home by paying down your mortgage. Never be underwater by owing more on an asset than it is worth.
11. Take advantage of investment opportunities and remember that diversifying and starting early are the keys to building wealth.
12. If you are currently working, open a Roth IRA now and a 401(k) when you get a full-time job.
13. Always consider taking advantage of good investment opportunities.
14. Give to charities you have researched and volunteer your time as your finances and schedule permit.
15. There are laws that protect the consumer from lender and seller abuse. If you have any questions about any financial decision, seek advice from a professional about the laws that protect you as a consumer.

Your Turn

Financial Literacy

List the five most important things you have learned from this text that will help you become financially literate.

1. _____
   _____
2. _____
   _____
3. _____
   _____
4. _____
   _____
5. _____
   _____

Chapter 11 Review and Assessment

Summary

11-1 Explain retirement planning.

Your retirement planning will involve many factors. You should plan to have enough retirement savings to replace a minimum of 80 percent of your annual working income. You can start saving small amounts of money now rather than having to save large amounts if you wait.

11-2 Discuss Social Security as supplement to retirement.

Social Security is a social insurance program run by the US government. You begin paying Social Security taxes when you begin working. Your employer matches the amount of taxes you pay. The benefits you receive at retirement will depend on how long you worked as well as how much you earned. If you were to become disabled or were to die, you or your family may be able to collect benefits.

11-3 Identify common retirement accounts.

Four popular types of common retirement accounts are traditional IRAs, Roth IRAs, 401(k) plans, and 403(b) plans.

11-4 Summarize estate planning.

Estate planning is arranging financial affairs so a person's wishes will be followed now and after death. A will is a legal document that states who is to receive a person's assets when that person dies. A trust is a legal document that authorizes a trustee to manage a person's estate on their behalf.

Review Your Knowledge

Choose the correct answer for each of the following.

1. ____ Which of the following is true of Social Security?
   A. It is a social insurance program.
   B. It is run by the US government.
   C. It is designed to provide benefits for retired workers and the disabled.
   D. All of the above.

2. ____ What is an amount of money paid into a retirement account?
   A. supplement
   B. distribution
   C. contribution
   D. rollover

3. _____ What is an amount of money withdrawn from a retirement account?
   A. supplement
   B. distribution
   C. contribution
   D. rollover
4. _____ Which of the following is true of a traditional IRA?
   A. The money you contribute is tax deductible.
   B. You do not need earned income to open an account.
   C. There is no limit on the amount you can contribute per year.
   D. The money you contribute is not tax deductible.
5. _____ Which of the following is true of a Roth IRA?
   A. The money you contribute is tax deductible.
   B. The earnings will be tax-free.
   C. You must withdraw money at age 72.
   D. You must be age 21 to open an account.
6. _____ A 401(k) plan _____.
   A. is an employer-sponsored retirement plan
   B. may include contributions from your employer
   C. has limits on how much you can contribute each year
   D. All of the above.
7. _____ A(n) _____ is transferring funds from a 401(k) account with one employer to a 401(k) account with a new employer.
   A. rollover
   B. distribution
   C. supplement
   D. appreciation
8. _____ A 403(b) account _____.
   A. is a tax-free retirement plan
   B. can be opened by anyone
   C. is designed for public school teachers and employees of certain nonprofit organizations
   D. All of the above.
9. _____ A(n) _____ is a legal document that states how your assets are to be distributed upon your death.
   A. PPO plan
   B. will
   C. insurance plan
   D. estate
10. _____ A person designated to carry out your wishes in distributing your estate upon your death is called a(n) _____.
    A. executor
    B. intestate
    C. premium
    D. beneficiary

Build Your Vocabulary

For each word or term, write the correct definition using your own words.

11. retirement account

12. tax-deferred

13. individual retirement account (IRA)

14. earned income

15. 401(k)

16. 403(b)

17. estate

18. estate planning

19. intestate

20. trust

Apply Your Math Skills

Calculate the answers to the following problems. Show your calculations.

21. You need $3,500 for an emergency. You decided to withdraw it from your traditional IRA but you are younger than 59 1/2. You are in a 17 percent tax bracket. How much will you receive as a net amount?

22. You have a Roth IRA and want to contribute as much as possible. You earned $1,570 working part-time during the school year. You also earned $1,200 babysitting. How much will you contribute to your Roth IRA? If you cannot contribute the maximum amount, how much more money would you need to earn to reach the maximum amount for 2023?

23. You contributed 6.5 percent of your $41,200 salary to a 401(k) last year. How much did you contribute? Your employer matched 50 percent of your contributions up to $5,000. What was the total contribution to your retirement fund?

24. You contributed 8 percent of your $70,450 salary to a 401(k) account last year. How much did you contribute? Your employer matched 50 percent of your contributions up to $3,000. What was the total contribution to your retirement fund?

25. Last year, you contributed 9 percent of your $45,690 salary to a 403(b) account. How much did you contribute? Your employer matched 100 percent of your contributions up to $3,500. What was the total contribution to the fund?

Glossary

401(k) Employer-sponsored tax-deferred retirement plan. (11)
403(b) Tax-deferred retirement plan available to employees of nonprofit organizations. (11)
529 plan Savings plan for educational expenses operated by a state or educational institution. (8)

A

academic degree Award given to a person by a college or university that signifies the person has successfully completed a course of study. (8)
adjustable-rate mortgage (ARM) Secured loan with an interest rate that can change periodically. (9)
allowance Condition for which a person qualifies, reducing the amount of income taxes withheld from gross pay; also *exemption*. (2)
amortization Process of making equal payments on a loan while reducing the principal. (9)
annual percentage rate (APR) Annual rate a lender charges for the use of credit. (6)
annual percentage yield (APY) Rate of yearly earnings from an account expressed as a percentage. (5)
apartment lease Contract that outlines conditions of an agreement to rent an apartment for a certain length of time. (9)
assessment Amount required by a homeowners association to pay for a major expense. (9)
asset Item of value that is owned. (1)
auto insurance See *car insurance*.
automated teller machine (ATM) Machine that allows a user to perform various banking tasks. (4)
available credit Difference between a card's credit limit and the amount of credit already used. (6)
average rate of return Average percentage of gain or loss of an investment over a specific period of time. (10)

B

bank Financial institution that receives, lends, exchanges, and safeguards money. (4)
bankcard See *debit card*.
bankruptcy Legal situation in which the courts excuse a debtor from repaying some or all debt. (6)
bear market Term used to describe falling stock prices or stock prices staying at a low level. (10)
beneficiary Person named in a life insurance policy to receive the benefits. (7)
bond Certificate of debt issued by a government or company. (10)
bounced check See *overdraft*.
budget Plan for the use of money based on goals, income, and expenses. (3)
bull market Term used to describe rising stock prices. (10)

C

capacity Person's ability to pay debt. (6)
capital Assets a person has. (6)
car insurance Property insurance that provides protection against financial loss related to a passenger car; also *auto insurance*. (7)
car lease Contract that allows a person to use a car in exchange for payment. (9)
career and technical college See *trade school*.
career plan List of steps needed to reach a career goal. (8)
cash advance Loan against the available credit on a credit card. (6)
certificate of deposit (CD) Savings account that requires a deposit of a fixed amount of money for a fixed period of time. (5)
Chapter 7 bankruptcy Eliminates most types of debt and stays on the credit report for ten years; also *straight bankruptcy*. (6)
Chapter 13 bankruptcy Allows a person with regular income to pay all or some debts to a trustee who will pay the creditors. (6)
character Person's reputation and willingness to pay debt. (6)

Note: The number in parentheses following each definition indicates the chapter in which the term can be found.

charitable contribution   Donation of money or gifts to a nonprofit organization or private foundation. (2, 3)
check   Written order to direct the bank to pay a specific amount to the person, business, or organization to whom the check is written. (4)
check card   See *debit card*.
checking account   Liquid bank account that allows the owner to make deposits, make online payments or transfers, write checks, and withdraw money. (4)
check register   Record of checking account deposits, withdrawals, online payments, transfers, checks, fees, and interest. (4)
collateral   Property a borrower promises to give up in case of default. (9)
collision coverage   Car insurance that pays for damage to a car caused by a collision with another car. (7)
community college   Two-year college supported by the government that offers associate degrees. (8)
comparison shopping   Gathering information about products to find the best option among similar ones. (6)
compound interest   Earning interest on the principal plus the interest already earned. (5)
comprehensive coverage   Car insurance that pays for damage unrelated to a collision. (7)
continuing education   See *professional development*.
contribution   Money put into a retirement account. (11)
corporate bond   Bond issued by a business to raise money for operating expenses or expansion. (10)
cosigner   Responsible person who agrees to pay the debt if you fail to pay. (6)
coupon rate   Percentage of interest earned on a bond. (10)
credit   Agreement in which one party lends money or provides goods or services to another party with the understanding that payment will be made later. (6)
credit bureau   Organization that collects information about the financial and credit transactions of consumers. (6)
credit card   Card that allows the holder to make purchases up to an authorized amount and pay for them later. (6)

credit history   Person's credit and financial behavior over a period of years. (6)
credit report   Record of a person's credit history. (6)
credit score   Numerical measure of a person's creditworthiness; also *FICO score*.
credit union   Nonprofit financial cooperative owned by and operated for the benefit of its members. (4)
creditworthy   Having the ability and willingness to repay debt. (6)

D

death benefit   See *face value*.
debit card   Card that allows the cardholder to electronically access funds to make purchases by having the money withdrawn directly from a checking account; also *bankcard* or *check card*. (4)
decision-making   Process of solving a problem. (6)
deductible   Amount that must be paid before the insurance company begins to pay on a claim. (7)
deduction   Amount subtracted from gross pay. (2)
default   Fail to pay a debt or other obligation. (6)
depreciation   Decrease in the value of an asset. (9)
direct deposit   Transfer of net pay to a checking or savings account. (2)
disability insurance   Insurance that pays a portion of income to a worker who becomes injured or ill and cannot work. (7)
discretionary income   Money that remains after regular or needed expenses are paid for; also *disposable income*. (3)
distribution   Money taken out of a retirement account. (11)
diversification   Spreading risk by putting money in different types of investments. (10)
dividend   Share of the company's profits received by its stockholders. (10)
dollar-cost averaging   Investing a fixed dollar amount at regular intervals without regard to the price at the time of the investment. (10)

E

earned income Money received from wages, salaries, tips, commissions, and other types of income. (11)

emergency fund Fund that consists of three to six months' basic living expenses kept in a liquid account for unexpected situations. (4)

employee benefit Service or item of value that employees receive from employers in addition to earnings; also *fringe benefit*. (2)

endorsement Signature on the back of the check to transfer ownership from the payee to the bank. (4)

entrepreneur Person who organizes and operates a business. (10)

equity Difference between what is owed on your house and its current market value. (9)

escrow account Account for holding money in trust for others. (9)

estate Value of a person's assets minus his or her debts. (11)

estate planning Process of arranging financial affairs so a person's wishes will be followed now and after death. (11)

executor Person who will manage the estate and be sure the deceased person's wishes are carried out. (11)

exemption See *allowance*.

expansion Upward trend in the stock market. (10)

expense Amount paid for goods or services. (3)

F

face value Amount payable upon the death of the insured person; also *death benefit*. (7)

Federal Deposit Insurance Corporation (FDIC) Independent agency created by the federal government to protect consumers by insuring their deposits at most banks and other financial institutions. (4)

federal income taxes Taxes on income collected by the US government. (2)

FICO score See *credit score*.

finance charge Interest paid by a credit cardholder to a lender for the use of credit. (6)

financial capability Ability to combine financial knowledge with the attitude, skills, and behaviors needed to use money wisely in a person's own life. (1)

financial goal Measurable objective related to acquiring or spending money. (1)

financial independence Having enough money for your basic needs and modest wants without work being a necessity. (10)

financial institution Provides services related to money. (4)

financial literacy Knowledge about basic topics related to finance. (1)

financial plan Set of goals for acquiring, saving, and spending money. (1)

fiscal responsibility Spending less than you make. (10)

fixed expense Expense that stays the same each month. (3)

fixed-rate mortgage Secured loan with an interest rate that does not change. (9)

FOMO Fear of missing out. (1)

foreclosure Process in which the lender takes possession of the house if the mortgage payments are not made. (9)

fringe benefit See *employee benefit*.

G

government bond Bond issued by the US Treasury Department. (10)

grace period Set number of days during which a bill can be paid before interest charges begin. (6)

gross pay Total amount of earnings; also *gross earnings* or *gross wages*. (2)

growth Increase in the value of an investment over time. (10)

H

health insurance Insurance that protects against financial loss due to illnesses or injuries. (2, 7)

homeowners association (HOA) fee Monthly or yearly fee for insurance, upkeep of the buildings and common areas, landscaping, snow removal, pool, and other amenities. (9)

homeowners insurance Property insurance that protects against damage to a house and its contents. (7)

I

income Money received from any source. (3)
individual retirement account (IRA) Personal savings plan that offers tax advantages for setting aside money for retirement. (11)
installment loan Purchase that is paid for in equal monthly payments for a specific period of time. (9)
insurance Service that is purchased to protect against financial loss. (2, 7)
interest Money paid for the use of money. (4, 5)
intestate Legal term for not having a will. (11)
investing Purchasing an item of value with the hope that it will increase in value over time. (10)
investment portfolio Collection of the investments a person has made. (10)

L

lessee Person who leases a car. (9)
lessor Dealership lending a car. (9)
liability Debt that is owed. (1)
liability coverage Car insurance that protects people who suffer injuries or whose property is damaged in a car accident. (7)
life insurance Insurance that provides benefits after the death of the insured person to people named as beneficiaries. (7)
lifelong learning Acquiring new skills and knowledge throughout life. (8)
liquidity Ease with which an asset can be converted into cash without losing value. (4)
local income taxes Taxes on income collected by a local government. (2)

M

Medicare Federal program that pays for certain healthcare expenses for older citizens and those with disabilities. (2)
mentor Someone who has knowledge and skills and shares them informally with an individual. (8)
money market account (MMA) Savings account that typically pays higher interest than regular savings accounts. (5)
mortgage Secured loan used for buying property. (9)
municipal bond Bond issued by a state, county, or city government. (10)
mutual fund Collection of professionally managed investments. (10)

N

need Something a person must have to survive. (1)
net pay Gross pay minus payroll deductions. (2)
net worth Difference between what is owned and what is owed. (1)

O

opportunity cost Value of the option given up. (6)
overdraft Check or transfer for an amount greater than the balance of the account; also *bounced check*. (4)
overdraft protection Banking service that ensures a check or transfer will be paid by the bank even if there is not enough in the account to cover it. (4)
overtime wage Wage amount paid for working more than 40 hours in a week. (2)

P

pay yourself first Concept that a person should budget for savings before budgeting for spending. (3)
payee Person, business, or organization to whom a check is written. (4)
permanent life insurance See *whole life insurance*.
postsecondary education Any education earned after high school. (8)
premium Amount paid for insurance. (7)
principal Original amount deposited. (5)
priority Value or goal that is given more importance than other values or goals. (1)
private mortgage insurance (PMI) Insures payment if the borrower defaults on the loan. (9)
professional development Improving or gaining new skills related to work; also *continuing education*.

proprietary school Privately owned educational institution that offers vocational or occupational skills but may not be under the authority of the Department of Education. (8)

R

recession Period of slow or no economic growth. (10)

regular savings account Savings account that pays interest and allows deposits and withdrawals. (5)

renters insurance Property insurance that protects against theft or damage to the contents of rented property. (7)

repossession Taking collateral when a borrower fails to repay a loan. (9)

Reserve Officers' Training Corps (ROTC) Military program offered on many college campuses that provides leadership training for commissioned officers. (8)

retirement account Personal investment account set up to provide income in retirement. (2, 11)

revolving credit Type of credit agreement that offers a choice of paying in full each month or making payments over time. (6)

risk Possibility that an unfavorable situation could happen. (7, 10)

rollover Process of transferring retirement savings from one qualified account to another without incurring penalties and taxes. (11)

Roth IRA Individual retirement account to which after-tax dollars are contributed. (11)

Rule of 72 Equation that estimates how long it will take to double an amount of money at a fixed annual interest rate. (5)

S

salary Payment for work expressed as a fixed annual figure. (2)

savings account Bank account used to accumulate money for future use. (5)

savings and loan association (S&L) Financial institution that earns money to pay interest on accounts by issuing home mortgages. (4)

savings plan Plan for using money to reach financial goals and increase financial security. (5)

security deposit Amount paid to protect a property owner or dealer against financial loss if a renter or lessee damages the property or fails to make payments. (9)

seminar Meeting or conference for exchanging ideas or learning new things. (8)

service fee Amount a person must pay the bank for having an account. (4)

simple interest Interest paid on the original amount deposited. (5)

social responsibility Behaving with sensitivity to social, environmental, and economic issues. (3)

Social Security Social insurance program operated by the US government that provides income for individuals whose earnings are reduced or stopped because of retirement, disability, or death. (2, 11)

state income taxes Taxes on income collected by a state government. (2)

stock Share of ownership in a corporation. (10)

stock split When a company divides its existing shares of stocks into multiple shares without changing the total value of the stock. (10)

student loan Money borrowed to pay college-related expenses. (8)

straight bankruptcy See *Chapter 7 bankruptcy*.

T

term life insurance Life insurance that provides coverage only for a specific period of time. (7)

time sheet Record of the time work began, the time work ended, and any breaks taken. (2)

time value of money Idea that the value of money decreases over time if it doesn't earn interest. (5)

trade-off What is given up when someone makes one choice over another. (6)

trade school School that teaches a skilled trade; also *vocational school* or *career and technical college*. (8)

trading Buying and selling stocks. (10)

traditional IRA Tax-deferred personal retirement account. (11)

trust Legal document that authorizes a trustee to manage a person's estate on their behalf. (11)

U

umbrella insurance policy Liability insurance that protects against losses not covered by other policies. (7)

universal life insurance See *whole life insurance*.

V

value Belief about ideas and principles a person thinks is important. (1)

variable expense Expense that changes from month to month. (3)

variable life insurance See *whole life insurance*.

vocational school See *trade school*.

W

wage Dollar amount paid per hour worked. (2)

want Something a person desires but is not necessary for survival. (1)

wealth Plentiful supply of money or valuable goods. (1)

whole life insurance Life insurance that is in effect for the life of the insured person as long as premiums are paid; also *permanent life insurance, universal life insurance,* or *variable life insurance.* (7)

will Legal document that states who is to receive a person's assets when that person dies. (11)

Index

529 plan, 167–168
401(k) and 403(b) plans, 246–248

A

academic degree, 163
account fees, 89–90
actual cash value, 141
adjustable-rate mortgage (ARM), 195–196
allowance, 24–25
amortization, 193
annual percentage rate (APR), 115
annual percentage yield (APY), 96
annuity, 149
apartment, renting, 190–192
apartment lease, 190–191
Are You Financially Responsible?
   budgeting, 57
   buying insurance, 151
   car purchase, 189
   financial goals, 251
   finding the right bank, 79
   finding the right savings account, 90
   handling credit cards, 118
   looking for the right investment, 228
   needs and wants, 8
   pay verification, 36
   preparing for education, 175
   retirement planning, 249
assessment, 197
asset, 8, 10
associate degree, 163
ATM. *See* automated teller machine (ATM)
auto insurance. *See* car insurance
automated teller machine (ATM), 66, 75–76, 113
automobile. *See* car
available credit, 115
average rate of return, 206–208

B

bachelor degree, 163
bank, 65–67
bankcards, 76
bankruptcy, 124–125
bear market, 213
beneficiary, 148
benefits
   employee, 34–35
   life insurance, 148
   military, 168
   Social Security, 26, 239–241

blank endorsement, 69
blue chip stocks, 214
bond, 219–221
   corporate, 220
   first investment, 224
   government, 221
   municipal, 220
bounced checks, 71
budget, 44
   advice for, 55
   college, 172–173
   creating, 53–57
   discretionary income and, 52–53
   expenses and, 46–51
   income and, 45–46
bull market, 213

C

capacity, 107
capital, 107–108
car
   buying, 182–187, 189
   expenses, 48
   leasing, 187–189
   value of, 187
career, 159–162
career change, 160
career clusters, 160–161
career plan, 160, 162
career and technical college. *See* trade school
car insurance, 136–140
   application, 138
   estimate by model, 139
   types of coverage, 137
car lease, 187
car loan, 182–186
   application, 183
   calculator, 185
   types, 182
Carnegie, Andrew, 33
cash advance, 113
cash value, 148
certificate of deposit (CD), 87–88
Chapter 7 bankruptcy, 125
Chapter 13 bankruptcy, 125
character, 107
charitable contribution, 33, 46
check, 70
check cards, 76
checking account, 68–73
   making deposits, 69–73

managing, 74–76
writing checks and transferring money, 70–73
check register, 74, 76
claim, 136
COBRA. *See* Consolidated Omnibus Budget Reconciliation Act (COBRA)
Coca-Cola Company, 218
collateral, 182
college, 162–165
   costs, 167
   effect on lifetime earnings, 164
   funding, 167–177
   military benefits for, 166
   trade school, 166
   two-year, 165
college access, 173
collision coverage, 137
common stock, 213
community college, 165
comparison shopping, 119
compound interest, 92–96
compound interest calculator, 96
comprehensive coverage, 137
condo, buying, 197–198
Consolidated Omnibus Budget Reconciliation Act (COBRA), 145
contribution, 241
copayment, 144
corporate bonds, 220
cosigner, 105
coupon rate, 219
credit, 105–108
   cost of, 114–116
   credit score, 110
   revolving, 116
   terms, 116–117
   three Cs of, 107–108
credit bureau, 109
   credit report, 109
   credit score, 110–112
credit card, 112–117
   application, 106
   cost of credit, 114–116
   credit terms, 116–117
   debt, 121–123
   payment calculator, 123
   proprietary, 113
   selecting, 114–117
   statement, 122
credit history, 109
credit limit, 114–115, 121
creditors, 125
credit report, 109
credit score, 110–112
credit terms, 116–117
credit union, 67
creditworthy, 105

D

death benefit, 148
debit card, 32, 76–78
debt, credit card, 121–123
decision-making, 120–121
decisions, purchasing, 118–121
deductible, 136
deduction, 24
   mandatory, 24–32
   mortgage interest, 192
   voluntary, 33–34
default, 109
deficit, 52
deposit slip, 69, 72–73
depreciation, 182
direct deposit, 32
disability insurance, 147
discretionary income, 52–53
disposable income, 52
distribution, 241
diversification, 208
dividend, 213, 217–218
dollar-cost averaging, 225
Dollars and Sense
   apartment rental, 192
   budgeting, 56
   car insurance policy, 140
   college access, 173
   credit card readiness, 124
   direct deposit or debit cards, 32
   first investment, 224
   identity theft, 79
   Roth IRA, 246
   savings plan, starting, 98
   SMART goals, 5

E

early termination fee, 188
earned income, 242
earnings, 17–23. *See also* income
   education and, 163–164
   overtime, 19–20
   salary, 22–23
   tips, 21–22
   wage, 17–18, 165
education
   lifelong learning, 174–175
   lifetime earnings and, 164
   postsecondary, 162–167
emergency fund, 66
employee benefits, 34–36
   disability insurance, 147
   401(k) and 403(b) plans, 246–248
   work from home, 35–36

Employee's Withholding Allowance Certificate (Form W-4), 25, 35
Employment Eligibility Verification (Form I-9), 35
endorsement, 69
entrepreneur, 205
Equal Credit Opportunity Act, 125
Equifax. *See* credit bureau
equity, 192
escrow account, 193
estate, 249
estate planning, 249–250
   trust, 250
   wills, 250
executor, 250
exemption, 125. *See also* allowance
expansion, 213
expenses, 46–51. *See also* car loan, housing, loans, mortgage
   categorizing, 47–48
   tracking, 49–51
Experian. *See* credit bureau
extensive decision, 118

F

face value, 148
Fair Credit Reporting Act, 125
Fair Debt Collection Practices Act, 125
Federal Deposit Insurance Corporation (FDIC), 66–67
federal income taxes, 24–26
Federal Insurance Contribution Act (FICA), 26
FICA. *See* Federal Insurance Contribution Act (FICA)
FICO score. *See* credit score
finance charge, 115
financial advisor, 209
financial aid application, 169
financial capability, 3
financial goal, 4–5
financial independence, 224–227
financial institutions, 65–67
   bank, 65–67
   credit union, 67
   savings and loan association (S&L), 67
financial literacy, 3, 4
financial plan, 3
fiscal responsibility, 225
fixed expense, 47
fixed-rate mortgage, 193–195
FOMO, 6
foreclosure, 192
Form I-9 Employment Eligibility Verification, 35
Form W-2 Wage and Tax Statement, 35
Form W-4 Employee's Withholding Allowance Certificate, 25, 35
franchises, 205
fringe benefits. *See* employee benefits

G

goal, 4, 7
governmental education loan, 168
government bond, 221
grace period, 113
gratuity. *See* tips
gross pay, 17
growth, 205–206, 214–216

H

health insurance, 33, 144–146
   HMO plans, 145–146
   PPO plans, 146
   PSO plans, 146
health maintenance organization. *See* HMO plans
HMO plans, 145–146
HOA fee. *See* homeowners association (HOA) fee
homeowners association (HOA) fee, 197
homeowners insurance, 141–142
housing
   buying a condo, 197–198
   buying a house, 192–197
   percentage of income on, 190
   renting an apartment, 190–192
hybrid employees, 35–36

I

identity theft, 79
impulse decision, 118
income, 45–46. *See also* earnings
   discretionary, 52–53
   earned, 242
income taxes
   federal, 24–26
   local, 30
   state, 29–30
individual retirement account (IRA), 242–246
   Roth, 244–246
   withdrawing money, 244
installment loan, 182
insurance, 33, 134
   car, 136–140
   disability, 147
   health, 33, 144–146
   homeowners, 141–142
   life, 148–149
   other types, 150
   private mortgage, 192–193
   renters, 142–143
   whole life, 148–149
insurance policy, 134
insurance protection, 134–136
interest, 86, 90–96
   calculating rate, 91

compound, 92–96
credit card, 112, 117
simple, 91–92
Internet Connection
career choices, 159–160
car insurance, 139–140
car values, 187
charities, 47
checking accounts, 68
compound interest calculator, 96
costs of education, 167
credit card payment calculator, 123
current market conditions, 214
debit cards, 77
federal employment forms, 35
FICO score, 110
insurance plan, 149
minimizing health care costs, 146
money management software, 56
money tips for teens, 3
mortgage calculator, 197
opening Roth IRA, 246
retirement planning for teens, 239
salaries, 23
savings accounts, 89
Social Security benefits, 241
stock quotes, 212
Truth in Lending disclosure statement, 126
wages, 165
intestate, 250
investing, 205
average rate of return, 206–208
basics, 205–208
examples, 225
first investment, 224
growth and, 205–206, 214–216
portfolio, 208–209, 223
saving for, 227
stocks, 209–219
investment portfolio, 208–209, 223
investment pyramid, 208

J

jobs. *See* career
Junior ROTC, 166

K

Kelley Blue Book, 137, 140, 186–187

L

lease
apartment, 190–191
car, 187
lessee, 187

lessor, 187
liability, 8, 10
bodily injury, 137
homeowners, 141
property, 137
renters, 142
stolen credit card, 114
liability coverage, 137
life insurance, 148–149
lifelong learning, 174–175
personal interests, 175
professional development, 174
limited decision, 118
liquidity, 66
living space. *See* housing
living will, 250
loan consolidation, 125
loans. *See also* mortgage
car, 182–186
student, 168, 170
underwater, 186
local income taxes, 30
long-term goal, 4, 6, 7

M

mandatory car insurance, 139
mandatory deductions, 24–32
federal income taxes, 24–26
local income taxes, 30
Medicare taxes, 27–28
net pay and, 31–32
Social Security, 26–27
state income taxes, 29–30
market conditions, 213–214
master degree, 163
maturity date, CD, 87
Medicare, 27–28
mentor, 174
military benefits
education, 166
educational funding, 168
minimum payment, 117
money management software, 56
money market account (MMA), 88–89
mortgage, 192
adjustable-rate (ARM), 195–196
calculator, 197
fixed-rate, 193–195
payments, 196
municipal bonds, 220
mutual fund, 221–222, 224. *See also* retirement account

N

National Credit Union Share Insurance Fund (NCUSIF), 67
needs, 5–6

net pay, 31–32
net worth, 8, 10
New York Stock Exchange (NYSE), 210

O

Occupational Outlook Handbook, 159–160
occupations. *See* career
opportunity cost, 120
overdraft, 71
overdraft protection, 71
overtime wage, 19–20

P

pay. *See* earnings; gross pay; net pay
payee, 69
pay slip, 32
pay yourself first, 46
permanent life insurance. *See* whole life insurance
personal identification number (PIN), 76–77
philanthropy, 33
PIN. *See* personal identification number (PIN)
point of service. *See* POS plans
POS plans, 146
postsecondary education, 162–167
   budget, 172–173
   college or university, 162–164
   costs of, 167
   funding, 167–171
   military, 166
   trade school, 166
   two-year schools, 165
PPO plans, 146
preferred provider organization. *See* PPO plans
preferred stock, 213
premium, 134
principal, 91
priority, 6
private mortgage insurance (PMI), 192–193
professional development, 174
proprietary credit card, 113
proprietary school, 165
purchases, debit card, 77–78
purchasing decisions, 118–121
   comparison shopping, 119
   decision-making process, 120–121

R

rate of return, average, 206–208
recession, 213
regular savings account, 86–87
renters insurance, 142–143
replacement value, 141
repossession, 182
required minimum distribution, 241

Reserve Officers' Training Corps (ROTC), 166
restrictive endorsement, 69–70
retirement account, 33, 241–249
   401(k) and 403(b) plans, 246–248
   individual retirement account (IRA), 242–246
   Roth 401(k), 248
retirement planning, 238–239, 249
revolving credit, 116
risk, 134, 205, 208
rollover, 248
ROTC. *See* Reserve Officers' Training Corps (ROTC)
Roth 401(k), 248
Roth IRA, 244–245
routine decision, 118
Rule of 72, 96–97, 205–206

S

salary, 22–23
savings account, 86–90
   certificates of deposit (CD), 87–88
   money market account (MMA), 88–89
   record, 87
   regular, 86–87
savings and loan association (S&L), 67
savings plan, 86, 98
scholarship, 168
school. *See* postsecondary education
secured loan, 182
Securities and Exchange Commission (SEC), 210
security deposit, 187, 190
seminar, 174
Series EE savings bond, 221
service fee, 68, 69
shopping, comparison, 119
short-term goal, 4, 7
signature card, 65
simple interest, 91–92
SMART goals, 5
socially responsible funds, 221
social responsibility, 33, 47
Social Security, 26–27, 239–241
special endorsement, 69–70
spending, weekly record, 49–51
state income taxes, 29–30
stock exchange. *See* stock market
stock market, 210
   market correction, 213
   NYSE, 210
   report, 212
stocks, 209–219
   blue chip, 214
   dividends, 217–218
   first investment, 224
   market conditions, 213–214
   quotes, 212
   reasons to buy, 214–217
   stock market report, 210

stock split, 218–219
  tracking, 216–217
  types, 213
stock split, 218–219
straight bankruptcy, 125
student loan, 168, 170
surplus, 52

T

taxable compensation. *See* earned income
tax-deferred, 241, 242
taxes
  federal, 24–26
  local, 30
  Medicare, 27–28
  refunds, 30
  Social Security, 26–27
  state, 29–30
  unemployment, 31
teaser rates, 117
term life insurance, 48
three Cs of credit, 107–108
time sheet, 18–19
time value of money, 90
tips, 21–22
trade confirmation, 209
trade-off, 120
trade school, 166
trading, 210
traditional IRA, 242
TransUnion. *See* credit bureau
trust, 250
trustee, 250
Truth in Lending Act, 125, 126

U

umbrella insurance policy, 150
unemployment taxes, 31
United States Distance Learning Association (USDLA), 165
universal life insurance. *See* whole life insurance
unsecured loan, 182
US Bureau of Labor Statistics (BLS), 159, 165

V

value, 6, 7
variable expense, 48
variable life insurance. *See* whole life insurance

vocational school. *See* trade school
voluntary deductions, 33–34
volunteering, 33, 47

W

W-4, Employee's Withholding Allowance Certificate form, 25, 35
W-2, Wage and Tax Statement form, 35
wage, 17–18
  by career, 165
  salary, 22–23
Wage and Tax Statement, W-2 Form, 35
Wall Street, 210
wants, 5–6
wealth, building, 8–9
weekly spending record, 49–51
whole life insurance, 148–149
will, 250
withholding tables, 24
workers' compensation insurance, 147
working from home, 35–36

Y

Your Turn
  account fees, 89–90
  career planning, 162
  car insurance application, 138
  car loan application, 183
  categorizing expenses, 48
  creating a budget, 55
  credit card application, 106
  decision-making process, 121
  deposit slips and checks, 72–73
  federal income taxes, 26
  financial aid application, 169
  inventory, 143
  investment portfolio, 223
  mortgage payments, 196
  net worth, 10
  renting an apartment, 191
  saving for investments, 227
  stock market report, 211–212
  three Cs of credit, 108
  time sheet, 19
  tracking spending, 51
  tracking your income, 46
  types of financial decisions, 119
  values and goals, 7
  withdrawing money from IRA, 244